Vera Weddige

A
Different
Heaven
and
Earth

SHEILA D. COLLINS

A
Different
Heaven
and
Earth

Judson Press, ® Valley Forge

A DIFFERENT HEAVEN AND EARTH

Library of Congress Cataloging in Publication Data

Collins, Sheila.
  A different heaven and earth.

  Includes bibliographical references.
  1. Women in Christianity. I. Title.
BV639.W7C57   261.8'34'12   74-2890
ISBN 0-8170-0700-8

Printed in the U.S.A. ⊕

To Freda
artist, mother—
the first liberated woman in my life.

And to my daughters, Jennifer and Megan,
that they may grow up free, and whole.

Acknowledgments

Since feminist theology is communal theology, I cannot begin to list all of those women, known and unknown to me, who justly deserve to be credited for the development of this book. I wish, however, to acknowledge a special indebtedness to those with whom I spent many hours in conversation and reflection, as we shared both ourselves and our ideas: Nelle Morton, Claire Randall, Dee Crabtree, Judy Davis, Sally Bentley, Jean Lambert, the women at the "Women Exploring Theology" conference at Grailville, 1973, and the women in the New York Ad Hoc Group on "Racism, Sexism, and 'Classism,'" chaired by Letty Russell. I am especially grateful for the help of Claire Randall and Sally Bentley in making materials available to me, many of which were not in published form, and to Susan Ross Clewell and Judith Plaskow Goldenberg for permission to use their work. I cannot neglect to mention my indebtedness to Mary Daly, whose defiant voice infused me with the courage to see and to speak out of a new reality, and to Kathy Engle and Rosalie Matsuoka for help in the preparation of the manuscript. I owe a special thanks to my husband, John, whose willingness to take over on the home front provided me with the time and energy necessary to write this book and whose wise questions served to keep me honest.

Foreword

I began this book as a reporting job. I set out to read all of the books and papers, attend as many of the theological conferences and workshops, and interview as many of the women involved in creating a new feminist theology as I had time for. Then, I had resolved to fit all the scattered pieces together into an intelligible and unified précis on the feminist theological movement.

The first chapter represents an attempt to outline a framework and to provide a justification for the feminist movement in theology from the third-party stance of the reporter. Other women were doing theology, I thought, and I was simply interpreting what I saw. Since I had left seminary several years ago after one year of study, I did not feel "qualified" to launch into an academic venture of my own in the field, but I could certainly report on what was beginning to happen.

Partway into the second chapter, which I had decided to entitle "Exorcising the Patriarchal Demon," a strange thing happened. I began to have trouble organizing the chapter. Something was blocking me so that I could no longer go on with the work. After many fitful starts and stops, several rewrites, much going back to do research in order to avoid sitting down with the manuscript, drinking several hundred cups of coffee, and finally experiencing panic at the approach of my deadline and nothing to show for it, I realized what had been happening to me. Instead of writing a chapter unveiling the patriarchal character of Judeo-Christian theology, I had been struggling to exorcise that patriarchal demon *from myself!*

I had wanted to find an orderly, logical mode of presentation for the second chapter. In my concern that traditional theologians and church folk not be turned off by some of the radical—perhaps heretical—things I would be reporting on, I had attempted to translate everything I saw into traditional theological language, or to use the intellectual tools which have long been at the service of theologians—logical argumentation, exegesis, hermeneutics, form criticism, apologetics—to make my case. But the material was recalcitrant. The more I tried to twist and shape it to fit into a recognizable mold, the more it slipped and wriggled out from under my grasp, until it stood on its own, proudly and defiantly Amazonian, as if to say: "Here I am; accept me on my own terms, or not at all!"

Then I realized I must slay the patriarchal dragon in myself, the demon that had kept me in bondage to logic, intellectualism, and to masculine expectations and approval.

With this acknowledgment came the further startling realization that I was no longer a reporter. In the course of researching the book, I and my subject had become one. No longer could I distinguish my feelings, my reactions, or my dawning convictions from those of the women on whom I was reporting. That false dichotomy between inquiring subject and intellectual object had been overcome, and I was beginning to theologize out of my own inner experience!

Suddenly the words of those women with whom I had talked came flooding in on me with the certainty of internalization: "Theology must come out of experience"; "Form cannot be separated from content"; "Theologizing can be done by anyone, with or without a theological degree"; "If women were ever to get into the pulpits in any numbers, the Book would no longer be kept from the people; the mysteries would be brought down from the cross and the pulpit for all to examine."

I became obsessed with the desire to investigate my own religious history as a woman—a history which had all but been obliterated by the past two thousand years of theological scholarship. Instead of taking the words of the female luminaries in the field at face value, I wanted to go back to the original sources myself: to the books on pre-

Christian and a-Christian religion and mythology, to descriptions of the religion of the Great Goddess, which preceded and was coexistent with the rise of Judeo-Christianity and may have lasted in modified form well up into the Middle Ages or later. I admonished myself for not having had the foresight to take Hebrew and Greek while in seminary so that I (as many women are now doing) could go back to the original Judeo-Christian sources to find there the seeds of enlightenment and liberation uncorrupted by a history of masculine editing and translating.

In order to get this book done, I have had to survey the field of feminist theological exploration rather cursorily and to come to some tentative conclusions. The book, however, is not what it started out to be. My own convictions are inextricably linked with those I have surveyed. Where I have depended on the scholarship and ideas of others, they are cited in the text or in notes. Some time after the first chapter, the reader may notice a subtle shift in person, from third to first person, reflecting the change in my relationship with the subject. I have left that editorial discrepancy in the text as a witness to the change which occurred in me as I became *engaged* with feminist theology.

I consider my personal (and communal) search for a new history and a new future only begun with this book. It will take me more than the rest of a lifetime to come to know what that history and future mean in face of this vast and terrifying cosmos. But this quest just begun has made theology come alive for me in a way that it never did in seminary. I present this book, then, as a personal testimony to the power of the epiphany of a new becoming.

Sheila D. Collins
New York, 1974

Contents

Introduction

At the end of *The Secular City,* Harvey Cox states that our transition from the age of Christendom to a new era of urban secularity makes irrelevant our previous language of God. What we must do, says Cox, is to "take up the work of liberating the captives, confident that we will be granted a new name [for God] by events of the future." [1] *The Secular City* was published in 1965. Today we may be entering an era where, if a new name for God is not yet readily apparent, at least the places where the transcendent is being met are being reconstituted, and there is the strong conviction that a new name will soon be heard. In the interim the work of liberation has been taken up by the captives themselves; and in that liberation struggle, waged by blacks, Hispanos, American Indians, Asians, and the silenced majority of women, can be found the seeds of a new, revitalizing theological understanding.

Add to this the recent acknowledgment by scientists of spiritual dimensions of the mind as a result of drug experimentation, and the discovery of the interrelatedness of all of life through an understanding of ecology, and we have the makings of a profound spiritual revolution.

To be sure, it is hard to find evidence of such an upheaval in

America today; but it is there—not on the surface of the culture, but bubbling underneath it and all around its edges, like a pot of water that is just about to boil. Characteristically, writers and artists have been quicker than others in our society to sense the first tremors of shifting cultural faults. Novelist and poet Joyce Carol Oates, in an essay in the *Saturday Review* entitled "New Heaven and Earth," acknowledges that which is only dimly felt:

> What appears to be a breaking-down of civilization may well be simply the breaking-up of old forms by life itself (not an eruption of madness or self-destruction), a process that is entirely natural and inevitable. Perhaps we are in the tumultuous but exciting close of a centuries-old kind of consciousness—a few of us like theologians of the medieval church encountering the unstoppable energy of the Renaissance.[2]

Barbara Ward, noted British economist and critic of technological society, echoes Ms. Oates's words in her address to the 1972 United Nations-sponsored Conference on the Human Environment:

> It is impossible to take part in this Conference on the Human Environment without wondering whether we may not be present at one of those turning points in man's affairs when the human race begins to see itself and its concerns from a new angle of vision and, as a result, finds new openings for action, for courage, and for hope. . . . One thinks of the intellectual ferment in China which, over two millennia ago, accompanied the end of the feudal ward and the establishment of the first great centralized Han dynasty. In more recent history men had almost to stand on their heads to realize that the sun did not go round the earth, but the reverse. This "Copernican Revolution" is the archetype of fundamental change by which men learn to rethink, totally, their place in the scheme of things. Our own epoch is, I believe, such an age again.[3]

Andrew Weil, a young doctor who has explored the inner world both through the use of drugs and without them, points in his book, *The Natural Mind,* to other forms of consciousness whose resources have been largely untapped in the Western rationalistic world. In *Where the Wasteland Ends,* Theodore Roszak sees in much of the present counterculture the seeds of a profound religious renewal which harkens back to what he calls the "old Gnosis," or the way of knowing which preceded the rise of Judeo-Christianity and the scientific world view. The immense popularity of Carlos Castaneda's books, *The Teachings of Don Juan, A Separate Reality,* and the *Journey to Ixtlan,* suggests the great hungering in our society for a new vision of the world.

The predominant theme among all these writers is the announcement of the death of old authorities and the emergence of forces which call us to participate in an altered form of consciousness or to find new criteria by which to order reality. This same theme has become the starting point for the liberation movements of Third-World peoples and of women.

Consciousness-raising (a term coined by the women's liberation movement) or *concientizacion* (a term coined by Paulo Freire and now used by many Third-World groups) is the process by which we begin to make a break with the old authorities and to come to a new vision of reality. The term does not connote a rather passive consciousness of oneself, as Descartes described consciousness. Rather, consciousness-raising is a process of dynamic reflection which impels one into action. It turns one's former perceptions of reality inside out, so that one can no longer live in the old world but must create a new one out of this new vision.

For each group which involves itself in consciousness-raising the direction of movement is similar, although the focus of one's perceptions may differ in detail. One begins the process with an awareness of division, alienation, limitation, and constriction. One then goes on to affirm one's liberation from those constrictions and to move toward a vision of wholeness and unity.

For many in our society—especially for women—the chief source of limitation and constriction has been the Judeo-Christian tradition and the culture which this tradition spawned. A few years ago, theological pundits pointed out that the God long associated with this tradition was not speaking to the realities of a modern, urban technological society. Men, such as John Robinson in *Honest to God,* Harvey Cox in *The Secular City,* and the "death of God" theologians, acclaimed the demise of the old, irrelevant God and called us to participate joyously in a celebration of the secular. But their call did not work. Cities have become places of alienation and fear, rather than arenas of hope and progress; and everywhere people are searching for some experience of transcendence, whether it be in the Jesus Movement, in communes, or in group encounters.

The reason for this may be that the vacuum left by the death of God could not be filled by a secular world which continued to operate on the same cognitive principles as the theocentric world it had left behind: a linear view of time, hierarchical patterns of relationships, abstract and increasingly technical language, and a view of human nature still based on a body-mind dualism. It is therefore not surprising that white, Western male theologians, still operating out of the same cognitive principles, could not replace the death of God with anything more spiritually satisfying.

It remained for those outside the intellectual structures embodied in most of traditional theology to point to new (or, in many cases, overlooked) realities and to provide the handles by which new meaning could be grasped and incorporated. Women have always remained outside the intellectual constructs erected by Judeo-Christian culture, and their coming to consciousness has sparked a renaissance in theological activity and exploration among them. As they become aware of the restrictions under which their lives have been led, women are offering a cogent and indicting critique of traditional Judeo-Christian theology and the role of the church.

The bulk of this critique can be found in unpublished papers which have been passed around from person to person in the movement—a method of communication which, in itself, bespeaks a break with the past. Some of this criticism has been collected into books, like Mary Daly's *The Church and the Second Sex* and *Beyond God the Father;* Elsie Culver's *Women in the World of Religion;* Rosemary Ruether's *Liberation Theology;* and *Women's Liberation and the Church,* edited by Sarah Bentley Doely. The rest has appeared occasionally in theological and religious journals. As women refine their criticism of Judeo-Christianity, they find it harder and harder to take meaning from the forms of worship and expression which embody the old theology. Increasingly, they are coming together to explore new avenues of worship, new forms of theological expression, and new images and symbols for some of the most basic concepts on which our Judeo-Christian heritage has been based.

Such explorations are taking place among college and seminary students, among church executive personnel, in consciousness-raising groups in local churches, in denominational women's caucuses, and in interfaith groups which have sprung up in several cities.

Three ecumenical conferences—called specifically to explore these new theological possibilities—have been exciting events in themselves and have had a ripple effect on all subsequent activity in the field. The first of these was called by the Alverno College Research Center on Women and was held at Alverno College in Milwaukee, Wisconsin, in June, 1971. There, twenty-two women met for two weeks to explore theology in light of their own experiences and understanding of life. The results of this conference, printed up in the form of "Notes," raise most of the basic questions with which women are grappling these days and suggest, tentatively, the direction in which future theologizing by women should go.

The second conference, attended by about sixty women and sponsored by Church Women United, was held at the Grailville Community in Loveland, Ohio, in June, 1972. Here the women began to answer (in profoundly meaningful ways for the participants) some of the questions raised by the Alverno group. A packet of materials entitled "Women Exploring Theology at Grailville" is the result of this experiment. Another conference was held in Grailville in June, 1973. A booklet entitled "Women and Theology" came out of this conference.[4]

The exploration is not over. Indeed, with these meetings, it has only begun. This book is an attempt, then, to assess in midstream what has been happening as women begin to *do* theology. I stress the word "do" here, for the method that women seem to be following is that of engaging in an action/reflection process *from* which theological insights *arise,* rather than *to* which they are *applied.* In one sense, my attempt to codify their insights in book form subverts the very nature of their enterprise; for it is of the essence of women's theology that form must mirror content. Religion is participation, not solely, or chiefly, discourse.

While the theological process described in this book will speak initially to women, it is not, in the end, so restricted a field. What women are now doing carries deep implications for the life of the total church and for the restructuring of society. For those who have ears to hear, let them hear!

To the Reader

Demythologizing has been a part of the academic theologian's stock-in-trade for a number of years. Yet experts tell us that myths never really disappear. They are merely rearranged or transmuted, or they go underground for a spell, only to reappear in another constellation. To deny the reality that the mythic world offers is to place ourselves at the mercy of myth, rather than to use it as a means of deepening our experience of transcendence.

Perhaps, in order to understand the greatest truths in a new way, we should not be demythologizing the tradition—that is, attempting to destroy the deeply emotional psychic bases upon which we have erected our systems of truth and the symbols which unite us with universal meaning—rather, we should be seeking to *re*mythologize those truths in a way that has personal and communal depth and meaning for us.

The following story is offered in the spirit in which it was conceived—as an exercise in remythologizing—tentative and unfinished, but suggestive of new ways of perceiving old truths. At the time in which it was written it represented for me the contention of two symbolic systems within my own understanding of faith-history. Since then I have shared it with other women doing theology who have also found it meaningful. Thus, it has assumed something of the nature of a communal myth.

Since the story reflects those ghosts with which I was wrestling in the second and third chapters of this book, you might want to turn back to it after having read those two chapters. In the meantime, relax, let down your defenses, and enjoy it!

A Tale
of Two
Deities

Once upon a time—a very long time ago—before there were anti-ballistic missiles or Apollo moon flights, pineapple bombs, or infrared sensors, long before there were B-52s, or even B-2s, automobiles, TV sets, radios, electric lights, or steam engines—long before the earth was scarred, scorched, and paved over by all these wonderful inventions, long before the air overhead was crisscrossed by wires and its color became a yellow pall, long before the waterways were choked with effluents and marine life deemed inedible, long before there were "masculine" ways of behaving which were rewarded and "feminine" ways which were punished, long before sacred and secular, inner and outer, me and Other, soul and body, mind and matter, intellect and emotion, up and down, black and white, first and second, young and old, light and dark, good and evil, life and death faced each other in an eternal enmity of metaphysical one-upmanship—yes, long before all this came to pass, there lived a Queen.

Her names were as numerous as the languages of her devotees. Some called her Ishtar and others Asherah; some called her Gaea and others Coatlicue; some called her Demeter and others Danae; but by whatever name she was called, she was honored. Ah, she was resplendent and awesome to behold. All the polarities twinkled interchangeably on her munificent bosom, like so many facets of a magnificent diamond brooch.

She was Sophia, Queen of the heavens, the source of all cosmic wisdom; she was Demeter, Mother Earth, womb of all fecundity and growth and the most delightful of sensual pleasures; and she was *Mater Dolorosa,* the grieving Mother, or Hecate, Queen of the mysterious netherworld, the place of rebirth and regeneration. Her symbols were the dove of peace, the serpent and the bull's horns of generativity, the precise justice of the double-edged ax, the cornucopia of plenty, the crescent moon of rebirth in time, and the pillar of strength and support.

The Queen's devotees included all the peoples of the earth, from Anatolia and the Aegean Sea north to Celtic Britain and west, across the ocean, to the land of the Aztecs. They were an agricultural people and in their devotion to their Queen maintained a life of rich harmonies. Planting and harvesting, consuming and storing, toolmaking and tool-using were acts of devotion with resonances in the mysterious and wonderful processes of the universe. The union of male and female was the plowing and planting of the seed. The fruit of that union— the newborn child—was celebrated as the spring grain, and the death of loved ones was the barrenness of winter itself.

At that time there was no work divorced from meaning, no play divorced from work, no production for the mere sake of consumption, no art "for art's sake." Poetry was not a mirror of life, for life *was* poetry; and ecstasy was found in the most usual of places.

Like the Queen whom they resembled, women in those times could be proud and strong, receptive and gentle, wise and gracious, or fierce and terrible, and always they were held in esteem. In fact, most activity centered upon their manifold arts and necessities.

In time the great Queen, out of her self-generating fecundity, gave birth to children who assisted her in blessing the world. Her daughters and, in turn, their daughters were legion. There were Artemis of the hunt; Isis, the virgin mother; love-struck

Psyche; Persephone, whose rape and abduction by Pluto caused her mother deep anguish; fierce Athena, protectoress of cities; Aphrodite, quintessence of love and beauty; and, oh, so many others.

Now the Queen in time also had a son who died once a year and was rescued by his mother from the underworld, and in this yearly drama resided the deepest meaning of all life. Eventually the son grew up and married his mother and the two of them reigned as consorts over heaven and earth, but with the Queen having a slight edge over her husband in the people's affections. After all, she was the source of all life and regeneration!

But one day a strange thing happened. The lover-son, who owed so much to his wife-mother, turned against her. Perhaps he was jealous, sensing that the people loved him a little less than they loved his consort-mother; or perhaps he had always been fearful of her uniquely fecundous powers which he could only imitate but never really equal. But for whatever reason, whether in a pique of jealousy or fear, he usurped her place in the heavens, cutting himself off from the earth, in which he proceeded to imprison the Queen. "From now on," he declared, "I am the Lord your God, King of all kings and Lord of all lords. You shall have no other deities before me! Furthermore, the earth is a mere substratum of my heavenly universe. You are to dominate it and to keep it under control." In order that no hint of the Queen's power be known among the people, the King ordered all of those who most resembled her to be kept subordinate and quiescent by men, who more nearly resembled the King. The Queen's daughters were declared prostitutes and whores, and their devotees were labeled "pagans" who must be conquered and subdued by the followers of the King.

The more power the King garnered to himself, the more fearful he became of losing that power, and the more dictatorial he became in protecting it. In order to strike fear into the hearts of the people lest they turn back to their Queen, he surrounded himself with fire and thunderbolts and roared down from his throne in the sky mighty warnings to the people. "Have you not known, have you not heard?" he boomed. "Has it not been told you from the beginning? Have you not understood from the foundations of the earth that it is he who sits above the circle of the earth, who stretches out the heavens like a curtain and who brings princes to nought?" And they were filled with fear and began to worship him slavishly, and their true origins were thus obliterated from memory.

The more the men worshiped this wrathful king, the more like him they became. They dressed up in armor and brandished swords against people they declared to be enemies of the King. They strutted around wearing fancy clothes and set up leaders among themselves. They held meetings in secret, from which women and children (because they resembled the Queen) were excluded. One kind of human activity—that which glorified the King—was set against that which had been instituted by the Queen, which was degraded.

But with the imprisonment of the Queen, life became hard and brittle for the people, so that the King was forced to make up stories to explain why they suffered so under his rule. "It is all the fault of the Queen," he said, "and her lascivious and rebellious nature. She overstepped her bounds; she disobeyed my divine command by opening the box of evils that I had forbidden her to open, by eating an apple from the one tree of which I had forbidden her to eat. As a result of her disobedience, you race of men will suffer until the end of time. There will be wars and rumors of wars, and the poor you shall always have with you. Men will have to work in the sweat of their brows and women will bear children in great pain."

And the people began to rebel, demanding a way out of this miserable state of affairs, but the King said: "Wait! I will promise you a new life and a new land at the end of time; but you must continue to worship me if this is to happen."

From her imprisonment in the earth, the Queen felt deeply the misery of the people. She decided to conceive another son who would enable them to ease the burdens they had made for themselves, since she could not act in her own right, having become such an object of debasement in their eyes. Not wanting this son to become all powerful like the first, she brought him forth in a stable, a place of low esteem.

When the Great Queen's son grew up, he began to teach the people many of those things they had all but forgotten during the Great Queen's imprisonment. He taught them that wisdom was not found in learned books nor in secret ceremonies, but in the heart of the child and in the simple justice of nature: in the sowing of seed, in the taste of salt, in the natural grandeur of the field lily, and in the fig tree's fruit. He taught them that the King's values and priorities were all distorted: that whoever exalts himself will be humbled and that whoever humbles himself will be exalted; that heaven is not won through great accumulations of wealth and power but through the efforts of the peacemakers and the pure in heart. He taught them that men could be gentle and compassionate (he even wept himself) and that women could be strong and capable again.

And the Great King's followers hated him for this, and they put him to death. He went back to his mother's womb, from whence he emerged and appeared to some women.

After seeing what a great impression this man had made on the people, the King became fearful of losing his power over them; so he decided to claim the son as his own. Thus he declared that he had sent this man down from heaven to be their Savior and that even now the Son was sitting at the right hand of the Father. Immediately the people mistook the King's sign †, the symbol of death, for the Queen's sign ♀, symbol of life generating from life, and the people began to worship the Son, as the Father. The Son's teachings were distorted to fit in with the Father's plans, or they were explained away as being nice thoughts but not too relevant to the world of hard realities. Women were counseled to take the Son's teachings to heart, and they did so, sensing in them a vague reminder of some other heritage.

But the Queen's power was not to be so easily stifled. The more rigid and dominating the King's followers became, the more powerful was her urge to break free from her confinement and to rejoin earth with heaven in one endearing cosmic embrace. Indeed, several times down through the years her spirit has broken free—in art, in poetry, in song, in bold women, and in gentle men—or wherever the polarities meet in dynamic interaction. But, alas, her spirit has emerged only to be burned at the stake, vilified, ignored, or—when all else failed—co-opted by the King's men.

Even now, as great penile missiles ring the earth in an apotheosis of kingly fear and mistrust, body is seeking to reclaim intellect, secular to reclaim the sacred, earth to reclaim its rightful place next to heaven, and man in woman is seeking to reclaim woman in man. Perhaps this time the Great Queen will break through into freedom. She is certainly trying!

1 Experience as the Crucible for Theology

"Hold your tongue!" said the Queen, turning purple.

"I won't!" said Alice.

"Off with her head!" the Queen shouted at the top of her voice. Nobody moved.

"Who cares for *you*?" said Alice (she had grown to her full size by this time). "You're nothing but a pack of cards!"

At this the whole pack rose up into the air, and came flying down upon her; she gave a little scream, half of fright and half of anger, and tried to beat them off, and found herself lying on the bank, with her head in the lap of her sister, who was gently brushing away some dead leaves that had fluttered down from the trees upon her face.

"Wake up, Alice dear!" said her sister. "Why, what a long sleep you've had!"

—Alice in Wonderland[1]

Theology—the attempt of humans to give shape and content to their experiences of the transcendent—arises out of the life of a people or, in the case of a systematic theologian, out of a particular person's life lived in a particular cultural milieu. Since the transcendent cannot be grasped or defined (and thus the experience of it transmitted) except by the human tools which are available to us, it is necessarily limited by the patterns of our speech and visual perception, by the concepts which speech makes possible, and by our history. Thus, theologies arise out of a cultural context; they are promulgated by means of culture; and they change because of changes in the cultural experience. Theology, says James Cone, cannot be separated from the community it represents.[2] Unfortunately, many theologians have forgotten this fact.

To say that all theologies are relative to the speaker who gives them voice and to the cultural milieu out of which he or she comes is not to say, as Marx and Freud did, that religion is merely an opiate and God a projection of the human imagination. As countless generations have witnessed, religious experience is real and pervasive. In its expression or transmission, however, such experience may often be inadequate, imbalanced, and sometimes even corrupted. Experience is the crucible out of which theologies arise. For the Hebrews it was the experience of the Exodus and deliverance into the Promised Land; for the apostles it was the experience of the life and death of the man Jesus Christ and the experience of exhilaration at the events of Pentecost; for Paul it was the experience on the road to Damascus; and for American blacks it was the experience of slavery and the subsequent liberation from physical and spiritual bondage to white society into authentic personhood.

Unfortunately, the history of the church is one in which theologies, like political ideologies, have been legislated rather than allowed to develop naturally. In the Middle Ages, theology, in the form of a system of logical arguments, was legislated for a society in which most of those who were expected to live by its tenets had neither the time nor the intellectual training needed to decipher its meaning. In more recent times, theologies, laden with archaic symbols, have been legislated from pulpit and podium to an audience whose social infrastructures no longer incorporate the original meaning of those symbols. What does it mean to a modern American to speak of God as "Lord" and "King" when American culture does not incorporate the concept of kingship? Much of the Western missionary effort abroad has been characterized by a failure to understand that the roots of theology must be in the experience of a people and that one cannot legislate concepts which a culture does not contain.

Often, when the theology being legislated has not given meaning to the experiences of a people, the proselytizers have fallen back on authority, as both the source and norm of their theology. For fundamentalists the authority is the literal interpretation of the Bible; for Catholics it is the church; and for many white Protestant theologians and clergymen it is their degree or status. The history of the church reflects a constant dialectic between the meaning of experience and the weight of authority, with authority usually the victor in official annals. But changes have occurred in theology, true meaning approximated, and growth obtained only when the weight of authority has been challenged—only when an individual or group has dared to say: "Wait a minute! My understanding of life, my experience, does not concur with what you tell me I must believe or what I must do."

Unfortunately, the insights of past reformers have often been systematized and rigidified by their followers, and thus distorted for future generations for whom these reformers are held up as authorities on the nature of faith. Thus, Paul's encounter with the Christ event was codified by him, and further by his followers, into a rather formal Christology, focused not on the truth to which Christ pointed, but on the figure of Christ himself. Subsequent theologians, assuming that they are basing their theology on something they call the "Gospel," are actually using Paul's interpretation of the Christ event as the source for the meaning of the Christian faith. This stands out quite clearly when one studies Barth's theology. Though proclaiming that we can only appropriate a knowledge of God through the Jesus of the Gospels, it is, in reality, the Pauline Christ that Barth talks about—a rather different man from the one who appears in the four Gospels. The cryptic nature of Jesus' remarks and the always paradoxical nature of his life and death defy neat schematization—yet men have consistently tried to systematize his meaning, to lock him into patterns, to shape him into creeds. In the same way, the radical essence of Martin Luther's stand became a rigid set of formulas for the Lutherans who followed after him. Those who only pointed to the truth became, themselves, the truth—the authoritative source from which all god-talk originates and the norm against which all experience must be measured.

The problem with citing authority as the source and norm for theological discourse is that the cultural biases of whatever theological authority one uses are almost always overlooked. It is in the very nature of an authority not to be questioned in this respect. Ultimately, theology speaks to the spiritual needs and longings of particular people in particular times and in particular places. These needs may change with place and time. If this assumption is correct, then the closer a religious expression or theology is to its source in experience—that is, the more the answers that are found approximate the questions that are asked—the closer it is to spiritual reality and the more meaning it will have for its adherents. The more redactions a particular form of theology undergoes, *without being informed by current experience,* the more likely it is to be tainted by unacknowledged cultural accretions which distort its original meaning and render it incapable of generating true faithfulness. To accept authority as the source for any theology always runs the risk, as Tillich has pointed out, of providing answers to questions that are not asked.

The conflict between experience and authority is a crucial one for women. Throughout the history of Judeo-Christianity, women have yielded to the coercion of authority, denying their own experiences and feelings in favor of some "higher authority"—e.g., God, as interpreted by men; the Scriptures, as interpreted by men; the tradition of the church, as molded by men; or some new theology developed by men. Women have been told that they could not study the Scriptures, pray certain prayers, or talk in public with men, and that their bodies were unclean, especially during menstruation and after the birth of a female child (the Torah and other Jewish teachings). Women were told to keep silent in church and to obey their husbands (Paul). They were told that they are inferior to men (Aquinas), or, if not inferior, then secondary (Barth); that their sole function in life is to produce children; that they are to have nothing to do with "divine service, the priestly offices, or God's word" (Martin Luther); that they must not speak out in public against the evil of slavery (many Protestant clergymen in the nineteenth century); that they are not worthy enough to be ordained to the priesthood (the Episcopal, Roman Catholic, and Missouri-Synod Lutheran churches); and so on.

For most women such injunctions became self-fulfilling prophecies, and women did remain silent in the churches, obey their husbands, think of themselves as inferior and unclean, and devote themselves to child rearing. But a great many women, throughout the history of the church, dared to accept their own feelings and experiences, dared to controvert authority and to search out and assert their own paths to the transcendent. Though usually overlooked in histories of the church, women, such as Deborah in the Old Testament, Mary the mother of Jesus, Mary Magdalene, Phoebe, Priscilla, St. Theresa of Avila, Joan of Orleans, Ann Hutchinson, Maria W. Stewart, Lydia Maria Child, the Grimké sisters, Mary Baker Eddy, Elizabeth Cady Stanton, and many others, made significant contributions to religious life and thought although, in many cases, their contributions are minimally recorded because of historical circumstances and the low status accorded women.

When one looks at the history of the church, one is amazed to find even what little there is about women such as these. So strong has been the anti-woman bias throughout Judeo-Christian culture and so powerful the forces of censorship which have denied women the right to speak, to record their thoughts, or to have their works published or kept alive, that it is by dint of unusual courage and extraordinary strength that such women have appeared in the history at all. St. Theresa of Avila, an unusual woman for her time, reflects on the anti-female bias of the church in the following words:

> When thou wert in the world, Lord, thou didst not despise women, but didst always help them and show them great compassion. Thou didst find more faith and no less love in them than in men. . . . We can do nothing in public that is of any use to thee, nor dare we speak of some of the truths over which we weep in secret, lest thou shouldst not hear this, our just petition. Yet, Lord, I cannot believe this of thy goodness and righteousness, for thou art a righteous Judge, not like judges in the world, who, being after all, men and sons of Adam, refuse to consider any woman's virtue as above suspicion.[3]

One wonders how many countless others like these were never recorded for posterity.

What is important about such women is that they provide an antidote to the traditional assumptions about women's nature and place in the cosmic scheme of things. Through their writings and what is recorded of their actions, we have a spotty, but nevertheless substantial, body of information on the experiences of women who defied authority to assert a different reality for themselves and their sisters.

Modern church women are discovering these soul-sisters of the past in a new and exciting way. What they find in the lives of a Phoebe, an Ann Hutchinson, or a Maria Stewart (an outspoken abolitionist, an advocate of education for women, and a deeply religious person) is a corroboration of most of their own innermost feelings and perceptions, of their own deepest religious aspirations. The discovery of their own history is, in effect, a form of revelation.

Modern women find a link with the past so easy because the geography of women's lives has remained surprisingly consistent through the years. There is an immediate empathy between women of any age who begin to think or act self-consciously, as the writer Anaïs Nin explains in her diary:

As I discover myself, I feel I am merely one of many, a symbol. I begin to understand women of yesterday and today. The mute ones of the past, the inarticulate, who took refuge behind wordless intuitions, and the women of today. . . .[4]

While men have discovered new continents and new theologies, changed the course of rivers and paved over continents, waged the wars and then allied themselves with "the enemy," women have, in the history books at least, been relegated to the same kind of secondary position vis-à-vis men in almost every civilized culture throughout history. "Look at the index of any cultural history," writes the social and literary critic Richard Gilman, and "the reader will almost always come upon the entry 'Women,' in nearly every case followed by some such phrase as 'position of,' for the very good reason that the history of men has been synonymous in the minds of nearly all historians with the history of civilization itself."[5] The place or role for women has been similar, then, whether we are talking about the twentieth-century woman or the first-century one. The role invariably has been that of "the Other," as Simone de Beauvoir has described it in her now classic book, *The Second Sex*. The place has inevitably been secondary, subordinate, or, in modern euphemistic jargon, supportive.

Take, for example, the statements about woman's role made by two theologians centuries apart:

Woman was made to be a help to man. But she was not fitted to be a help to man except in generation, because another man would prove a more effective help in anything else.

(Thomas Aquinas)[6]

Why should not woman be the second in sequence, but only in sequence? What other choice has she, seeing she can be nothing at all apart from this sequence and her place within it?

(Karl Barth)[7]

When women, at different times and in different places, listened to their own consciences and began to live out different roles from the one delineated in the statements above, they were severely put down with the force of "religious" authority. In a pastoral letter written in the 1830s by the Council of Congregationalist Ministers of Massachusetts, Angelina and Sarah Grimké were warned against speaking out on behalf of abolition with the following argument:

We invite your attention to the dangers which at present seem to threaten the female character with widespread and permanent injury. The appropriate duties and influence of women are clearly stated in the New Testament. Those duties, and that influence are unobtrusive and private, but the sources of mighty power. . . . The power of woman is her dependence, flowing from the consciousness of that weakness which God has given for her protection. . . . But when she assumes the place and tone of man as a public reformer . . . she yields the power which God has given her for her protection, her character becomes unnatural.[8]

In a similar reliance on biblical authority, New Testament professors at Uppsala, Sweden, issued the following statement in response to the demand for ordination on the part of women in 1951:

We, the undersigned, professors and lecturers in the field of New Testament exegesis at our two universities, hereby declare as our definite opinion, based on careful investigation, that ordination of women would be incompatible with New Testament thought and would constitute disobedience to the Holy Scriptures. Both Jesus' choice of apostles and Paul's words concerning the position of women in the congregation have significance on principle, and are independent of circumstances and opinions conditioned by any particular time in history. The current proposal that women should be admitted to the priesthood in the Church of Sweden must therefore be said to meet with grave exegetical obstacles.[9]

A similar position was taken by Pope Paul in his *motu proprio* on women in 1972.

In a pamphlet entitled *The Equality of the Sexes and the Condition of Women*, Sarah Grimké replied to the warnings of the Congregationalist ministers by categorically rejecting their version of God's will with her own simple conviction that God created men and women to be equal.

I ask no favors of my sex. I surrender not our claim to equality. All I ask of our brethren is that they will take their feet from off our necks, and permit us to stand upright on the ground which God has designed us to occupy. . . . To me it is perfectly clear *that whatsoever it is morally right for a man to do, it is morally right for a woman to do.*[10]

For Sarah Grimké and her sister it was a clear and simple contradiction to say that a righteous God who forbade the institution of slavery would maintain that women were inferior to men and were to remain in their place. Her convictions were born out of her experience as a woman and out of the counsel her own conscience kept with the faith.

Today the appeal to authority is not quite as blatant as it was when the Congregationalist ministers lashed out at the Grimké sisters. In the Catholic and Episcopalian traditions the denial of ordination to women often takes the form: "We can find no scriptural reason *to ordain* women," while in those denominations which have granted ordination, the barriers to women's full participation in the life of the church are far more subtle, resting on precedent, church polity, or a claim that "qualified women can't be found."

Members of The Lutheran Church—Missouri Synod are not as

subtle. Their position against women's ordination is clearly stated, being rooted in the doctrine of the "orders of creation," by which the roles of men and women are everywhere and at every time to be fixed and separate. The Reverend Peggy Ann Way, however, finds that while liberal churchmen deny the validity of this old-fashioned doctrine, they continue to act on its premises. Based on the authority of Scripture, this theology of the supraordination of men and the subordination of women is so deeply ingrained in the masculine consciousness, she feels, that it continues to operate even after the authority base has been shifted to a more sophisticated interpretation.[11] Mary Daly compares theology to an organism, in which a disease infecting one part quickly spreads to another. "It is not enough to cure a symptom," she declares, for it only disguises the fact that the disease is present at deeper levels, "ready to manifest itself in other forms."[12] This is what has happened in the development of liberal Protestant (as well as Catholic) theology.

To speak of theology is to speak of the deepest roots of man's conceptual and intellectual framework. It is the framework which enables him to define himself in relation to the stimuli that constantly impact him. Thus it is no surprise that traditional theology, with its male God and *his* orders of creation and with its myths and doctrines purporting to show that woman is responsible for sin, has always been the ultimate authority for keeping woman in her "place." Like Elizabeth Cady Stanton, who as early as 1895 and again in 1898 published *The Woman's Bible* to refute scriptural arguments for the inferiority of women, many modern church women find appeals to theological authority patently absurd. Like their proverbial heroine, Alice in Wonderland, women are waking up to a new reality, in which the old authorities, like so many packs of cards, no longer have any power to limit or define their existence. If, they contend, the authority of Scripture or of church history is one which insists on women's subordination, then it is an authority based on erroneous assumptions about the nature of human life and its ultimate destiny. It is an authority too jaded by the necessities of masculine culture to be able to be the bearer of truth.

The question of authority is the key for those who have grown up under the secure canopy of a revelatory tradition. What happens when one begins to question the stability of the poles and stays which have kept that sacred canopy aloft?[13] Two options are being exercised by women as they begin to do their own theology.

Taking the first option, one can question the validity of some of the scaffolding, pointing out that it is lodged in sand rather than stone. Perhaps some of this scaffolding will have to be torn down and replaced with other, more secure, supports; but the sacred canopy is left intact. Women who pursue this line of inquiry accept the timeless validity of the Judeo-Christian God-revelation but attempt to correct the content and direction of that revelation—discerning the kernel of truth, the revealed Word, from the distorting cultural accretions which have grown up around it. In exercising this option, women are calling for a new hermeneutic or method of interpretation, based on the principle that God's Word can never be construed to imply their own inferiority to men. Through a renewed interest in historical biblical scholarship, women are discovering that the Word has indeed been distorted by culture. Certain elements of the message have been almost completely ignored or disregarded by the church, while more tangential concerns have been elevated to the level of ontological truth. We will see how this distortion came about through the mistranslation of particular Hebrew and Greek words and through the creation of myths and doctrines to reify, or objectify on the level of the sacred, what were essentially social or political constructs— just as the king's power in the Middle Ages was objectivized as "divine right" in order to reinforce the economic-political system of the Middle Ages.

The women who take this first option are reformers, in that they leave the Judeo-Christian canopy intact. But the reformation they envisage is every bit as powerful, if not more so, as the cataclysm which shook the church in the sixteenth century. Indeed, if the church were to take them seriously, it might find itself turned quite completely inside out.

The second option open to women who begin to question Judeo-Christian theological authority is simply to bypass that authority and to find other sources of validity for one's desire to seek the transcendent. Women who pursue this path are part of that "cognitive minority" Peter Berger describes as those "whose view of the world differs significantly from the one generally taken for granted in their society." [14] Choosing this option places one outside of the "givens" of one's cultural, theological, cognitive milieu. It allows one to raise questions about the god-experience that have never surfaced before because the perceptual and intellectual constructs in which previous theological scholarship operated did not allow their possibility. Raising such questions is like asking a doctrinaire Marxist why God allows evil. The concept of God is simply not within the Marxist cognitive framework. Not only does this "cognitive minority" raise questions which have never been raised before, but also it seeks answers to them, again, outside of the cherished authorities of Scripture, church history, denominational polity, and most theological scholarship.

While its tools, like those of the modern existentialist theologians, are largely derived from disciplines other than theology—from anthropology, depth psychology, archaeology, history—its object is not simply one of correlation as Tillich's was, but it is the discovery, or recovery, of an entirely new dimension of religious life. Its categories, therefore, are not those of philosophy but those of the poet, the mystic, the myth-maker, and the women's liberationist. If this last phrase strikes a jarring note, it is because the general public has not yet discovered the tremendous spiritual power of the women's liberation movement. The media-projected image of the demanding, strident, politicized woman is a distortion of the more numinous force which is at the heart of the movement.

The approach of this cognitive minority is revolutionary. Some might call it heretical, or even mad, but more and more women are flocking to this approach in their retreat from patriarchal structures. The search is exciting, and a trifle scary, for the way is uncharted. There are no canons and few norms against which to measure one's discoveries. The women's movement with its shared *Weltanschauung* does, however, provide that "countercommunity of considerable strength" which Peter Berger points out is necessary if cognitive deviance is to survive against the onslaught of the majority's world view.[15]

Because of the support of other women, those who flout traditional theological authorities find their way pregnant with possibility. Reflecting on her ministry, Peggy Ann Way expresses the joyously open sense of possibility which feminist theologians feel:

> I consider the authority of my ministry to be rooted in the authority of possibility. I am delighted at this point of my life that I don't have any safety or niches in Scripture or in history or in myth or in structures; I am delighted in my present understanding that the authority of my ministry is rooted in futures and in possibilities, and in a Faith experienced so profoundly that "nothing in all Creation shall separate me from the love of God which is in Christ Jesus our Lord . . ." not even Scripture, or history, or myth, or structure, or the masculine consciousness.[16]

Because the theology of the feminists refuses to adhere to

authoritative methods, traditional theologians may be tempted to label it "untheological" or "unscholarly" and thereby dismiss its contents. When this occurs, feminists are likely to respond the way Mary Daly did to a critic at Yale Divinity School who objected that her lecture was not "theology." "I couldn't have cared less whether what I was doing was or wasn't theology in his terms," she has stated. "As far as I was concerned, I was involved in a search for God. The label does not matter." [17]

The sources from which both reformist and revolutionary feminist theology arise are the life experiences of women and the reflection on these experiences which has come out of the women's liberation movement. The movement has given women a taste and feel of their burgeoning spiritual power, and out of this movement has emerged a new language, a new naming of the world, which is beginning to be appropriated in the service of a search for God.

In taking their cue from human experience, feminist theologians ally themselves with the existentialist theologians, like Tillich, rather than with the orthodox or neoorthodox school as exemplified by Karl Barth. Indeed, "Kerygmatic theology" denies, by its prior assumption of a unique and changeless revelation, the very wellsprings of the feminist search.

There is an important difference, however, in the kind of human experience used by the feminists and the Tillichians as a base from which to derive questions of meaning. Tillich's failure to identify the concrete reality behind his categories of being and nonbeing, alienation, estrangement, salvation and his attempt to find the denominator common to all of human experience in the highly abstract jargon of philosophy, renders his theology meaningless to most of those who are caught up in very concrete expressions of nonbeing and estrangement. Moreover, his failure to recognize the almost universal fact of sexual hierarchy and oppression allows the structures of sexual oppression to remain intact and vitiates the potentially radical and liberating thrust of his theology.

The feminist use of "human experience" as the matrix out of which theological questions are formed is specifically the experience of women who have come of age in the women's movement. While this experience has radical and far-reaching implications for all of humanity, it does not, at the beginning, presume to speak for the generic "human condition." Rather, it is professedly and without apology partisan. The terms it uses to talk about the human experience—such terms as "sisterhood" as opposed to "brotherhood," "consciousness-raising" as opposed to "conversion," "herstory" as opposed to "history," and many others—have concrete referents in the lives of those who use them. Feminist theology in relation to the universal is rather like the good novel or drama, whose characters shine with the spark of human recognition, not because the author set out to create an *Everyman,* but because she described particular human lives.

While the questions to be asked arise out of experience, the answers that are being arrived at are found in a variety of places; certainly they are not found in any divine decree, creed, or systematic theological treatise. Some of the answers (I would prefer to call them "directions" to indicate their dynamic rather than static or fixed nature) come out of the past—in the pre- and extra-Judeo-Christian cultures of the world. Others are found buried in the Judeo-Christian heritage itself but are likely to have been disregarded by church historians and theologians. Still others are found in the dynamic interaction of women as they get together to do theology. Many of the answers (if such there are) have not yet been found, but a process is at work in which partial answers are arrived at, while new questions are being generated.

Perhaps for the future there can be no theology—that is, no systematized body of knowledge about God—but only *theologizing,* that dialectical process of action/reflection which generates ever new questions. Paulo Freire has called this process of action/reflection in the political sphere *praxis.* The application of *praxis* to theology would mean the demise of the "theologian" in the sense of a man who develops in an ivory tower or theological seminary a systematized body of knowledge which is thereafter linked with his name. Rather, there would be many people *theologizing* out of their own experience and that of the community in which they find themselves.

This trend away from theology and toward theologizing is already apparent among both feminist theologizers and various Third-World groups. An example of the latter is to be found in a statement issued during a "Workshop on Theology in Action," held by a number of Asian church leaders in Manila in September, 1972:

> Theology begins with the experience of actual struggles, sufferings and joys of particular communities. Each of these struggles and sufferings is filled with meaning and deep human aspirations. When we speak of involvement, we are speaking of it within concrete human suffering and aspirations. We seek to make sense of experience, explore its human meaning, and discern the Spirit of Christ.[18]

While there are many women writing theological papers and books, there is no evidence of a "theologian," in the old sense, among them. Women see themselves engaged in a communal process in which women with theological degrees as well as women without them are exploring together mutual ground. The essence of the women's theological movement is that of a shared search for transcendence. It is self-consciously communal in style and in purpose, as all deviant world views must be in order to survive and win credibility.

The body of cognition and feeling, the world view being developed by women, runs counter to that set of assumptions, priorities, methods, and experiences which has dominated the Judeo-Christian world since the time of the early patriarchs. In this sense, the movement is anti-Christian, though it is profoundly religious. In order to get on with our own business, however, we have found it necessary first to exorcise this patriarchal demon from our midst. It is with the exorcism of patriarchy that the next chapter begins.

2 Exorcising the Patriarchal Demon

Exorcising demons is an ancient and venerable religious tradition, practiced by Christianity's chief medicine man (the Christ) as well as by his pagan precursors and successors. It is not often, however, that demons have been exorcised from entire cultures. Women today are attempting to exorcise the demon of patriarchalism from Western culture, and one of the ways in which they are doing this is by exorcising patriarchalism from the Judeo-Christian religious tradition which has shaped so much of the conceptual patterns as well as the values and customs of Western culture.

Since the first task of the exorciser is to call the demon by name, so women are calling that demon which has been in possession of the Judeo-Christian imagination for most of the last two millennia "patriarchalism."

The term "patriarchy," or "patriarchal," came into general parlance in the latter part of the nineteenth century, with the rise of sociology and anthropology as academic disciplines. In searching out the basis for common law and current customs in the roots of civilization, the majority of nineteenth-century scholars came to the conclusion that the first and highest form of social relations was marked by the dominance of the father of the clan over the wife and mother—hence, patriarchy. For proof of the correctness of patriarchy as the primordial and "natural" form of human relations, such scholars usually pointed to the biblical account of human origins—especially the story of Adam and Eve—to the customs of the ancient Jews, in which woman was but a chattel to her husband, and to the *patria potestas* of Roman law, in which the father exercised power over his children.[1]

If proof such as this were not enough, these scholars had only to look to the current social situation of middle- and upper-class American and European women to validate their assumption of the superiority of men and the need for strict sex-linked roles. For here, in popular culture, praised in every popular book and from every pulpit and podium, was the demure, corseted Victorian woman, content with her role as wife and mother so long as she could believe in her power to rule the world through rocking the cradle.

That this view of the superordination of men and the subordination of women was neither historically correct nor even a realistic view of the, then, current social situation appeared not to bother the upholders of the patriarchal theory of human origins. No matter that the Greek and Roman antiquarian Johann Bachofen had published *Das Mutterecht* (1861) in which, after long and patient research, he had come to the conclusion that the mother was the original center of the family and had assumed a dominant role in early societies and in the development of civilization. No matter that, following the work of Bachofen and the American anthropologist Lewis Morgan, Frederich Engels had linked the historical development of patriarchy with that of property rights and the discovery of the male's role in procreation. No matter that lower-class women had always carried physical and emotional burdens as great as their mates—perhaps even greater because of the added burden of childbearing. No matter that middle-class women were rising up *en masse* during the nineteenth century to declare their dissatisfaction with their limited sphere of life and their determination to assert their equality with men. Such women were not "real women," it was argued. They were eccentrics or "unfortunates" who were defying the God-given role for which they had been made.

The theoretical base for a different view of reality supplied by the male allies of the feminists—such men as John Stuart Mill, Bachofen, Morgan, Engels *et al.*—was inevitably ignored, if not ridiculed, by the majority in both the academic and popular culture.

One doesn't have to look back to the nineteenth century, however, to see the predominance of the patriarchal mind-set. In spite of the impact of the women's movement in recent years, there are still those who believe that women are inferior to men, that they are peculiarly suited for certain circumscribed roles in society, that they are to be loved and protected, but that their thoughts, abilities, insights, talents, and qualities are not to be given equal weight with those of men in the world outside the home. And heaven forbid that they just might be superior to men in chairing a committee, pastoring a congregation, or ruling a state! Patriarchalism has been peculiarly endemic to the discipline of theology.

In the sense in which it will be used in this book, patriarchalism refers to more than the socially prescribed hierarchy of sex roles. The term will be used to connote the whole complex of sentiments, the patterns of cognition and behavior, and the assumptions about human nature and the nature of the cosmos that have grown out of a culture in which men have dominated women.

Patriarchal thought is characterized by being objective rather than subjective, rational rather than intuitive, linear rather than circular or organic, logical rather than mystical, dissecting rather than unifying, abstract rather than concrete. Patriarchal behavior is cool and unemotional rather than warm and emotive, expedient rather than purposeless, aggressive rather than passive, unreflective rather than reflective. Patriarchal institutions tend to be ordered along hierarchical "chains of command" or "lines of authority" rather than being communal and anarchic; they are exclusive rather than inclusive and are goal directed rather than maintenance oriented.

What I have been describing sounds very much like our culture's definition of "masculinity" and "femininity," and to a large extent it is.

We should not make the mistake, however, of equating patriarchalism with the "nature" of the male, and its opposite with female "nature," for it is clear that in our changing society there are many patriarchal women and many men who exhibit the opposing or "feminine" patterns. And there have always been individuals or whole groups of people who have been expected to exhibit some characteristics of the opposite sex. The artist, for example, whether male or female, has been seen throughout most of Western history as more intuitive than logical, more emotional than rational, more unifying than dissecting. Similarly, the clergy have been expected to assume many of the so-called "feminine" traits, such as nurturance and maintenance functions, inclusiveness and emotional warmth in human relations.

Patriarchalism, then, refers to a metaphysical world view, a mind-set, a way of ordering reality which has more often been associated with the male than with the female in Western culture. While patriarchalism is only one of perhaps two or more ways of ordering the raw data of experience, it has tended to pass itself off as the *only way*. It has said of itself: "I am the very nature of things." Because it is only one way of looking at reality, it is therefore a false way, for falsity, as Mary Daly has pointed out, "often consists in partial truths being taken as the whole truth."[2]

Why have the majority in our Western culture bought the patriarchal world view? One can, of course, cite numerous examples of individuals or whole groups who have continued to hold on to a set of assumptions about the world that fly in the face of contradictory evidence. One thinks of those who, in the fifteenth century, continued to believe that the world was flat. To cite a modern example, those who continue to believe in "monolithic, expansionist communism" in spite of the contradictory evidence presented by the Communist regimes of Russia, China, and North Vietnam are examples of such a phenomenon.

Patriarchal thought and customs, however, have outlasted almost all other forms of self-delusion, and the feminist is bound to ask: Why? Perhaps part of the answer lies in the tremendous hold which Judeo-Christian religious tradition, with its implication of cosmic veracity, has had over Western culture until recently.[3] Judeo-Christianity grew out of a patriarchal culture and its basic expression continues to this day to be characterized by a patriarchal ethos. Since the subjugation of women has been a worldwide phenomenon, we can assume that the other so-called "higher religions" played a similar role in legitimizing and reinforcing patriarchal thought and customs in the cultures in which they were dominant. We are chiefly concerned, however, with what took place in the West.

Much of the tradition has been demythologized in recent years. The existentialists began the process; Bishop John Robinson in *Honest to God* dealt it a crushing blow, while Harvey Cox and the "God is dead" theologians finished it off—or so they thought. But although the essential content of the Christian myths and doctrines were shown to lack efficacy in the modern, urban, technological world, the essentially masculine outlook of the faith, curiously enough, was never demythologized.

As Jung has demonstrated, symbols, myths, and images, much more than concepts, have a powerful role to play in the shaping of the human personality and, quite possibly, in the shaping of the state; for myths and symbols touch the deepest chords of our unconscious and come to affect behavior in ways that we may be totally unaware of, at least on a conscious level. Thus, although theologians have demythologized Christianity to some extent, its patriarchal myths, symbols, and images continue to infect the human imagination and to shape the culture. While it may no longer be fashionable in some intellectual circles to speak of "God, the heavenly Father," transcendent power is still imaged in the mind as a male being. The proof that this is so is revealed in the fact that almost no theologian has dared to use a feminine pronoun in referring to the Godhead. To do so would seem ludicrous, and perhaps even blasphemous!

The most fundamental failure of modern liberal theology has been its tendency to ignore the male-female relationship and the part it has played in the construction of the Judeo-Christian *Weltanshauung*. In its inability to step outside of its own deepest roots and to look at these roots from a different perspective, modern theology—including the sub-theologies of hope, of the future, of play, etc.—fails to be radically enlightening or liberating. By talking about estrangement, injustice, and oppression, but failing to make explicit the forms of estrangement, injustice, and oppression which inhere in the age-old relation of the sexes, modern theology merely perpetuates the existence of these sins in the culture which it spawned.

What has been so consistently ignored by theologians may point to a deeper truth which is at the very heart of the religious enterprise. By calling the demon of patriarchalism by name, we are able to separate it from its matrix in the religious imagination and to discern what effects it has had on the development of the Judeo-Christian world view. In calling this demon forth out of its host, the feminist movement is thus opening humanity up to a truly revolutionary cleansing and healing process. Mary Daly, a feminist theologian, has called the women's movement "very possibly the greatest single hope for the survival of religious consciousness in the West."[4]

In order to exorcise this demon, we will have to use a different set of tools than the ones normally used by theologians in discussing their subject. As we have seen, theology up to this point has been incapable of providing the intellectual stance necessary to examine its most fundamental assumptions. Most theology has been apologetic; that is, it has attempted to explain, justify, or defend the contents of some given faith to the faithful—or to the faithless, as the case may be. For our purposes, however, a willing suspension of belief is required. The Judeo-Christian enterprise must be seen, not as revealed truth of an ontological nature, but as a certain body of knowledge, developed by a certain segment of the human community during particular socio-economic-political-historical circumstances and having a particular function for the group of people for whom such knowledge operated.

The analysis of the role and function of religion delineated by Peter Berger in *The Sacred Canopy* is a useful cognitive tool with which to approach this task of exorcism. Berger, a well-known sociologist, points out that the most important function of any society is that of "nomization" or *naming* the world. Out of the myriad impressions, feelings, sense stimuli, and experiences that *homo sapiens* is bombarded with, our species is compelled— almost by the force of instinct—to impose an order on reality, to name the world. To fail to order experience would be to live in anomic terror. Conversely, says Berger, to inhabit a society, to order one's life according to the meanings imposed by that particular society, is to be "sane."

The set of social institutions and products which humans create in the process of imposing meaning on the world is culture. In time, culture comes to assume an objectivity above and beyond its human creators—a kind of ontological givenness which is impervious to questioning. It is then internalized by its human creators and comes to assume the character of being "in the nature of things." It acquires, says Berger, a "self-legitimating facticity." Thus, the "family," "democracy," "communism," "Christianity," the "English language," and so on have all acquired an ontological status apart from the human situation which gave rise to them.

Since culture is ultimately a product of human interaction—a human imposition of meaning upon the cosmos—it is inevitably bound to change or to be challenged. When a challenge appears, in whatever form, the self-legitimating facticity of the particular social order can no longer be taken for granted, but must be explicated and defended both for the sake of the challengers and those meeting the challenge.

Challenges to a particular world view can take many different forms. The most basic challenge comes with the impingement on consciousness of the fundamental anomic terror of chaos or meaninglessness, as experienced in sleep, in drug-induced altered states of consciousness, in the death of a loved one, or in the destruction of an ordered reality as brought about by an earthquake or a political upheaval. The challenge can also occur with the juxtaposition or imposition of an alternative world view to the one held by a particular society. The cultural shock experienced by missionaries and anthropologists who are not adequately prepared to meet up with a different world view is an example. Similarly, the determination by many women to claim equal status with men—thus to assert a different set of assumptions and operating principles for human relations—is for some a frightening challenge to the time-honored "givenness" of woman's inferiority. The shock waves which the women's movement has generated throughout Western society, and the ridicule or vehemence with which it has been attacked in some quarters, are indicative of the fear of anomic terror which occurs whenever old certainties and supports are seriously challenged.

Berger distinguishes three different levels of legitimation which are brought to bear by a society whenever a challenge is made to a particular *Weltanshauung.*[5] The first legitimation is on the pretheoretical level. It is the simple, traditional affirmation: "This is how things are done"; or "That is the way life is"; or the parent's response to the child's acultural question: "But *why* do I have to do that?" "Because *I* said so!"

The second level of legitimation is incipiently theoretical and occurs in the form of proverbs, moral maxims, and traditional wisdom which may, in turn, be translated into myths, legends, or folktales. Such stories, told from one generation to another, bear time as a legitimating factor, plus emotional and imaginative weight in the way they are told. For example, the traditional wisdom that "girls are fickle" is given further imaginative credence in the myth of Eve's seduction by the serpent.

The third level is theoretical; that is, specific sectors of the social order are explained and justified by means of specialized bodies of "knowledge." To use, again, our example of sex-linked characteristics: woman's ostensible fickleness, inconstancy, or inferiority (and, therefore, the need to keep her out of the social world as much as possible) are legitimized by Freud's theory that "anatomy is destiny." In regard to this level of legitimation, it is interesting to note that Freudianism—which has been credited by feminists with the psychological crippling of women—developed at about the time that the earlier movement for women's emancipation was beginning to shake the very foundations of Western culture.[6]

An even higher form of theoretical legitimation is represented by political ideologies and by religion. Through the broad sweep of these all-embracing constructs (some more all-embracing than others), the totality of humanity's institutions and products are legitimated on a cosmic scale. Religion has been the most effective legitimation of all because it mediates for humanity the threat of meaninglessness (evil, chaos) to the socially constructed world. Religion defines and gives a meaningful place to what is most baffling about the human experience. In doing so, it provides a shield or sacred canopy against the terror of the universe.

As Berger reminds us, all legitimation serves to maintain reality as it is defined in a particular human collectivity. This means that specific institutions and roles within a given society are endowed with cosmic status which sets them above and beyond their historical particularity. "The institutions are thus given a semblance of inevitability, firmness and durability that is analogous to these qualities as ascribed to the gods themselves."[7]

Just as the order of society is linked to the all-embracing sacred order of the universe by religion, so religion links that which goes against that order with the "yawning abyss of chaos"—"the oldest antagonist of the sacred."[8] To go against the order of society as legitimated by religion (to deny its cosmic reality) is to make a compact with the primeval forces of darkness—and those who go against it are then seen as either evil or mad. Thomas Szasz, in *The Manufacture of Madness,* his brilliant comparison of modern psychiatric institutions with the institution of the medieval Inquisition, points out that the witch and the person diagnosed as mentally ill today are merely social deviants who question or deny the world view legitimated by the Christian church in the Middle Ages and now by the modern religion of psychiatry.

With Berger's analysis of the role and function of religion for society in mind, we are now ready to examine in more detail the patriarchal character of Judeo-Christianity and to point out the way in which it functioned for the society which gave it birth and which it, in turn, legitimized.

A sociological approach to the study of theology makes it possible for the student to examine the emotional, psychological, and philosophical presuppositions of the major concepts and images inherent in that theology from a position other than that of the believer. Let us first, then, try to state with as much clarity and simplicity as possible, the salient philosophical world view which Judeo-Christianity postulates. Such an attempt is frought with the danger of being overly simple or stereotypic in its analysis, since obviously the proliferation of churches and the thousands of scholarly books on Christian theology indicate that there is no one body of doctrine or belief that can be said to represent "the faith." On the other hand, the very fact that it is so often referred to as "The Faith" or "Christianity" or that its believers are referred to as Christians does indicate a certain body of beliefs held in common.

The central belief that Christians hold in common is the idea that there is a transcendent power or being—a some *thing* outside of human comprehension and experience—and that power or being has the characteristics of being omnipresent, omnipotent, and infinitely good. Secondly, that being whom man has named God is creator of the world, the ground of all being. As such, he gives order to the universe. Man understands that order and how to live in accordance with it through two revelations or epiphanies of God to his human creatures. The first was his revelation to the Hebrew people through several miraculous events which took place starting in the dark prehistory of man's evolution and were recorded in what has come to be known as a sacred book of history—the Old Testament. The second and most important revelation for all time was God's incarnation in Jesus of Nazareth who lived in a region of the Near East about two thousand years ago. Through Jesus Christ's life, but more importantly through his death, God has given signals to humanity about how it is to order its life and how it is to think about the two great and mysterious abysses—birth and death—which encompass man's existence on this earth.

According to God's revealed plan, man is born in order to glorify his creator. He is the most important creature among all that God created, and in his position of dominion over all other creatures he mirrors God's dominion over the world. Thus, he is made in the "image" of God. But humanity's existence is also marked by a condition variously called original sin, the Fall, or estrangement (in modern existentialist jargon). According to this theory, man has been *given* the freedom to disobey God, and when he does this, he commits sin. Sin, then, is the human equivalent of cosmic evil or disorder—a turning away from the order or chain of command imposed by God. What causes man to sin is his pride—his failure to remember that he is not God but a creature who is to obey the God-given order set down in the holy books and exemplified in the person of Christ. But man has a way out if he chooses to disobey God. God incarnated himself in Christ and was crucified so that man will not be forever doomed for his sins. In the manner of the scapegoat of early Hebrew cultic worship, Christ took upon himself the "sins of the world."

Therefore, we no longer need to fear death or suffering because Christ has shown that they are not the final answer. In Christ we also have a model by which to pattern our lives so as to glorify God and beat the rap of death.

Thus does Judeo-Christianity order our experience into a more or less unified whole—providing props against the cosmic terror of chaos with the assurance of God's love in the gift of his Son.

Let us now examine some of the cognitive principles apparent in this world view, as a basis for defining the social and psychological functions this world view has played in the lives of the faithful.

THE VIEW OF HISTORY, TIME, CHANGE

The first philosophical assumption inherent in the world view of the Christian is that all saving knowledge, all reality of ultimate importance is ordered by the events which took place in Palestine several millennia ago. In fact, all historical value derives from the particular periods and places recorded in the Scriptures.

While the mysterious prehistory of the ancient Aegean world may be of interest to scholars and archaeologists, it has no saving value for the Christian. He can learn nothing that is of real worth to the ordering of his present life through a study of the religion and politics of classical Greece, through a study of the science of the early Egyptians, or through a study of the folkways and magical fertility rites of antique neolithic villages. Nor for that matter are Buddhism, Hinduism, Taoism, or any other "isms" of any real significance. Instead, the ways in which the Christian's society is to be ordered have their source and eternal paradigm in the ways set down in the Old and New Testaments—but particularly, for the Christian, in the New Testament. In fact, so bound up is history with the events recorded in the Gospels, that all time in Western Christendom is calculated from the birth of Jesus.

In this view, religiously expressed meaning which predates the central events embodied in the Judeo-Christian hagiography is pejoratively labeled "primitive" or "pagan" and, with those labels, dismissed. The polytheistic pantheons of the ancient world are somehow not as "advanced" as the single God, Yahweh, of the Old Testament; and the wrathful Yahweh of Jewish tradition, in turn, is considered not as mature a concept as that of the self-sacrificing heavenly Father of the New Testament. Wolfhart Pannenberg, considered one of the more progressive of the modern Christian theologians, continues a long-held Christian assumption in the following statement: "The archetypes of myth arose in the history of man's experience of divine reality, and just as surely were these myths refuted by the same process of historical change."[9] Two assumptions, both refutable, are implicit in that statement: (1) Historical fact is more advanced than mythic or archetypal thinking, and (2) early religious concepts and practices are *refuted* by the events of history—hence, history equals progress.

But for the Christian, history means progress only in relation to the Christ event. Religious expression, whether old or new, which exists outside of the Judeo-Christian patterns of cognition is ignored, considered inferior, or in some cases it is evil—the "work of the Devil."

Since all historical value for the Christian derives from or is related to a specific historical past (the incarnation), Christian eschatological theory thus views the future as a fulfillment of that past. Just as Jesus was seen as the new Adam, so the future will be a fruition, a fulfillment of the events set into motion in the first century A.D. History, then, in the Christian world view, is a progressive, linear movement from first cause (God) to effect (the eschaton) in which the promises made in the past will be redeemed. Once the doctrine of creation *ex nihilo* was interpreted allegorically rather than literally, Christian history was easily reconciled with Darwin's evolutionary time scheme in which the earlier event was viewed as a more primitive precursor of the later. So easily do the two views of history—the Christian and the scientific—blend together, that one wonders what all the fuss was about. Of course, this view of history as progression from lower to higher was brought to its logical conclusion in the work of Teilhard de Chardin.

The linear view of time and history can be contrasted with two other views of time and change which, for the most part, Christian theology ignores. The first is the cyclical view, which has its paradigm in the seasonal changes of the earth. In this metaphysic, time is revolving or circular, birth leading to death and death becoming life again. A modification of the cyclical view of time and change is that expressed in ancient Chinese wisdom in the concept of the Tao. Here, the ordering principle of the universe is summed up in the interlocking relationships of two primary cosmic principles, *yin* and *yang,* which, like the seasons, are opposite poles that flow in and out of each other and are dependent upon each other for their existence. Modern atomic science and mathematics incorporate this theory of change; the disciplines of ecology and ethology have discovered it; and the Jungian school of psychology has legitimated it with respect to human dynamics.

Still a third theory regarding time and change—more an option or a possibility for reflection on than an ordering principle like the first two—posits the idea that change can occur spontaneously and cataclysmically. What occurs afterward may not bear any relationship to what went before. This theory of change is a window on that dark chaos against which the other two ordering principles are posited. If change can occur in this way, then there is no order to history, no guiding principle to the universe. Anything is possible. The absurd dramatists of recent years—Becket, Arrabal, and company—have explored this idea; Immanuel Velikovsky in his books *Worlds in Collision* and *Earth in Upheaval* has presented an astonishing body of evidence and speculation that such cataclysmic physical changes could have occurred to the planet in the not too distant past; and the sciences of astro and subatomic physics are beginning to find more irrationality at the heart of the cosmos.

GOD AND THE IMPERIALISTIC CONSCIOUSNESS

No matter how modern theologians have tried to demythologize and deanthropomorphize the mysterious order for which humanity yearns, it has invariably been envisioned as a "being," a some-*thing* apart from our material matrix. Throughout most of Judeo-Christian history, of course, it has been more particularized than a "being." It has been a male being—a Father, Lord, King, or Master. God's maleness, it was argued, was not derivative, however, but was in the very "nature of things," just as his other qualities of infiniteness, omnipresence, and omnipotence were.

Man's nature derived from God, not God's from man. The categories were temporal: man is finite, but God is infinite. The categories were also spatial: God is the supreme Other, *to* whom man looks *out* and *up*. Man defines himself only in relation to an Other from whom he is different. He is similar, too, but much more different—for the categories are also value laden: God is supremely good, but man, well—he is burdened with a sinful nature.

For most of its history, the Christian doctrine of the relation between God and mankind has been one of dichotomy and polarity: Man versus God; me versus not-me. This subject-object split is apparent in the very first words of faith that the Judeo-Christian learns: "In the beginning God created. . . ." God and his creation are separate. This creation myth is distinctly different from those of other cultures and religions—for example, those in which heaven and earth are created through a warring of the gods, or those in which the world comes into being by the splitting off of the divine principle from itself—and this fact has had a particular function for the shaping of Judeo-Christian culture, as we shall shortly see.

Most of the earlier attempts by theologians to bridge the gap between God and man were dismissed as heresies; and although modern theologians have emphasized God's immanence and his continuous acting *in* and through history, it is the subject-object split which continues to act upon the popular Christian mind. The average Christian prays *to* God in a radically different sense from the way in which the Buddhist meditates.

The Christian's mode of defining himself—by focusing on his difference or distance from an Other—has had far-reaching social reverberations. Simone de Beauvoir, in her classic book *The Second Sex,* has called this process the "imperialism of the human consciousness" and has laid the subjugation of women to men throughout most of history, at the feet of this ostensibly ontological necessity of human development.

> She [woman] is defined and differentiated with reference to man and not he with reference to her; she is the incidental, the inessential as opposed to the essential. He is the Subject, he is the Absolute—she is the Other.[10]

De Beauvoir criticizes Engel's thesis that the oppression of women came about as a result of the institution of private property and the possessiveness and tendency to dominate that the law of primogeniture engendered. Instead, she asserts, "If the human consciousness had not included the original category of the Other . . . the invention of the bronze tool could not have caused the oppression of women."[11]

Although her work is considered a classic on the subject of the relation between the sexes, de Beauvoir is, I believe, mistaken in her analysis. Having been groomed in the European patriarchal intellectual tradition, she was unable to believe that the mature human consciousness could define itself in any other way than by separating itself from an Other which is valued as good or evil, superior or inferior. Without denying the necessity of the consciousness in some way to differentiate itself from other consciousnesses, it does not necessarily follow that values need be attached to that differentiation. Eastern cultures have certainly stressed other forms of consciousness; the women's movement is proving that one's identity can be established by focusing on similarities rather than differences; and the Chinese revolution has demonstrated that the transcendent, ambitious, dominating ego is not a necessary development in the progress upward from ape to man, from "primitive" to "civilized," but is very much a product of the kind of institutions and cultures which mold it.

Berger's analysis of the role religion plays in legitimating social constructs is crucial here. Might not the tendency to define the self in relation to a subordinate or superordinate Other and to consider this gestalt an immutable "fact of nature" be predicated upon the God-man relationship at the heart of the Judeo-Christian religious tradition?

Let us look at the cultural situation in which such a paradigm was born. Judeo-Christianity, with its concept of transcendence as a "Lord," "King," "Almighty Father," omnipotent, holy "Other," was born in the culture of a seminomadic tribe, whose wandering life and final settlement in Palestine depended on the physical strength and leadership of strong males. In the popular mind, their tribal god, over a long period of time, came to take on the character of the male leader, or potentate, who enforced rules and regulations, maintained discipline, sat in judgment over disputes, and led the tribe into battle.

The religion of the Canaanites (the ancient Near Eastern inhabitants of Palestine against whom the Israelites saw themselves in opposition and from whom they eventually had to conquer the land) was characterized by a wholistic world view, in which the salvation of the individual was bound up with the community and the community with the renewal of the earth. The divine pantheon of these peoples included both gods and goddesses, the principle figures being the goddess Asherah and her son or husband Baal, whose death and resurrection were enacted annually in cultic ritual, often with priestesses serving as ritual prostitutes. Canaanite religion thus reflected female principles as well as male and was tied to the earth and to sexuality.

For a long while the cult of the patriarchal, other-worldly Yahweh of the Israelites existed in Palestine alongside the cult of Baal-Asherah; and the Old Testament records the many attempts that were made by Israelite purists to purge the culture of these "corrupting" influences. E. O. James reports: "On the wall at Mizpeh temples of Asherah and Yahweh appear to have stood side by side in the ninth century B.C., and to have survived until the city was destroyed." [12] Archaeological relics of the goddess cult are to be found throughout the region, indicating its persistence until the postexilic period in which Yahwism emerged "purged of its Canaanite and Mesopotamian accretions." [13]

Against this background, Israel's faith was struggling to define itself. Some time after the Babylonian exile of the Jews, probably in the first millennium B.C., Yahwism emerged, shorn of its feminine and bodily influences (except in the subordinate image of Israel as the bride of Yahweh, dependent on and submissive to her Lord), and cut off from its connection with the seasonal renewal of the earth. This trend can be seen most clearly in the prophets, but it can be "found in the Psalms, the liturgy of the temple cult, as well." [14] The old earth festivals were reinterpreted to refer to historical events in the Sinai journey, and renewal/salvation was projected onto a messianic future. [15] The concept of God as the male Lord of Hosts, presiding over a fallen and sinful people—a God who was as different from man as man was from woman—triumphed at last. The objectifying patriarchal consciousness, defining itself in relation to an Other either superior or subordinate, had thus established itself in the Hebrew imagination.

This process of objectification was brought to its ultimate conclusion with the development of Hellenic Platonism and its incorporation into Christian theology in the first few centuries A.D. Through this syncretization, the purely spiritual world and body-negating *logos* of the Greek philosophers was wedded to the transcendent Lord of Hosts to form the divine *Logos* of which the apostles John and Paul speak.

Thus, the ultimate Other, the source of all truth, goodness, beauty, and order was even more removed from the vicissitudes of human affairs and the changing cycles of nature, birth, growth, and death. Since God could only be known by the intellectual soul through the exercise of pure reason and will, the body and its contrary necessities were seen as that which pulled man away from God—i.e., "the spirit is willing, but the flesh is weak." The body, therefore, was evil. It was the principle of disorder which revolts against spirit. Since women had always been more associated with the body (through menstruation and childbirth), they were objectivized by the Church Fathers as the embodiment of the antithesis of God. Woman, in effect, was body, as this passage from Thomas Aquinas's *Summa Theologiae* indicates:

> Father and mother are loved as principles of our natural origin. Now the father is principle in a more excellent way than the mother, because he is the active principle, while the mother is a passive and material principle. Consequently, strictly speaking, the father is to be loved more.[16]

All the basic dualities, Rosemary Ruether has pointed out—"the alienation of the mind from the body, the subjective self from the objective world, the individual from the community, and the spirit from matter"—are summed up in the alienation of the masculine from the feminine which reached its dichotomizing apex in the patristic theology of the church. "The psychic traits of intellectuality, transcendent spirit and autonomous will that were identified with the male left the woman with the contrary traits of bodiliness, sensuality and subjugation."[17] Society has yet to recover from this alienating influence.

THE HIERARCHICAL WORLD VIEW

The idea or doctrine of the "orders of creation" upon which so much of Judeo-Christian tradition rests is a natural development of the dichotomizing consciousness which defines itself in opposition to an Other, either superior or inferior. In this doctrine, all of creation is ordered into a hierarchical pattern of relationships, which may be schematized by a ladder with God on the top rung followed by the Angels, Jesus, Men, Women, Children on down to the lowliest creatures at the bottom.

As we have seen, in the masculine culture of ancient Palestine, God took on the characteristics of the male leader. Since women were, for the most part, camp followers in a nomadic culture, they came to be seen as secondary creatures to males, who assumed more of the characteristics the society had projected onto their God. In ancient

Hebrew society, woman was in every sense a secondary creature, in many respects a mere chattel of her husband. Not only was she secondary, but because of the superstition about menstrual blood and the earthiness of childbirth, she was ritually unclean, having to spend great periods of her life in seclusion. By law and custom women were excluded from both the privileges and responsibilities of religious life. Only males could speak to and for God, and only males were the rightful inheritors of the Jewish name and tradition—the true Israelites.[18] The discovery of the Dead Sea Scrolls some years ago has "provided us with further evidence for the strictly masculine structure of Jewish religious life."[19]

Thus, the socially functional predominance of the males in primitive Hebrew society—i.e., the need for the nomadic tribe to have confidence in strong male leadership and to have women who would bear children for the continuance of the race—was eventually externalized into a fixed "order of existence" ostensibly created at the beginning of time by a divine masculine God. This cosmic order of creation, in turn, was the major factor which gave the divine legitimation to all of the laws and customs which kept women subordinate to men.

The divine sanction for a hierarchical ordering of creation was impressed upon the imagination through myth and symbol. The myth of God's creation of the earth, of man as his crowning achievement and woman as a secondary helpmate, made to fill Adam's loneliness, has played a powerful role in the Christian imagination down through the centuries. In spite of the more egalitarian view of the postexilic priestly editions of the Old Testament ("so God created man in his own image; male and female he created them"), it has been the rib, the apple, and the serpent which have continued to influence the Judeo-Christian view of the roles of the sexes and their part in creation.

As the doctrine of the orders of creation became solidified in Christian tradition, it provided a world view that was simple and secure. With each part of creation having its own specified rung on a hierarchical ladder of values, confusion (i.e., chaos) need not obtrude its terrifying countenance. Each creature had its own place and knew its duties. Any aberrance from that scheme was labeled evil, or "unnatural," because this was deemed to be the very order of creation itself. The scheme which had emerged in the era following the death of Christ might look something like this:

God = Goodness, order
Angels
Jesus
Men
Women
Children
Beasts
Plants
Earth
Evil, Chaos

As God is the ruler and creator of his world, so man is to rule woman who is beneath him. She, in turn, rules children who are beneath her. This hierarchical image of the ruler and the ruled, the superior and the subordinate, is clearly exemplified in the following prescriptions of Paul:

> But I want you to understand that the head of every man is Christ, the head of a woman is her husband, and the head of Christ is God (1 Corinthians 11:3).

> Wives, be subject to your husbands, as to the Lord. For the husband is the head of the wife as Christ is the head of the church, his body, and is himself its Savior (Ephesians 5:22-23).

By analogy, then, man is woman's savior; only by being subject to him in matrimony can woman achieve redemptive grace. This idea of marriage—that woman finds fulfillment in and through a man—has continued to rule the lives of women down to the present and has been the source of much unhappiness and depression when women have realized at some point in their lives, that being subject to a man has not brought about that happiness they had sought for so long.

But this hierarchical paradigm has had other ramifications throughout Western society, for it has been the cognitive basis for almost all of our human relationships. Those who have identified themselves with God have used the paradigm to rationalize their subjection of others. The idea of man's domination of the earth, a notion which many now see as having led to our destructive rape of nature, is based on the orders of creation. So, too, was the king's "divine right" to rule over others, his "subjects." The slavemaster's right to oppress beings he considered inferior was based on the slavemaster's view of himself as higher up on the ladder of creation than the slave; while the slave's unrebellious subjection was due to his internalized image of himself as ontologically (in the order of creation) inferior. In this respect, it is interesting to note the direct parallel between the subjection of woman to man and the subjection of slave to master. Gunnar Myrdal has pointed out in an appendix to *An American Dilemma* that when a legal status was needed to justify the institution of slavery in the seventeenth century, the slaveholders turned to the English laws then extant which prescribed the subjection of women and children, and to certain passages in the Holy Scriptures. The feminists' claim that the idea that the subjection of women to men is the primordial form of all subsequent oppressive and alienating relationships may have its corroboration in evidence like this.

The superior-subordinate gestalt is deeply ingrained in Western culture and traditions. It is written into the laws which restrict the legal power of woman and determine her economic and emotional dependence on men; it governs society's view of children as inferior beings (the usual euphemism is "immature") who are to be subject to adults no matter how poorly the adults behave. (Children in our society have almost none of the rights accorded their elders in the Constitution—not even the right to life, liberty, and the pursuit of happiness! They can be incarcerated without ever having committed a crime as defined by adult standards, and they are denied the right to counsel and due process of the law.)

The superior-subordinate paradigm has governed almost every conceivable human relationship: that between husband and wife, parent and child, boss and employee, priest and parishioner, president and people, teacher and student, principal and teacher, affluent and poor, white and black, brown, yellow, or red, American and foreigner. It is a pecking order in which the direction of flow is from superior to subordinate, and not the other way around. At its best it is paternalism; at its worst, tyranny.

This primordial cognitive pattern is so deeply internalized in Western consciousness that it is hard for most people to conceive of a society in which this paradigm would not govern human affairs. Threats to its existence uncover the latent fear of anarchy or chaos, and the status quo is rationalized in the same hierarchical terms—the fear that the oppressed if given power will become, in turn, the oppressor. This fear of the dissolution of hierarchical roles was illustrated for me recently in conversation with a Methodist bishop at a meeting I attended in which a number of clergy and their spouses were questioning the bishop on his system of appointments. The possibility of a co-pastorate was raised, and the bishop was asked whether he would be willing to consider such an arrangement, one in which two people had equal status and equal duties. The bishop replied that such an arrangement could not possibly work, that two adults could not work together as equals! One would have to be made the senior pastor and the other the associate. "The buck has to stop somewhere" was the bishop's justification. The same attitude is expressed by many men when confronted with a coequal marriage arrangement: "But somebody *has* to wear the pants in the family," is the reply.

These examples illustrate the complete internalization of that hierarchical world view developed so long ago in ancient Palestine. As I have pointed out, this world view was first given cosmic significance in the Old Testament images of God and in the Law alleged to have been handed down from God to Moses. It was further legitimized in the first few centuries A.D. when Hebrew thought was infused with Greek Neoplatonism, establishing still other hierarchies—that between soul and body, mind and matter. All along the way, of course, the hierarchical model was concretized in taboos, in law, in customs, and in language, thus shaping for subsequent generations the very patterns of perception itself.

Far from being antithetical to the religious outlook of Judeo-Christianity, modern science built upon the psychic foundation set by religious tradition, with its hierarchy of values and relationships, its dichotomizing and imperialistic consciousness always ready to assert its own being in opposition to an inferior Other which it could subjugate and manipulate. Theodore Roszak has shown the relation between science and Judeo-Christianity most clearly in his book, *Where the Wasteland Ends:*

> The melodramatic confrontation between Galileo and the Church (usually misread), often obscures the truth of the matter. What was most revolutionary about the revolution was not the struggle with Christian religious psychology, but with its overlay of inherited Aristotelian concepts. . . . What science did was to extract from western man's religious psychology its well-developed idolatrous disposition and to elaborate the experience of nature that lay within it—at first with every expectation that this fresh worldview would serve piety, not detract from it.[20]

Playing out Roszak's thesis, what was social Darwinism but the old "orders of creation" denuded of its religious imagery? Or what was Freudianism with its hierarchical relationship between id, ego, and superego but the translated relationship between nature (woman), man, and God? Indeed, there is very little practical difference between

Freud's dictum on women that "anatomy is destiny," and Aquinas's statement that the mother is to be loved less because she is the "passive" and "material" principle.

GOD, MAN, AND DIVINE DESTINY

Another assumption or ruling concept integral to the patriarchal nature of Judeo-Christian theology is the concept of God as the other-worldly ruler and shaper of his creation. While much scholastic ink was spilled over the attempt to reconcile the doctrine of creation *ex nihilo* with Darwin's theory of the evolution of the species, the conflict was essentially a spurious one, for the doctrine of the orders of creation had already paved the way for the incorporation of God's creative power with the evolutionary scheme of beginnings. Thus, to this day, the assumption remains that God is somehow responsible for what happens on earth—even for the evolutionary process itself—and that he has a plan, a destiny that humans can buy into, if they choose.

An image which recurs throughout the Old Testament to sum up the relationship of God to his creation is that of the potter and the clay. God was seen as the molder, the shaper, the manipulator, while man was the raw material to be shaped. This image also lurks behind the story of Adam's creation. The familiar hymn, "Spirit of the living God . . . melt me, mold me, fill me, use me," reflects this primordial image.

For Calvin, this mold or plan was fixed, or predetermined, for each person. Modern theologians are more subtle in their interpretation, believing in the need for a theology which reflects an openness to the future. Yet even in the work of a theologian of the future, like Pannenberg, the image of the potter and the clay lurks suspiciously in the background. Listen to Pannenberg's words:

> God's futurity was hidden in the beginnings of human religion. . . . When man asserts himself against the future, he misses his authentic existence, betrays his *destiny* to exist in full openness toward what is *to be,* and abdicates his participation in God's *creative* love.

> The process of history is God's *instrument* in the education of humanity, bringing man to the awareness of his historicity and thus completing his creation [italics mine].[21]

How free from the notion of predestination are these statements by a theologian who claims to turn conventional ideas of time inside out?

This image of God as the divine manipulator or shaper (and its corollary that man is to fill or fit that shape or fulfill that destiny for which he was made) has several psychic and social ramifications. First, it limits vision and the possibility of dramatic newness. If man has a destiny, then all the theological talk about "finite freedom" (Tillich's term) or "free will" has little substantial meaning. In spite of Pannenberg's claim to be completely open to the future, the language and images operating beneath his rhetoric belie his ostensible openness to radically new possibility. We have the familiar picture of the theoretician's intentions at odds with his declarations, rather like the mother who allows her teenage daughter the "freedom" to stay out late on a date and then sits by the door all night worrying until the daughter comes home.

Moreover, if one believes that man has a specific destiny to fulfill, he is tied to role models and forms of identification which some group or person at some particular point in history has decided is the pattern of behavior which best fits that destiny. Throughout history men have taken upon themselves (though ostensibly speaking for God) the authority to define another's destiny for them, often with tragic and oppressive results. This is especially apparent in the "destiny" set out for women by men speaking on God's behalf. For example, Paul: ". . . and man was not created for woman's sake, but woman for the sake of man . . ." (1 Corinthians 11:9, NEB). Or John Knox: "Woman in her greatest perfection was made to serve and obey man, not to rule and command him."

In Karl Barth's theology of the creation *(Church Dogmatics)* we find an example of the idea of divinely ordered destiny carried to its penultimate conclusion. He begins thus: "What God's command wills for man and woman is that they should be faithful to this their human nature and to the special gift and duty indicated in and by it." This human nature, he goes on to explain, is summed up in their creation as male and female. Admirably (or so we think!) he goes on to say that being male and female does not mean that society's typologies of "masculinity" and "femininity" are to be accepted as normative of behavior.

They may have value in other directions, but they are certainly not adapted to be a valid law for male and female, and we can only cause the greatest confusion if we try to exalt them into such a law and use them as such. . . . The specific differentiation particularly of male and female which are at issue in the *divine command* and its *requirement of fidelity* lie somewhere above and beyond the sphere in which such typologies are relatively possible and practicable. [italics mine—but notice the language!]

Then, after one-half page spent refuting the idea of immutably fixed sex-linked roles, Barth concludes with the following astonishing about-face!

> Just because the command of God is not bound to any standard it makes this distinction [between the sexes] all the more sharply and clearly. This distinction *insists* upon being observed. It *must not* be blurred on either side. The command of God will *always* point man to his position and woman to hers. In *every situation*, in face of every task and in every conversation, their functions and possibilities, when they are obedient to the command, will be distinctive and diverse, and will *never* be interchangeable.

Further on, acknowledging the incipient feminist movement, he elaborates on this distinction:

> The essential point is that woman must always and in all circumstances be woman; that she must feel and conduct herself as such and not as a man; that the command of the Lord, which is for *all eternity*, directs both man and woman to their own proper sacred place and *forbids* all attempts to violate this order.[22]

It is interesting to examine Barth's use of language. The phrases and terms used to describe God's purposes are those of coercion, manipulation, and a kind of harsh immutability: "divine command," "requirement of fidelity," "insists," "always," "in every situation," "never," "for all eternity," "she must," the divine command "forbids," the order must not be "violated." Here God is even more than a shaper and molder, a friendly potter; he is a divine totalitarian!

Throughout most of Judeo-Christian history, separate roles or spheres for men and women have been justified on the basis of divine destiny. Woman had her sphere in the home. Her divinely instituted destiny was to bear and raise children and to serve her husband, while that of her mate was to provide for the family and to carry on the affairs of the society. This separation of roles and spheres was upheld by learned theologians as well as by theological popularizers, as this nineteenth-century Methodist minister in a book of advice to young women indicated:

> What is the sphere of woman? Home. The social circle. What is her mission? To mold characters—to fashion herself and others after the model character of Christ.... Her place is not on life's great battle-fields. Man belongs there. It is for him to go forth armed for its conflicts and struggles, to do fierce battle with the hosts of evil that throng our earth and trample upon its blessings. But woman must abide in the peaceful sanctuaries of home and walk in the noiseless vales of private life.[23]

Aside from the pompous, paternalistic tone of such admonitions, the idea of divinely sanctioned roles has led men to the expression of much cruelty toward women who did not, or would not, fit into this mold. Single women were and still are the brunt of much derisive humor and disapprobation, not to speak of economic and social discrimination, because they are not fulfilling themselves with Kinder and Küche. In doing research on female involvement in missions in the nineteenth century, Elaine Magalis found that women were severely put down by their male overlords in the church when they determined to do more for missions than knit socks and mittens:

> Women would come long distances to churches and find the doors bolted; many meetings were held on church steps. Sometimes husbands simply forbade their wives to become involved, and failing that, locked them in their bedrooms for the duration of any meeting.[24]

In an essay on the historical significance of the nineteenth-century feminist movement, Theodore Roszak has intriguingly suggested that in threatening traditional sex roles, the movement caused such a severe cultural trauma that it may actually have provided the psychic groundswell for the unleashing of violence in World War I. Far from being a quaint human interest story, as most historians have pictured it, Roszak finds evidence throughout every level of turn-of-the-century European culture that the movement was the most explosive social force of its day, precisely because it was the one social relationship that men and women took to bed with them every night. What happened when woman's traditional place was threatened was the eruption of a tremendously violent and vitriolic male backlash, resulting in an ever-increasing war mentality, a projection of male anger onto the world scene. "Compulsive masculinity," Roszak points out, "is written all over the political style of the period."[25]

The assumptions operating in the idea of divinely sanctioned sex roles are further reflected in the following statements. The first was spoken by an elderly Italian Catholic who lived in the building next door to mine in New York City. Pointing to the picture of his wife who had died many years before (her picture was enshrined in his living room alongside a life-size statue of the Madonna), he said: "You know how much my wife loved God? She loved him so much, she bore me twelve children." And, in an address to women at Nürnberg, on September 14, 1934, Hitler declared: "Woman has her battlefield. With each child that she brings to the nation, she fights her fight for the nation."[26] The subtle transformations between God, man, and state have not been lost on modern feminists.

Indeed, this all too easy tendency to identify the state with a manipulating, shaping God or with God's destiny has been too much a part of patriarchal history. It does not require a great leap in imagination to realize the links between God's destiny for man and that "manifest destiny" which provided the justification for the imperialistic expansion of white men to the western frontiers of America during the nineteenth century. Nor does it require less logic to see the well-intentioned but ill-conceived theory of the "white man's burden" of British colonialism as stemming from the Englishman's identification with God and his mission or destiny to "save" the heathen. Nor, again, is it too far removed to speak in the same vein of the destiny of the Aryan race which inspired a nation of Germans during the 1930s or the mission of America ("one nation under God") to save Southeast Asia from communism and to "make the world safe for democracy." The basic cognitive patterns for these distortions were set in motion several millennia ago with the vision of the Supreme Being of the universe as a shaper, molder, and creator of human destiny:

> Have you not known? Have you not
> heard?
> Has it not been told you from the
> beginning?
> Have you not understood from the
> foundations of the earth?
> It is he who sits above the circle of
> the earth,
> and its inhabitants are like grasshoppers;
> who stretches out the heavens like a
> curtain,
> and spreads them like a tent to
> dwell in;
> who brings princes to nought,
> and makes the rulers of the earth
> as nothing.
>
> Isaiah 40:21-23

THE MYTH OF FEMININE EVIL

"What is man that thou art mindful of him?" asked the psalmist, to which the feminist must add a coda: "And woman, that thou didst disdain her so?" For thousands of years man has speculated about the nature of his species: Are we more like the beasts or like the angels? Why do we suffer and inflict suffering on others? Do we have a purpose in the universe, or are we set down in the midst of an absurd cosmos to fret out a meaning for ourselves? For thousands of years men have done the speculating while women have lived out the prescriptions arrived at as a result of that speculation.

The most consistent answer to come out of the Judeo-Christian tradition regarding the nature of the human race has been the description of humanity as "fallen"—as from some higher or more perfect state—immersed in sin, tainted with some weakness which invariably tempts us away from our better natures. And the most consistent cause for mankind's fallenness has been laid at the feet of woman! In spite of the modern existentialist theologians' attempts to describe the state of fallenness as "alienation," "estrangement," or "existential anguish," the myth of feminine evil continues to plague the imagination of many Christians. One of the reasons for the Anglican Church's refusal to admit women to the priesthood, claim Emily Hewitt and Suzanne Hiatt, authors of *Women Priests, Yes or No?,* is an underlying strain of male fear of and antipathy toward women, which manifests itself in both fascination and distrust. The authors, both ordained deacons, seeking ordination to the priesthood, are well qualified to speak of their male colleagues' attitudes toward women.

But others have also pointed to the strain of misogyny that runs through the Christian tradition and which has tainted the manners, morals, customs, and laws of Western society right down to the present. The reader is well-versed, I'm sure, in the many faces of Eve which tantalize us from TV screens and magazines, which are implicit in "dirty jokes," in mothers' remonstrances to teenage daughters, and in laws that grant more credibility to the rapist than to his victim.

In an appendix to *The Woman's Bible,* Elizabeth Cady Stanton points out that the "real difficulty in woman's case is that the whole foundation of the Christian religion rests on her temptation and man's fall, hence the necessity of a Redeemer and a plan of salvation. As the chief source of this dire calamity, woman's degradation and subordination were made a necessity." [27] Stanton goes on to say that if we can accept the story of the Fall as merely a myth, then "we can exonerate the snake and emancipate the woman!" Unfortunately, Miss Stanton's knowledge of the function of myth was a little shortsighted. In spite of the fact that the story has been dehistoricized and understood as myth in our time, its images and events still strongly affect the emotions. The image of the Fall in generic terms has been exposed and even taken apart as myth, but the myth of feminine evil imbedded in the story remains to be examined.

As we have seen, the idea of women's inferiority became incorporated in Hebrew law and religion probably as a result of woman's necessary social subordination in the exigencies of nomadic life in early Palestine. In hunting and nomadic societies, a woman's physical disabilities, because of menstruation and childbirth, would be quite evident. Rosemary Ruether, citing the work by H. R. Hays on the myth of feminine evil in hunting societies, points out that all the taboos and rituals of uncleanness against women which are exhibited in these societies were incorporated and canonized in the Torah and Talmud and from there passed on into Christianity.[28] Thus, the exclusion of women from the hunting lodge is translated into their exclusion from the inner court of the temple and from participation in the Jewish prayers and rituals. The male hunter's fear of woman's blood as "bad manna" or as a terrible wound which might be likely to infect him becomes incorporated into laws which prescribe periods of ritual purification for women during menstruation and after childbirth (longer periods were prescribed after the birth of girls).

As Berger has shown, social constructions are projected cosmically into myths, laws, and finally metaphysical world views which then turn back upon the society which externalized them, assuming the force of cosmic truth and shaping the consciousness of future generations. In time, then, women, who had started out in Hebrew society as necessary but, perhaps, secondary partners in the masculine world of tribal nomadic life, came to be seen as unclean, inferior creatures to some extent responsible for the evils that beset the community. Against the background of the more feminine and sexual religion of the Canaanites, woman's "uncleanness" was even more pronounced in the male Hebrew mind. Women were necessary for the procreation of the race, but it was the male seed, merely housed in the female's body, which was important. At some time during Israel's long history the male's discovery of paternity occurred. It seems here to go hand in hand with the subordination of women, for the male seed plays an extremely important role throughout the Old Testament.

Textual criticism has shown that the subjugation of women and their coming to be seen as responsible for evil was a gradual process, fraught with frequent contradictions which are to be found in the texts themselves. We do have the stories of Deborah and Miriam, two strong women whose leadership roles probably reflect a very early period in the history of Israel in which the sex roles were not as differentiated as they were to become later on. Even in strands of text composed by one editor we find subtle contradictions. For example, the J or Jahwist (Yahwist) strand, probably written in the ninth or eighth century B.C., contains the story of Eve's transgression; but this strand also includes Genesis 4, in which women are mentioned without prejudice in the lineage of the nation. (The names of the daughters were later omitted from the genealogies, since only men were the true Israelites.) The P or Priestly strand, which was probably written during the Jewish exile in Babylon some time in the fifth century B.C., includes the statement that men and women (equally it is presumed) are made in the image of God ("male and female he created them"—Genesis 1:27); but this strand also includes the major genealogy of Israel's origins (Genesis 5) which lists only the names of sons.

One could argue that the story of Adam and Eve does not so much blame women for the problems of the world as it is an attempt to explain the "why" of evil (an etiological statement) using the example of weakness of will (i.e., woman) which was closest at hand to the Hebrew psyche. Indeed, it is not until Paul's writings that we find the notion of a "Fall" from some original state of righteousness as normative of the human condition.

Nevertheless, the seeds of woman's subjection and of her predilection to evil are to be found in Hebrew culture and Hebrew religious tradition, even if they were not carried to their logical conclusion until much later.Throughout the Old Testament, images of the feminine which have come down to us are either those of Israel as the subordinate and obedient bride of Yahweh (an image which Paul was later to pick up as normative of the wife's relationship to her husband) or as the disobedient Israel, whoring after false gods.

> Lift up your eyes to the bare heights, and see!
>   Where have you not been lain with?
> By the waysides you have sat awaiting lovers
>   like an Arab in the wilderness.
> You have polluted the land
>   with your vile harlotry.
>   Jeremiah 3:2-3

Similarly, the few examples of actual women in the Old Testament which have come down to us are either those of the temptresses—the Delilahs and the Jezebels—or the pure and obedient ladies—the Ruths. Woman as temptress or as subservient maiden has been the major contribution of Judaism to the Western world's conception of the feminine; while evil as disobedience, the overstepping of limits, has been the concomitant result. The myth of the Garden of Eden, with its powerfully sensuous imagery, provides the psychic base for these and later theological developments.

It was in some of the writings attributed to Paul, but more especially in the theology of the Church Fathers, that the myth of feminine evil achieved its most expressive apotheosis. In late classical times, the Hellenic world had undergone a patriarchal revolution similar to that which had occurred in ancient Palestine, although there is some speculation as to whether the lives of actual women were nearly as restricted as they were in Judaism. At any rate, the assertion of the masculine consciousness over the feminine can be traced in Greek mythology and is seen as an expression of contention in the plays of Euripides and Aeschylus.

The soul-body dualism, as it emerged in classical Greek philosophy, provided a convenient channel through which the incipient male-female dualism could be expressed; and this is exactly what happened. Paul's asceticism, his statements on the subordination of women, his pronouncement on marriage ("It is better to marry than to burn"), and his doctrine of Christ as the divine *Logos* were translated by the Church Fathers into a rigidly dualistic anthropology, in which man was equated with the mind, the soul, and with God, while woman was equated with the body, with materiality, and with sexuality—hence with all that degraded the soul and pulled it away from the divine.

In the Church Fathers the development of the myth of feminine evil is closely connected with, if not dependent on, the struggle of these men with their own sexuality in a cultural world in which the body and its functions were ontologically degraded. Augustine's own conversion was so closely connected with his conquest of sexual desire that he could never quite dissociate this desire from sin.[29] "Thus I polluted the stream of friendship with the filth of unclean desire and sullied its limpidity with the hell of lust," he related in his *Confessions*.[30] For Augustine, woman stood for the bodily "side" of man (Adam, in the Hebrew text, meant both man and woman) which was taken out of man solely to be a helpmate to man and to enable the race to procreate itself. Woman is, "in her nature," body, only a *relative being,* whereas the male possesses the full image of God.[31]

Since woman was the object of the carnal desire which pulled man away from God, which disrupted the orderly subordination of body to mind in classical ontology, she came to be seen as the initiation of that desire, as a temptress, a siren, a lurer of men to their destruction. Jerome and Tertullian lashed out with vehemence at women as the seducers of men.

> Do you not know that you are [each] an Eve?... *You* are the devil's gateway: *you* are the unsealer of that forbidden tree: *you* are the first deserter of the divine law: *you* are she who persuaded him whom the devil was not valiant enough to attack. *You* destroyed so easily God's image, man. On account of *your* desert—that is, death—even the Son of God had to die.[32]

Here is the myth of feminine evil brought to its logical conclusion: woman as the source of all evil for which Christ as Redeemer had to come. At least in regard to Tertullian, Elizabeth Cady Stanton's analysis is an understatement!

This view of women and sexual activity presented some basic problems for the Church Fathers, for how were they to reconcile the obvious need for the race to procreate itself with their view of carnality as sin? And how did they reconcile their friendship with real women with their misogynistic attack on the principle of "woman"? Their solutions to this dilemma present some interesting cases of schizophrenic thinking. For Augustine, Rosemary Ruether points out, "the man is exhorted to love his wife's spiritual nature, but to despise in her all her bodily functions as woman and wife."[33] For most of the Church Fathers coitus was seen as necessary for the production of children and was tolerated when performed in the married state, but only as a kind of lesser evil, even though theoretically it was good because ordained by God. Virginity, then, became the way to true spirituality.

Many women during this time took the church's preaching on virginity to heart, including even women who had already married. But instead of seeing these women as having overcome the same kinds of temptations as they had themselves, the Fathers responded with still more ambiguity. In a letter to a woman who had exacted a vow of continence from her husband and who had begun to dispose of her property, Augustine reproved her for acting with such boldness and against her "nature" as woman, which was to be submissive.[34]

Those unmarried women who flocked to the celibate life as the means of salvation were seen as somehow transmuted into males as Ruether indicates:

> It becomes characteristic of the Fathers, the ascetic writers especially, to speak of the virgin as having become "male," by transcending the female nature, physically and psychically. The very possibility of redemption through spiritualization is thus, for

woman, "unnatural"; a transcendence of her "nature"; whereas the male ascetic is seen as being restored to his natural male spirituality through redemption. This view extended itself into a debate over the sexual character of the risen body. It was natural to conclude, therefore, that in the resurrection from the dead, there would be only males, females being transformed into males.[35]

This degradation of the female nature, both physical and psychic, led to absurd and cruel repressions of the feminine in Christian culture. Those who aspired to the holy life had to strip themselves of any hint of their femaleness. Thus were begun the nun's confining habit and the suppression of sexuality and sexual enjoyment in females (the sexual double standard) which have lasted even down to today. The witch-hunts of the Middle Ages, in which thousands of persons (mostly women) were put to death under the aegis of the church, stem directly from this view of woman as carnality personified, as the temptress who lures man into sin; and the Catholic church's continued exclusion of women from the priesthood as well as the hardheartedness of the hierarchy's ban on contraception and abortion can all be laid at the feet of the theological view of woman and sin as it developed in the early Christian church.

Unfortunately, the Protestant Reformation did little or nothing to reform the misogyny of Christian theology. Luther regarded marriage with a little more acceptance, but saw it as God's gift to mankind to protect the virtue of chastity against the insatiable sins of the flesh, while women's sole purpose in life was to beget children. Calvin likewise saw marriage as instituted for the begetting of offspring and as a guard against incontinence; and John Knox wrote a book entitled *The First Blast of the Trumpet Against the Monstrous Regiment of Woman.*

The Puritan theocracy of New England was especially harsh on women, carrying out witch-hunts and discouraging their right to have any kind of spiritual wisdom or insights of their own. The story of Ann Hutchinson is a particularly poignant one to read. Here was a strong, spiritual woman who had taken Luther's notion of the priesthood of all believers to heart (not deigning to think that "priesthood" meant that only males could serve the Lord). When the authorities in the Massachusetts Bay colony realized that Mistress Hutchinson was spreading the word of the power of the "in-dwelling Christ" to groups of women (and some men) who were meeting in her home, they moved with ruthlessness to crush this aberrant spirit. They attacked her both through the civil court and in a religious trial, falsifying her words, denying her the right to introduce evidence in her own defense, and causing her untold physical hardship. She was pregnant during the civil trial and was not allowed to sit down until she was nearly fainting. Eventually, Ann Hutchinson was banished from the colony in disgrace, and her most ardent supporter, Mary Dyer, was later hanged. "The frequent claim that Christianity elevated the position of women must be denied," Rosemary Ruether states. "It actually lowered the position of women relative to the more enlightened legislation of later Roman society, as far as the married woman was concerned, and elevated woman in her new 'unnatural' and anti-female role as virgin."[36]

The image of woman that has come down to us through the elaboration of Christian doctrine is threefold: woman as temptress or witch; woman as body-negating virgin; and woman as wife-mother, the begetter of children and servant of her husband. As alluded to earlier, it was woman as temptress which undergirded the development of the doctrine of sin and the Fall, and its corollary the doctrine of redemption or salvation. While woman as temptress lives on in the imagination of Western man, coloring and distorting his views of sex, marriage, women co-workers, and his attitude toward his wife and daughters; woman as responsible for evil, for the Fall, has been dropped from modern theological discourse. Theologians today know better than to blame woman for everything that is wrong—or do they?

While the vitriolic attack of a Tertullian seems like an anachronistic absurdity—blaming woman for Christ's death—it is still disobedience, or pride, which is at the heart of the Christian doctrine of sin.

The coerciveness of the Father and the disobedience of the creature remain operational images. In a recent book on theology and technology published by Friendship Press, a number of prominent theologians and scientists made the following rather generalized statement: "Sin is pride, self-will, anger, insolence toward God and his creation."[37] Again and again (Tillich's more enlightened view of sin as "estrangement" notwithstanding) sin as pride, disobedience, and self-assertion is preached from pulpits, recited in prayers, and testified to in devotional literature.

Linked with this conception of sin as disobedience is its opposite— love, as obedience, self-sacrifice, taking no thought of oneself, living for others. Jesus is held up as the role model for Christians to follow in this kind of self-sacrificing love. He is "the man for others" as certain modern theologians have explained it, and this quality of living for others was "manifested supremely on the Cross."[38]

Now a curious thing happens when we conceptualize sin as disobedience or pride; for what do such concepts mean but the overstepping of limits and boundaries? And for whom has Western culture always set boundaries and limits? For women!

As we have already seen the Judeo-Christian doctrine of sin was the end product of a long series of conceptualizing events which occurred in male-dominated societies. These events started with the externalization of a patriarchal, other-worldly God who shaped and molded human destiny, and they culminated in an elaborate schema of the created order in which woman was, by virtue of her ontological place in that order, "naturally" prone to temptation, to the sin of pride, self-will, and disobedience. Man, by virtue of his closer relationship to God on the ladder of creation, had less to rebel about. In exercising his creative, managerial, and intellectual prowess, he was only living up to the image of the dominant, managerial, rational God in whose likeness he was made.

Because of the way in which Judeo-Christian symbols, myths, and images have shaped the very perceptions of Western man, where sin has been defined as pride, self-will, or disobedience, it has always functioned to keep women submissive, underdeveloped, and perpetually guilty. On the other hand, the preaching of this doctrine has allowed most men the freedom of self-expression, self-assertion, and the power to dominate and subjugate others.

Valerie Saiving Goldstein, in an essay which has had wide currency among feminist theologians, delineated the way in which Western culture, particularly in the modern era, has "emphasized, encouraged and set free precisely those aspects of human nature which are peculiarly significant to men."[39] Thus, the culture has stressed the necessity of man's separation from nature (so as to manage and subdue it); it has demanded his separation from the vegetative, self-giving, and participatory nature of childbearing and child-rearing (attention to such functions naturally slows productivity in the material world); and it has insisted on definition of the self through differentiation and competition, through transcendence over others rather than through self-transcendence. Pay, then, is based on productivity or on the recognition and status conferred on those who beat out others in the athletic, monetary, and academic games men play.

While the culture has lauded motherhood and women's virtues in name, it has, in reality, worked to deny these functions or virtues any kind of reward or status. Women's work—bearing children, caring for and nurturing the family—has never been paid for, as feminists have often pointed out. The woman who attempts to claim a reward for her work over the years as a housewife—by using her experience as a basis for seeking political office or obtaining a job—finds that she has absolutely no standing in the masculine world of "position," "experience," "degrees," or "status."

Until recently, the world of most women has been a different world from the one which men experience. Having been tied to the home and the family, with its 24-hour-a-day demands on one's time, energy, and patience, and its lack of status and direct financial rewards, women's temptations have not been the same as men's, as Ms. Goldstein points out:

> . . . the specifically feminine forms of sin—"feminine" not because they are confined to women or because women are incapable of sinning in other ways but because they are outgrowths of the basic feminine character structure [perhaps "cultural pattern" would be a more appropriate phrase] have a quality which can never be encompassed by such terms as "pride" and "will-to-power." They are better suggested by such items as triviality, distractibility, and diffuseness . . . dependence on others for one's own self-definition; tolerance at the expense of standards of excellence; inability to respect the boundaries of privacy; sentimentality, gossipy sociability, and mistrust of reason—in short, underdevelopment or negation of the self.[40]

In other words, women's sins are not the result of too much pride and self-will, but not enough of them. Her sin is not disobedience but a too willing obedience to the will and dictates of others. Yet, throughout Judeo-Christian history the sin of pride and disobedience has been preached to women who have accepted it as normative of the "human situation," not realizing that it was an expression of the excesses of the masculine (patriarchal) ethos and so did not serve to explain the temptations of their own particular cultural situation.

Thus, the story of Eve's transgression becomes every woman's transgression against her husband, her father, her boss, or whatever other male figure happens to be identified in her mind with the patriarchal God to whom she is supposed to be obedient. The myth lingers on beneath the now abstract rhetoric of pride, self-will, and even "estrangement"—where that word is insufficiently explained.

The harm that has been done to women with the perpetuation of this doctrine cannot be underestimated. At the very least, women have accepted the "correctness" of this explanation for human evil at the expense of their own full development as human beings. Let us consider just one aspect: the development of the intellect. Numerous psychological and sociological studies have shown that in the late teenage years, women's academic performance (which had earlier been ahead of the performance of their male contemporaries) begins to fall behind that of the male, in apparent preparation for their role as subordinates in the marriage relationship. Time and again, women in consciousness-raising groups have confessed the fact that as young women in the dating and mating game they had felt compelled to repress their intellectuality and to "play dumb" in order to be acceptable to men. It is a truism that strong, competent women have often been shunned as "castrating females." After conducting extensive psychological studies of bright college women, Dr. Mattina Horner, now president of Radcliffe College, came to the conclusion that women, in terms of intellectual and career achievement, actually *fear* success and behave in ways that prevent them from being successful. What is at work here is a fear of disobeying the male norm for subordination which has been set up for them.

Many women have internalized the myth of Eve's disobedience so deeply that they are continually plagued by excessive guilt whenever they feel the desire to do something for themselves—to go beyond or to renege on their prescribed role as mother, wife, or servant. One of the most frequent expressions of pain heard in consciousness-raising groups is the expression of feelings of guilt. These feelings erupt in great disproportion to the acts which occasion them. Housewives often feel guilty when their husbands "help out" at home; they feel guilty when they get angry with their children or when they want some time "for themselves." They feel guilty if they find that they don't enjoy the role of housewife or mother, and they feel guilty about wanting to go back to work. Psychologist Erik Erikson has described the preschool years as the period in which the child's increasing self-autonomy precipitates a conflict between initiative and guilt. In order to grow into a mature human being, the child must resolve this conflict in favor of purposive initiative. But the perpetuation of the Judeo-Christian paradigm expressed so vividly in Eve's eating the apple (of the tree of *knowledge!*) has served to keep many women in a perpetual state of preschool infancy in which their guilt is never resolved.

For some women, the guilt over their desire to be both women and self-actualized human beings has been intolerable. Feminist psychologist Phyllis Chesler, in her book, *Women and Madness,* indicates how this conflict literally drives women crazy:

> Women are impaled on the cross of self-sacrifice. Unlike men, they are categorically denied the experience of cultural supremacy, humanity, and renewal based on their sexual identity. . . . In different ways, some women are driven mad by this fact. Such madness is essentially an intense experience of female biological, sexual and cultural castration, and a doomed search for potency. The search often involves "delusions" or displays of physical aggression, grandeur, sexuality, and emotionality—all traits which would probably be more acceptable in female-dominated cultures. Such traits in women are feared and punished in patriarchal asylums.[41]

If sin is pride, disobedience; then, by definition, love in the patriarchal schema is obedience (to God's will), self-abnegation. Sacrificial love in the Christian tradition was most fully expressed in Christ's death: "Nevertheless, not *my* will, but *thine* be done" (italics author's). The Christian is exhorted over and over again to submit himself (herself) to the Father's will.

The Christian church transformed the Old Testament idea of a communal covenant between God and his people into the individualistic doctrine of salvation by grace. "For God so loved the world that he gave his only begotten Son, that whosoever believeth in him should not perish, but have everlasting life" (John 3:16, KJV). Jesus was the quintessential expression of that self-sacrificial love which gives of itself completely, even unto death. Whereas the Jew was saved by the adherence of the community to Yahweh's law, the Christian is saved by his individual recognition of Christ's sacrifice for him: "This is my body which is broken for you, take and eat remembering that Christ died for you and feed on him in your hearts." (See Luke 22:19; 1 Corinthians 11:24.)

The doctrine of Christ's sacrificial self-giving, of his death and crucifixion, is perhaps the central element of the Christian faith. Although we give lip service to Easter and resurrection—that is, to life and regeneration—it is death (the cross) which occupies center stage in the life and symbolism of the Christian church. It is not, however, a healthy coming to terms with our own mortality, but a dwelling on the voluntary giving up of life by someone else. We celebrate this sacrifice (Communion) every week in some churches, less often in others, but certainly more than the once-a-year ritual which is given over to a celebration of life and joy.

The early church's interpretation of Jesus' death as an atonement or a "propitiation for the sins of the world," as one Communion liturgy puts it, is merely a reinterpretation—elevated to the universal level—of the ancient ritual of blood sacrifice, by which the primitive community purified itself of evil and suffering by pouring out the blood (the vitalizing agent) of a human or animal. The giving up of life to promote and preserve life and purity has been the fundamental principle throughout the long and complex history of the ritual of sacrifice.[42]

The doctrine of the crucifixion brings together three strands of ancient Hebrew tradition. The first is the eating of the Paschal Lamb (Christ = the Lamb) to celebrate the sealing of the covenant between Yahweh and his people. In this tradition a ritually perfect lamb or kid was killed in the spring (Easter-Passover) and during the night was eaten with bitter herbs and unleavened bread, while its blood was smeared on the doorposts and the lintel in remembrance of Yahweh's passing over the houses of the Jews in his slaughter of the Egyptians. The essential purpose of the rite, explains E. O. James, was that of imbibing sacramentally the inherent vitality (the blood and flesh) of the victim.[43]

The second Hebrew tradition which presages the crucifixion was the Day of Atonement ritual in which the sins of the Israelite community were symbolically placed on a goat, the (e)scape goat, which was then sent out into the wilderness to bear the evil away from the community and thus to purify it. The third strand from which the doctrine of the crucifixion derives its meaning is found in the image of the Suffering Servant of Isaiah 53, a development of Jewish thought which combined the Day of Atonement ritual and the Passover Lamb into the vision of a human who would suffer for the sins committed by the community and thus would make atonement for them:

> He was oppressed, and he was afflicted,
>   yet he opened not his mouth;
> like a lamb that is led to the slaughter,
>   and like a sheep that before its
>   shearers is dumb,
> so he opened not his mouth.
>   Isaiah 53:7

> Yet it was the will of the Lord to
>   bruise him;
> he has put him to grief.
>   Isaiah 53:10

The ritual of blood sacrifice, or of scapegoating, has been a common practice in many of the religions of the world, and while its origins are lost in the mists of history, several explanations for its development have been offered. One explanation for this strange phenomenon has been offered by Jane Ellen Harrison. The religious impulse, she asserts, is directed toward the conservation and promotion of life through two kinds of rites: *expulsion,* or getting rid of evil, and *impulsion,* securing and conserving the good.[44] Expulsion, the way Harrison uses it, may correspond to Berger's description of the way in which societies seek to shut out or expel that which threatens the social order—i.e., chaos.

Harrison traces the beginnings of sacrifice, and eventually our notions of sin, sacrament, and sanctity, to the rise of totemism and tabu in primitive society. The primitive family, she explains, had to do something about the constant warring of males for possession of the female, otherwise no order or advance was possible. Eventually, instead of killing each other, a tribal totem (a plant, animal, or human) was ritually killed and tabus were established around the female. Totemism, from which sacrifice thus springs, consists of group distinction and has its roots in sexual jealousy.[45]

Another explanation for blood sacrifice has been suggested by some anthropologists and psychologists and seems to be substantiated in anthropological studies of primitive tribes. It is well-known among anthropologists that one of the most prominent features of primitive psychology is the male's horror of and fascination with menstruation. Perhaps primitive man, connecting this regular bloodletting of women with their natural fecundity (the male role in procreation was not realized by primitive man), attempted to imitate this connection with life and generation with his own bloodletting rituals. The initiation rites of many primitive tribes involve the mutilation and bloodletting of the young boys in apparent imitation of the naturally occurring rites of women. Joseph Campbell has pointed out that in the puberty rites of the Central Australian Aranda peoples, the wound inflicted on the boy's penis is actually referred to as a "penis womb or vagina," and the blood that is drawn from this wound corresponds in the men's imagination to the menstrual blood of the women. By going through an initiation, the boy thus achieves a kind of identification with his mother at the same time that he separates himself from her by joining the adult male society.[46]

Both of these explanations for bloodletting thus stress the masculine nature of their origins. While the doctrine of Christ's once-and-for-all atonement is a far cry from the slaughter of a man or animal engaged in by primitive tribes, it is not terribly far from the

Jewish rite of circumcision by which only males were initiated into the body of Israel. And it still bears the traces of that masculine compulsion to let blood as a means of ensuring life as the words "Christ died that you might have life" would seem to indicate. And if this compulsion for bloodletting is not a masculine character trait, then why is it that many men claim that they have never felt so "manly" as they have in war; that most of our heroes have been warriors and soldiers (bloodletters); and that pacifism is so often labeled cowardly and "feminine"?

Although Jesus is proclaimed as the "Prince of Peace," it is not his militant pacifism which the church has held up, but his participation as the victim in the act of sacrificial bloodletting. The scapegoat syndrome, as some feminists refer to it, continues to plague the Christian imagination. It is interesting to note that the times and cultures in which the blood-imagery of Christ's passion have been most prominent are those cultures which have been most repressive of the feminine in their common life. For example, those countries in which the Catholic church is most powerful, Spain, Italy, Mexico, etc., continue to stress the agony and blood-imagery of the passion, while not so coincidentally denying woman a role in society's public life. Similarly, the crucifixion played a prominent role in the life and thought of the New England Puritan theocracy while women were severely subjugated. On the other hand, groups, such as the Friends, which have been more open to the feminine principle in their life and polity have not dwelt as consistently on Christ's death as on his life and teachings.

Feminists are raising serious questions about the role played by the idea of sacrificial love in Christian culture. After all, it arose out of the view of human nature as sinful, fallen, and disobedient, as we have seen, a patriarchal notion born out of the dominance of masculine consciousness and dependent on the myth of Eve's transgression for its psychic validity. Some feminists also find the idea of blood sacrifice and vicarious suffering, which lies behind the doctrine of the atonement, repugnant and absurd.

Perhaps we could accept the strange notion that to preserve life, someone has to give it up if we could see that the doctrine of Christ's sacrifice has made a difference in the Christian's behavior. But has it? Where is the evidence? Has this role model of self-sacrificial love made it possible for Christians to be more loving, more compassionate, more caring, and more altruistic than others?

Sociologists Rodney Stark and Charles Y. Glock find that among Protestants whom they have studied there is a slight negative correlation between orthodoxy—adherence to traditional beliefs and practices—and ethical behavior—"loving thy neighbor" and "doing good for others."[47] Psychologist Gordon Allport and his partner J. M. Ross found more intolerance and less humanitarianism among regular church attenders than among those not affiliated with any church.[48] Indeed, there is probably greater evidence to indicate that the teachings of the church have led to abuses rather than to blessings, if we consider the fact that the Inquisition, the Crusades, and the witch burnings were all carried out in the name of the crucified Christ, not to mention the wars which have been perpetuated by "Christian" nations down through the centuries.

Instead of preventing the proliferation of scapegoats, the church's emphasis on the crucifixion may actually have created them. Thomas Szasz, a radical psychiatrist, provides some valuable insights into how this might happen:

> It is fruitless to exhort men to be self-sacrificing. Indeed, the more the scapegoat suffers and the more blame he takes upon himself, the more guilt he may engender in those who witness his suffering, and the more onerous is the task he imposes on those who aspire to justify his sacrifice. Christianity thus asks more of a man than he can do. In the few, it inspires saintliness; in the many, it often promotes intolerance. The moral aim of Christianity is to foster identification with Jesus as a model; its effect is often to inspire hatred for those who fail—because of their origins or beliefs—to display the proper reverence toward Him. The Judeo-Christian imagery of the scapegoat—from the ritual of Yom Kippur to the Crucifixion of Jesus as the Redeemer—thus fails to engender compassion and sympathy for the Other. Those who cannot be saints, and who cannot transcend this awesome imagery, are thus often driven, in part by a kind of psychological self-defense, to identifying with the aggressor. If man cannot be good by shouldering blame for others, he can at least be good by blaming others. Through the evil attributed to the Other, the persecutor authenticates himself as virtuous.[49]

Women are particularly sensitive to the way in which the suffering servant image has functioned in the Christian tradition, for we have invariably played that role within the family and vis-à-vis man in the larger society. What we have found is that the role neither saves us nor serves to make those around us more altruistic. Consciousness-raising is allowing many women for the first time to come to terms with the way in which their acceptance of the suffering servant role model has deadened them and blighted their spirits, leaving them bereft of a vital center once those for whom they have lived (husband and children) are gone. And in carrying the sins of the male half of the world on their own shoulders, women are discovering that they have allowed men to escape from the responsibility of bearing their own burdens and of coming to terms with their own sin and guilt.

The scapegoat or projection mechanism does neither the scapegoat nor those who use the scapegoat any good. Parishioners often cast their ministers in the role of the suffering servant. The minister is supposed to be holier, more perfect, and more humble and self-negating than those in the congregation. Yet we know that where this attitude prevails, the parishioners do not change their own life-styles to become holier and more self-sacrificing. Often, when the minister refuses to play this role, he finds himself without a congregation, or at least in trouble with it.

The scapegoat syndrome appears wherever one class of people dominates another. Thus, blacks have long played the role of the suffering (shuffling) servant for whites. But when blacks began to cast off this role in the late 1960s and to react in anger and sometimes violence to the racism which was oppressing them, they found themselves without white allies. A recent *Harper's*/Quayle poll of the racial attitudes of a cross section of Illinois voters concluded with the following remarks: "To perceive blacks as victims does not, it seems, lead whites to sacrifice anything tangible to help the victims. The notion of sacrifice, added to the burden of guilt, almost guarantees resistance and rationalization." [50]

Thus, the suffering servant role model, a product of the patriarchal consciousness, has functioned to perpetuate that very dichotomy and alienation between human beings that the tradition claims to overcome. In accepting that particular interpretation of the Christ event as normative for their lives, women have participated in their own crucifixion. As feminists, we must exorcise that image from our midst in order to discover the roots of that true reconciliation which can only come about between equals.

3 Herstory

The liberation movements of various ethnic groups, as well as that of women, have all pointed to the need for a reinterpretation of history. Just as the neurotic who has internalized the oppressive parent within himself must go back to the origins of the trouble in his childhood, so the oppressed group, if it is to move from a condition of oppression to one of liberation, or from self-contempt to self-actualization, must go back to its origins in order to free itself of its psychic chains.

There appear to be three steps in the process of rewriting history which are required but are not necessarily distinct or consecutive. The first involves a critical look at the historical tradition in which the oppressed group was placed and a rejection or exorcism of what was negative for the group in that tradition. This stage finds its parallel in traditional psychotherapy in the patient's regurgitation of his painful childhood experiences of shame and guilt and the rejection of the oppressive parent within his own psyche. This stage is accompanied by anger and resentment, and an objectification of the enemy as an identifiable party or entity outside the self, for example, when the patient in therapy blames his parents for his problems or when black Americans blame the "White Devil" for their oppression. If this stage is never transcended, the patient (or group) is locked in a mood of perpetual anger and frustration, never able to take the reins of his or her own life and to grow into maturity and self-actualization. The venting of anger is, however, a necessary step. If it is not released, it turns against the self, thus destroying it.

Almost every woman in the movement, from an awareness of oppression and frustration to a sense of liberation and fulfillment, has gone through this period of anger. In feminist jargon it is often jokingly referred to as the "rage stage." In a sense, the previous chapter represented a venting of spleen against the enemy of patriarchal Judeo-Christianity. If its judgments seemed harsh and unfair, too one-sided or distorted, it is because the enemy has first to be objectified, regurgitated, and denounced, before any reconciliation with it can come about and a more wholistic view developed. Much misunderstanding by middle- and upper-class whites of Third-World peoples, as well as much misunderstanding by those who denounce the women's movement, comes about as a result of the failure to recognize the necessity for anger in the movement from oppression to liberation.

The second stage which must occur in the process of liberation is the development of a positive history of the oppressed group. Here, the group comes to see that all history is relative to the historian and that in order to come to a more complete understanding of its own potential for affirmation, it must *write* its *own* history. Thus, we find black groups seeking their authenticity in the African heritage and calling for a *black history* and a *black theology;* we see Hispanic-Americans finding the roots of their uniqueness in the birth of *La Raza Nueva,* the "new race" that was born out of the cultural and racial blending of European, African, and Indian; we find American Indians discarding the accoutrements of the white man and returning to the tribal lore and religion of their ancestors; and we see women establishing a "women's history, with a different time line, perspective, and explanation for events and affirmation than that normally found in patriarchal histories. Sometimes we refer to this history as *herstory,* in order to distinguish it from the history of patriarchal culture which, while pretending to be a universal form of knowing is, in reality, *his* story.

Traditional Freudian psychotherapy, which was based on a highly patriarchal ethos (on the denigration of the *id,* the body, the irrational, and the unconscious in favor of the ego and the superego—

that is, the controlling and repressive functions), was often never able to bring the patient beyond the first stage, beyond a discovery and regurgitation of the problem, holding that to expose the source of the problem was to cure it. Jung, however, realized that to become whole, one has to reintegrate one's history—that particular past of one's childhood experiences—with the collective past of the culture or race, which Jung termed the "collective unconscious." The past is never totally negative. One can always find seeds of the positive in one's past which can be nurtured and used as food to fuel a healthy future. The so-called humanistic psychologists, as well as the radical psychiatrist, R. D. Laing, have acknowledged the necessity to cull out from the wasteland of madness or neuroticism those sparks of the positive which can be built upon. They merely affirm for the individual's case what oppressed groups have been doing instinctively and collectively.

Western religion has been intimately concerned with history. The rituals of the Judeo-Christian tradition almost entirely consist of acts of remembrance: the Passover, the Exodus, the Covenant, the Incarnation, the Last Supper, the Crucifixion, and the Resurrection are all remembered and relived symbolically in the great celebrations of the temple, synagogue, and church. Indeed, what are the Old and New Testaments if not a rewriting of the historical record?

Judeo-Christianity may be a little too historicity-centered, Christianity even more so than Judaism. In Christianity, Theodore Roszak points out, "matters of fact became the basis for articles of belief and doctrine—as if no other reality than that of the historical record could hold truth."[1] Judeo-Christianity's literalism has been its source of endurance (the revelation in time and space has always been the source of legitimation for the faith), but this literalism is also its most disappointing failure. A tradition which is bound so exclusively to facts becomes hollow and lifeless once the symbolic resonances in the facts fail to find expression in the common life of those who gather to celebrate them. A strenuous act of faith is therefore required by a tradition whose truth cannot be known through immediate experience.[2]

As long as the personal or communal life of the faithful Jew or Christian paralleled the deeper meaning of the history, that life was easily translated into salvific categories. For the European Jews, the daily indignities and occasional pogroms suffered at the hands of the dominant class only solidified their faith in a God who had once brought them out of similar bondage and would do so again. It is perfectly natural that the theology of the black church and of the old spirituals should find expression through the symbols of the Old Testament. When the black slaves sang "Go down Moses, down into Egypt-land," they were not thinking of the Hebrew Moses of centuries past, but of their own black Moses who would deliver them from the hands of the slave owner into the promised land of the freedman. Quite properly, the symbolic content of history resonated in their own experience.

Similarly, those stern Calvinists who made it to America's shores, and who outwitted storms, famine, and sickness to do it, could truly believe that they were of the elect, for hadn't they gone through a kind of crucifixion and resurrection of their own? No wonder so many of the young people who flock to the Jesus Movement come to this experience of faith from the morass of the drug culture. Their experience of personal salvation from a life of sin (i.e., drugs) is real for them. Their own experience reflects the "saving grace" of the incarnation.

But what happens when our experience no longer seems to correspond to the experiences recorded in Judeo-Christian history? I suspect that the key to Christianity's failure to tap the religious life-roots of the average middle- or upper-class American may lie in its exclusivistic insistence on historicity. The lives of most affluent Americans simply find few correspondences with a faith which insists that they are all sinful and therefore in need of a savior. Perhaps it is a regrettable fact, but nevertheless fairly evident, that most Americans feel little sense of sin, and therefore little need to be saved from anything. Still less do they feel themselves to be oppressed or in bondage and in need of deliverance. Too many Americans are already living in the land of milk and honey, and though they find it wanting, they are not likely to give it up for the promise of something less physically but more ethically heady.

Certainly, there are areas in which these affluent Americans hurt, and there are all kinds of unarticulated longings; but the answers traditionally supplied by the Christian church no longer seem to fit the questions, or at least the *ways* in which the answers are supplied no longer meet real needs. The questions that many seem to be asking are: how can I deepen and enrich my life? How can I find meaning in my work? How can I find joy, release, and spontaneity in my personal relationships? To deepen and enrich one's life may mean to get in touch with those hidden and denied areas of oneself, to open oneself to the unconscious and to manifestations of the sacred in the world around us. Perhaps the current interest in Eastern religions, in psychedelic drugs, in the human potential movement, and the almost compulsive vacation-time pilgrimage to the wilderness are not the foolish aberrations of a post-Christian civilization, as some would see them, but a fervent, though not always clearly articulated, search for the kind of religious knowledge that Western Christianity has increasingly denied us.

The herstory of women, a necessary and vital foundation for our entry into self-actualization, comes at an appropriate time, for it opens up to Western society those areas of transcendence which have been systematically ignored in the Judeo-Christian theological tradition.

As women, we can claim few historical *facts* of our own. We have a paucity of recorded heroines to whom we can look as role models; only a very few of us could be said to have swayed nations or toppled governments; we have more often been the Muse of artistic creation than creators in our own right of the world's artistic treasures; the epiphanies which have come down to us have almost exclusively been cast in male imagery, and our prophets and saviors have reflected but little that has been native to us. What, then, is women's herstory? To what source of affirmation in the past do we look?

Women's herstory cannot be history as we have known it. According to the dictionary, history is a "systematic, written account of events," "a record of facts," "a narrative." Women's herstory, on the other hand, and in particular our religious herstory, is neither systematic, nor written, nor factual, nor narrative, nor *event*-ful. Instead of beginning with an event, as Judeo-Christian history begins with Yahweh's revelation of himself to the Hebrews, women's herstory begins—if we can even say that there is a beginning—in the dark prehistory of the ancient world, in a time whose only record consists of strange images and symbols cut into the stone walls of Paleolithic caves, etched into the surfaces of shards and clay bowls, or imprinted in men's ambivalent fears of and fascination toward women throughout the ages. Unlike the systematic way in which the genealogies of the early Hebrews are listed in the Old Testament, women's genealogies take great leaps back and forth through time and around the map. For the most part, our religious ancestors exist in the imaginations of known and unknown artists, in the "delusions" of "mad women" and "witches," in strange and exotic remnants of myth, and in dreams.

Those who have uncovered the religious associations of the feminine have done so because of a talent for uncommon speculation and the ability to see organic and poetic convergences between disparate phenomena. They have not been noted for their passion for "objectivity," logic, or "correctness." These writers, both men and women, have been acknowledged with skepticism, amusedly tolerated, or ignored by the larger academic community of religious scholars. Rarely has their work been taken with any measure of seriousness by those in the academic community whose business it is to discover and describe our religious heritage.

Women who are seeking to understand and incorporate a religious heritage which, for the most part, has been denied us are finding vital meaning in the works of such people as Johann Bachofen, Elizabeth Cady Stanton, and the other authors of *The Woman's Bible,* from depth psychologist C. G. Jung, and his disciple Erich Neumann (*The Great Mother*), from Berta Eckstein-Diener who, under the pseudonym of Helen Diner, wrote a heretical account of the origins of culture *(Mothers and Amazons),* and from numerous art historians, anthropologists, archaeologists, and writers on comparative religion who have uncovered the growing body of evidence which indicates the female to have been at the very heart of the cultural/religious enterprise.

Let's engage in some herstory now. Our quest is predicated on the thesis that throughout history humans have expressed life's meaning (or perhaps we might say life has been revealed to us) in terms of polarities or dualities: light/dark, up/down, sky/earth, right/left, active/passive, mountain/valley, life/death, good/evil are but a few of the myriad of antipodal poles between which life has been thought to flow. The most common paradigm in which these dualities have been expressed is the sexual one, possibly because sexual anatomical and functional differences were the most primordial, the most obvious, and the most persistent of all of the differences known to the human race. That life has been expressed in terms of a "masculine" or "patriarchal" principle and a "feminine" or "matriarchal" principle does not mean that these terms are to be equated with qualities that are uniquely innate to men and to women, inherited, as it were, in the genes. As anthropologists have amply demonstrated, norms for what is masculine and what is feminine have varied greatly from culture to culture; nevertheless, some form of sex differentiation is always present.

The masculine principle and the feminine principle, then, are to be thought of as two differing sets of responses to the "givenness" of raw experience. The ancient Chinese symbolism of the *yin* and *yang* expresses this dual meaning of life. Jung and his disciples refer to them as the great archetypes—the archetype of the Great Father and the Great Mother—which Jungians claim are the psychic heritage of the human race and which are known by every succeeding generation. Claude Lévi-Strauss, the French anthropologist, refers to them as binary structures of the human mind. In all of the ancient religions, this duality of meaning was represented by gods and goddesses, each symbolizing differing constellations of images, meanings, and responses to the mystery of life.

Many have justifiably objected to defining life in terms of dualities or polarities, pointing out that life is much more complex than that and contains infinite variations of gray. They are correct when they point out that people who see things in "black and white terms," that is, in extremes, tend to be narrow-minded and to exclude vast areas of pertinent data.

At the beginning of the current women's liberation movement, women sought to erase sexual differences, pointing out with justification that actual females did not fit the stereotypes the culture had defined for them. We objected to this stereotyping chiefly, I believe, because the "feminine principle" with which we had been identified had been devalued throughout most of recorded Western history. I suspect that if the "masculine" characteristics of aggressiveness, competition, differentiation, intellectuality, and unemotionality had been ridiculed and negatively reinforced in our culture, and if the opposite "feminine" qualities of receptivity, emotionality, intuitiveness, and inclusiveness had been valued and rewarded, we women would have been quite willing to claim "femininity" as our own!

After initially rejecting the feminine, we are now beginning to realize that the qualities with which we have so long been associated and which previously were used against us are now worth saving and elevating. They are the very qualities that our overly masculinized, competitive, hierarchical society needs. Indeed, attention to them could be the basis for a renewal of our communal life and may be the only means of saving our planet from imminent destruction.

But I am getting ahead of the story! What is important for us to understand here is not the debate over whether "masculine" and "feminine" are innate or inherited conditions but whether they are useful as points of reference around which to gather data in order to explain certain cultural and religious phenomena. I prefer to think of them as two different ways of responding to life which are equally accessible to males and females but which have tended to be separated according to gender by our institutional arrangements.

Since just about every known culture organizes itself around certain dualities, we can assume that the structuring of experience around dualities is a basic human enterprise—as basic as thinking itself. The ancients knew that experience comes in twos. They were constantly surrounded by evidence of such duality: male and female, sky and earth, sun and moon, light and darkness, life and death spoke to them of divine forces. As life has become more complicated, we have tended to forget or deliberately to ignore such seemingly simplistic thinking. We speak now in generics—about the "human condition" or about "mankind." We devise complicated theories about this "human condition" and clothe these theories in highly technical language so that only a small percentage of the populace, after rigorous training, will be let in on the secrets. Yet underneath this grand universalizing and this deliberate mystification lurk the same old mythic dualities. Elizabeth Janeway has written a book *(Man's World, Woman's Place)* to elucidate the ways in which the male/female dichotomy and the myths in which it is elaborated continue to operate at every level of our culture.

Ancient and primitive peoples may have more wisdom than we do when they insist on seeing things in twos. Bachofen and later Helen Diner recount that the ancients, and primitive tribes today, have intuitively associated the left side with the female principle and the right side with the male. (Why does Christ sit at the *right* hand of God, the Father?) Ethnologists, folklorists, and those who have studied comparative religions have pointed out that where solar worship (male god) predominates, the right side is preferred, whereas when a lunar cult is prevalent (the moon was associated with the female), the left side is preferred.[3] The male principle has almost always been associated with the sun, with light, with rationality and the intellect, whereas the female principle has been associated with the moon, with darkness, magic, the emotions, and the unconscious.

Surprising as it may seem, modern research on the brain may be corroborating what supposedly less civilized cultures than ours have always known. Through studying hundreds of clinical cases in some of which the two hemispheres of the brain (the right and left) were deliberately severed, scientists have been able to differentiate the functions of each. The left hemisphere, which controls the right side of the body, "is predominantly involved with analytic thinking, especially language and logic. This hemisphere seems to process information sequentially," a necessity for logical thought. The right hemisphere, which controls the left-hand side of the body, "appears to be primarily responsible for our orientation in space, artistic talents, body awareness, and recognition of faces. It processes information more diffusely than the left hemisphere does, and integrates material in a simultaneous, rather than linear, fashion."[4]

Intuition versus logic? Female versus male? Perhaps we have much to learn from the ancient religions. To ignore the masculine/feminine duality is thus to ignore a crucial analytical tool for discovering the basis of social, political, and ecclesiastical systems as well as the functions of symbols and myths. Christianity, by purporting to be a universal religion which speaks to the entire "human condition," is thus predicated upon an untruth. Its "universality" hides the fact that it is almost totally dominated by the masculine side of the male/female duality, as I attempted to indicate in the previous chapter.

Our attention must now turn to that other pole, the one symbolized by female imagery and personified in the form of a goddess. Before the Father God, Yahweh, of Judaism was canonized, perhaps as many as 30,000–70,000 years ago, the female principle was worshiped throughout the world—if we can deduce such a theory from the thousands of female figurines which are the most persistent archaeological finds throughout the ancient world and the earliest form of art.[5] Because of the enormous breasts and pronounced pubic areas of most of these early female figures, and because most scholars and archaeologists worked under the assumption that the human race had, from its earliest beginnings been dominated by men, these female figurines were dismissed as mere fertility charms and the deeper religious significance (as well as cultural significance) of this apparent anomaly remained unexamined.

Before most of the breakthroughs in archaeology had been made, however, Johann Bachofen, tracing changes in myth, language, customs, and law, had come to the conclusion that the female was the real center and source of civilization and that, naturally, it was her powers that were held in religious awe.

In recent years, archaeological evidence tending to support the broad outlines of Bachofen's theories has been amassed, and more is forthcoming. It seems that some form of goddess worship occupied the life of the human race for at least fifteen times as long as Christianity has been in existence. Female figurines have been found all over the Mediterranean world and as far away as Britain and the Americas. They date well back into what we used to think of as the days of the "caveman," and they are found right up to the beginnings of the Christian era.

Some of the figures are abstract, symbolic representations of the female breasts and genitalia, while others are the refined and graceful figures of goddesses and real women. Some of these relics are extremely beautiful, while others have a fierce and terrifying presence.

Archaeological digs made throughout the 1960s in a region of Turkey known as Anatolia have, more than any other discovery, refuted past calculations of the stages of civilization and have more firmly corroborated Bachofen's theory as to the primacy of the feminine at the beginnings of history. What these discoveries have suggested is that our notion of prehistory has to be pushed back even further than we had reckoned it earlier. The excavations at Mersin, Halicar, and Catal Hüyük date back as far as 7000 B.C., and some on the Anatolian plain as far back as 9000 B.C. What they show is a civilization which was more technically advanced than any of which we had had any previous notion. Moreover, there were no signs of war or violence; women appeared to be regarded highly, and a goddess was the chief deity. The excavations also indicate the presence of symbols related to the goddess which link this civilization with others in the Aegean, Europe, and Britain.[6]

A recent article in the *New York Times* caught my attention, for in it was reported the latest archaeological discovery regarding the preeminence and diffusion of the goddess religion. It seems that marine archaeologists, exploring off the coast of Israel, had found a Phoenician shipwreck somewhat north of the Israeli city of Haifa. The ship contained more than two hundred figurines of the Phoenician goddess Tanit, the only known female deity of the Phoenician world. According to Dr. Elisha Linder of the University of Haifa, this discovery of the Tanit figurines—"the first of their type" ever discovered—should assist archaeologists in determining how widespread the worship of Tanit was. "Previously, archaeologists had found only drawings and symbols of the goddess and impressions on bronze coins, and these" had come primarily from Carthage, in North Africa. The shipwreck was estimated to have occurred in the fifth century B.C.[7] Thus, 6,500 years after the goddess religion reigned supreme in Anatolia, it was still going strong in another region of the Near East, and this right next to the cradle of Judaism, with its patriarchal God!

In recent years, interest in the mother goddess has increased among some segments of the academic community, although the religious implications of the evidence have never fully been explored. Jungian psychologists have long been interested in the "feminine principle" as it has manifested itself in religious iconography, in art, in myth, and in symbol down through the ages, and they have demonstrated that the feminine is an extremely important part of our psychic makeup which must be recognized and incorporated by both men and women if we are to live well and fully. Erich Neumann's book, *The Great Mother*, is perhaps the most comprehensive rendering of the (Jungian) psychological meaning of the feminine, while M. Esther Harding's work, *Woman's Mysteries*, carries the implications a step farther. Writers on myth and anthropology, like Sir James Frazer *(The Golden Bough)*, Robert Graves *(The White Goddess)*, Robert Briffault *(The Mothers)*, Joseph Campbell *(The Masks of God)*, and others have gathered together the evidence pointing to the unique role of women in the secular and religious life of different cultures. They have then attempted to draw up some theories based on this evidence.

In 1959, before the Anatolian discoveries, the distinguished religious historian E. O. James put together most of the evidence then available on the goddess cult in the ancient Mediterranean world. In his work *The Cult of the Mother Goddess*, he traces the evidences of the cult from the earliest Paleolithic artifacts through its numerous manifestations throughout the Mediterranean world right up to the veneration of the Virgin Mary in the Roman Catholic Church and the remnants of goddess-worship rites which can still be found in the folk festivals of Europe and Great Britain. While James's approach is an historical one (he makes little attempt to probe the deeper psychic and religious meaning of the phenomena he presents), he shows the extent to which feminine symbolism and imagery affected the life of almost every civilization, and how such symbolism was transformed and muted but never totally eradicated in the Christian era.

Unfortunately, James's book is entitled "The *Cult* of the Mother Goddess." The term "cult" usually connotes a lesser, more localized, generally faddish manifestation of religiosity than that found in the so-called "higher religions" of Judaism, Christianity, Islam, and Buddhism. We think, for example, of various occult cults which are to be found in pockets throughout the country today, or of the "cult of personality" with which certain leaders are wrapped in glory for a while. A cult is something that is ephemeral—not universally true or meaningful. Goddess worship, as described by historians with a patriarchal mind-set, has invariably been described as a cult. Thus, it is dismissed as a mere aberration of the "primitive" mind which was later to be superseded by the "true" revelation of divinity, first in the Father God, Yahweh, and later in his Son, the Christ.

Recently, I turned back to a textbook on the history of Israel which I had used in seminary to see how the Near Eastern religions (which featured goddesses) were portrayed in relation to the rise of Yahwism. My recollection of the way in which Yahweh's rivals in the ancient world had been portrayed was a negative one. What I found when I returned to the book more than corroborated my vague earlier impression, for here was the goddess worship of the ancient world characterized as "paganism," as a mere "fertility cult," as "idol worship" (idolatry), and as a localized cult of the status quo, lacking any transformative character. In contrast to pagan "nature deities," Yahweh is portrayed as infinitely more lofty, powerful, and universal. A short passage from the book, one of many in this and similar texts, underscores the way in which we have become prejudiced against our religious heritage:

> However much importance her cult might assume, and however mechanically it might be prosecuted, Israel could never properly regard the cult as a technique for coercing the divine will. Nor could she, though it survived in popular practice, make place for magic (e.g., Ex. 20:7; 22:18). Yahweh was no benign maintainer of *status quo* to be ritually appeased, but a God who had called his people from the *status quo* of dire bondage into a new future, and who demanded of them obedience to his righteous law. Israel's faith, thus grounded in historical events, alone in the ancient world had a keen sense of the divine purpose and calling in history.[8]

Notice the subtle use of such pejoratively loaded phrases as "magic," "ritually appeased," and "coercing the divine will" used to describe, by implication, the pagan religions against which Yahwism was set.

In spite of his use of the term "cult" in the title of his book, E. O.

James affirms the universal character of the religious phenomena he is describing. Earlier scholars (with the exception of those we have already noted, namely Bachofen, Briffault, etc.) had taken the proliferation of names for the goddesses in various cultures and times as an indication of a multiplicity of localized cults. But an increasing body of scholars is coming to the conclusion that whether she is recognized as Demeter in Eleusis, as Isis in Egypt, as Inanna-Ishtar in Sumeria, as Astarte in Syria, as Tiamat in Babylon, as Athena in Athens, as the Magna Mater in Phrygia and in Rome, as Coatlicue in Mexico, or as Kali in India, the goddess is really one. What most scholars regarded as primitive polytheism turns out to be but the local variants of a single religious impulse! Therefore, Yahweh's claim to the title of sovereign God needs to be critically reexamined.

Why and how the goddess came to assume such religious importance in the life of the ancient world and why her rule was overthrown have been the cause of much speculation. In 1971, a book was published which has only in the last year begun to send shock waves through the women's movement. *The First Sex,* written by Elizabeth Gould Davis, an obscure librarian from Sarasota, Florida, attempts to answer the question of why and how goddess worship came into existence. In an astonishing amalgamation of sound documentation (drawn from hundreds of sources), personal observation, experience, and sometimes wild speculation, Ms. Davis presents the theory that the world was once inhabited by a matriarchal race in which men were subservient to women; that this "lost civilization" preceded the beginnings of recorded history as we know it and may have been wiped out by some worldwide conflagration, such as the myths of the Great Flood and Great Fire or the sinking of Atlantis indicate; that this civilization was highly developed and civilized; and that with the patriarchal revolution a regression in civility, peacefulness, and justice ensued and a deliberate subordination of women was the result. "The goddesses of historical times," she speculates, may have been "but the reflected memory of the ruling hierarchy of a former civilization."[9]

While meticulous scholars can find much that is faulty in Ms. Gould Davis's book—e.g., she draws sweeping conclusions from limited evidence; her prejudices and partisanship are too much in evidence; she is uncritical of her sources and tends to ignore contradictory evidence—one must admit that her book opens doors to inquiry which most have never dared to open before and the book raises serious questions for those who are interested in getting to the bottom of the age-old controversy between the sexes. At the very least, her speculations are no more fantastical than the theories postulated by countless patriarchal historians, anthropologists, and theologians who have written for the past two millennia and who have ignored or devalued the part played by woman in the development of culture and in the shaping of religion. Indeed, Elizabeth Gould Davis's theories on the development of taboo, exogamy, circumcision, patrimony, and fetishes, and her reinterpretation of the myths of Oedipus, Orestes, Adam and Eve, etc., seem to explain some of these strange phenomena better than previous attempts have done. The idea that there was once a patriarchal "revolt" or "revolution" which, over a long period of time and in differing ways in various regions of the world, overthrew a previously matriarchal world view is not so improbable when we consider that the opposing dynamic, the challenge of the patriarchal world view by the feminist one, is in process today.

What did that matriarchal world view look like and what does it have to say in our quest for religious meaning? To answer these questions is to embrace an altered view of time. It is to see the symbolic connections between the religious symbols and practices of different cultures at various stages of development and in vastly different eras. It is, in short, to be ahistorical, acritical, and heretical. But truth, as the earliest Christians came to learn, is not always revealed in expected ways.

Whether the enormous evidence of goddess worship now available represents the tail end of a lost civilization in which women held power, as Ms. Gould Davis contends, or whether the goddess cults merely represent the universal awe in which agricultural peoples held the fecundating powers of woman and the earth is perhaps beside the point. The theme which interests us here is that the feminine principle was at one time *the* source of all religious feeling and devotion. So long lasting and so powerful was this impulse that the goddess religion—if we are to understand the numerous warnings of the Hebrew prophets against idolatry—was the most effective rival to Judaism and, from the second century on, was one of the most effective rivals to Christianity as well.[10] We shall now attempt to outline some of the themes which were operative in the various manifestations of the goddess and to discern what, if any, significance they can have for us in the twentieth century.

Since we are accustomed to linear thinking, it might help to outline a time scheme for this herstory before we begin to examine its major themes and meaning. The chronology can only be very broad, since we are tracing an impulse which appears in various guises throughout a multitude of cultures and across many stages of civilization.

If we disregard Elizabeth Gould Davis's theory that an advanced civilization existed before the dawn of what we know as history and stick, instead, with those traditional notions of time advanced by present archaeological research, we come out with the following rough chronology:

1. Prepatriarchal culture: ?–4500 B.C.

This period corresponds to the Paleolithic and Neolithic periods described by archaeologists and anthropologists. It is marked by an abundance of female goddess figurines and female symbolization. Only toward the end of this period do the male morphology and symbolization begin to make themselves felt. The sociology of the period, which, of course, can only be induced from rather inconclusive evidence, indicates a matrilineal, matrilocal clan or tribal organization, since the male role in procreation had not yet been discovered. Probably, as Bachofen thought, it was the females who provided the stabilizing influence for the clan or tribe, while males related to the primary family unit (mother and children) somewhat peripherally, just as many low-income black males (having been deprived of their patrimony by the institution of slavery and continued racism) relate to the black matriarchal family unit today. It was probably women, too, who learned to domesticate fire and plants, to weave, to make pottery, and to organize an aesthetic field. In such a social pattern one cannot speak of class systems or hierarchies—terms which necessitate the development of the concept of private property and the rise of city-states.

2. Early patriarchy: 5000 B.C.–600 B.C.

This period extends very roughly from the end of the high Neolithic period to the development of the city-states and larger civilizations of the ancient Near East. It is marked by the domestication of animals (by which men may have discovered their own role in the mating process), the emergence of small industry, written history, private property, kingship and aristocracy, an organized priesthood, and patriarchal kinship, by which women were eventually to be reduced to economic dependency. It must be remembered, however, that these events did not occur in a straight, chronological sequence. This period saw the continuation of female religious symbolism, but a new element, the male, began to be added. At first the male symbolization was definitely subordinate to the female, but as time advanced, it became more and more dominant until it finally eclipsed female symbolization in the following period.

3. Patriarchy triumphant: 600 B.C.–present.
The rise of classical civilization in the Aegean and Mediterranean world brought with it the triumph of the masculine consciousness over the feminine, which included a triumph of man over nature, mind over matter, rationality over ecstasy, and a definite social subordination of women to men. Myths were reversed to indicate the reversed social status of the sexes, and female symbolization was devalued and eclipsed in the religious literature and life of the people.

With that very general chronology in mind, we are now ready to explore the various themes associated with goddess worship.

THE MOTHER GODDESS

The impulse which was earliest and most persistent in goddess religions was the sacred awe in which humans held the phenomenon of birth, a phenomenon with which women were most intimately connected. Before the male role in procreation was appreciated, and long before the Hebrew Father God created the heavens and earth by fiat, the earliest creation myths pictured life as having emanated from the womb of a Great Mother, who produced her offspring parthenogenetically.

"For the Greeks . . . it was Ge or Gaia, the Earth-goddess, who first gave birth to Ouranus, the heavens, and they then became the primeval pair, begetting the innumerable family of gods" who, in turn, produced the human race.[11] The Egyptian goddess, Nut, has been called "the old one, who gave birth to the sun and laid the seeds of God and men," or "the mother of the morning sun, the creatress of the evening sun, who existed when there was nothing and who created what was after her."[12]

The first deity of the prehistoric Sumerians (who were later to blend with the Semites to create the great Babylonian empire) was the goddess, Geštin, or Geštin-anna, an unbegotten, genderless earth-mother, who produced heaven (Anu) and all of life as a virgin.[13] In still other myths, the primeval life-force is a cosmic egg, which eventually divides to form the heavens and the earth. The egg is a distinctly feminine symbol, representative also of the womb.

In much of the early archaeological material we find the goddess associated with or symbolized by a circle (egg, womb, cycle), a spiral (the birth canal), a triangle (the pubic region from which new life emerges), or the moon (symbol of cycle, season, plenitude, death followed by rebirth, etc.).

Scholars are uncertain as to how or why the earliest Paleolithic drawings were done deep within the recesses of mountain caves, approachable only through narrow hazardous passages, but many are now concluding that these drawings were connected with a religious ritual, possibly for the increase of crops or animals, possibly to relate man to the deep mystery surrounding birth and death. At any rate, the ritual could have involved an experience of birth from the womb, the round cave room symbolizing the womb and the long narrow passage through which one enters the cave, the vagina.

Were the cave paintings and numerous early figurines (as well as the earliest mythic figures) the product of a feminine religious consciousness? Did women produce them to celebrate their own numinous powers? Elizabeth Gould Davis believes that these earliest forms of art were the efforts of women to make the world brighter;[14] others, however, feel that they may have been the work of men, an attempt to incorporate the naturally occurring religio/magical powers of the women. Who can say? Perhaps it was a combination of the two.

At any rate, "there can be no doubt," writes comparative mythologist Joseph Campbell, "that in the very earliest ages of human history the magical force and wonder of the female was no less a marvel than the universe itself."[15] E. O. James puts it another way when he remarks, "As in the procreation of children so in the origin of all things, it was the self-fertilizing female principle that was the operative cause in fecundity,"[16] a fecundity which was the paramount order of existence for primitive peoples.

Thus, from the beginning we find the dominant religious symbolism to be the feminine: earth as the Great Mother, the source of all life and fruitfulness and woman as earth, womb, life vessel. From this primordial symbolization has derived all of the other associations of woman with the earth and with the body.

How this religious elevation of the feminine affected the lives of actual women during these ancient times we can only conjecture. Ms. Gould Davis feels certain that such evidence of woman's importance points directly to her high status at one time in the civilizations of the world. Joseph Campbell feels that it must have given women great power which it has been the concern of men ever since to break and subdue. Bachofen believed that women were the source and center of all civilizing activity, while Wolfgang Lederer, H. R. Hays, Jane Ellen Harrison, and Theodor Reik, among others, find the development of taboo, totemism, and sacred rite and ritual to be attempts on the part of males to rationalize and channelize their envy of woman's inherent magico-religious power.

While we will never really know what the actual status and role of women was in those ages when goddesses reigned supreme, it does not seem logical that where woman's inherent powers were the *only* symbol of religious devotion, she could have enjoyed anything less than supreme respect. Perhaps such conjecture, however, is beside the point. The question we must deal with is: how do *we* relate to this piece of historical evidence? What sense, if any, do we make of an image of creation as birth from the womb and woman as the Great Earth Mother? Making sense of this image is fraught with peril for us, because it is precisely this association of women with the womb and the earth which we women have been fighting against. Isn't this the image that St. Augustine had of us when he called the mother the "passive and material principle" who is to be loved less than the active father? Mother, after all, comes from the Latin *mater,* meaning matter, matrix. Again, Freud wrote in regard to women that "anatomy is destiny." All along, our ability to give birth has connected us with what is passive, receptive, and static. Our place in life was assigned to us on the basis of our physiognomy, to the exclusion of those other parts of us that are not directly related to our female "nature."

Let us look, again, at the image of Mother Earth and at the religious impulse which lay behind it. When we go back to the period when the mother goddess was the only, or the dominant, symbol of deity, we see it in an entirely different gestalt. So much of our negative reaction as women to the image comes from the way in which it was interpreted for us by a patriarchal culture, which cut the earth and the natural world off from its transcendent and numinous roots, turning it into mere matter which was to be subjugated and dominated by the superior masculine intellect and will.

The mother goddess of the ancient world was no such pallid creature, however, but the powerful source of all meaning and mystery, all sorrow and ecstasy. Out of her womb all life emanated, and into the bowels of this earth goddess life repaired to await its rebirth.

What must it have meant to envision the creation of the world as birth from the womb? Just think of the difference between that kind of conceptualization and the one we are most familiar with: creation from the Word. The former image is an organic one, drawn from an observation of the natural world, a world in which the phenomena of childbirth is open and natural, messy and miraculous, won through great effort, but ecstatic in its final phases. When childbirth ceased to become an operative religious symbol, it became a stigma of uncleanness to be hidden and feared. Creation from the Word, on the other hand, is an abstract, magical image. Celebrated by theologians as an extremely elevated notion, it is actually one of the primary notions of creation entertained by the human infant who, by naming something, believes he has created it; and just as the human infant believes that everything in the world is created for him, so does the biblical writer view all of creation as made *for* man.[17] Man can therefore dominate and subdue it without compunction.

On the other hand, in the world which was born of the Great Mother, virtually every animal, bird, rock, and plant had a message for humans which could be read. The goddess worshipers recognized the conjunction between human and vegetable life. The earth was resonant with symbolic meaning. The open furrow was the vulva and the new grain the child. That is why, in some of the myths, the goddess is known as the "corn mother" or the "vine mother." The ground is the womb from whence all life—animal and vegetable— arises and to which it repairs at death. Earthly life is encompassed by a mystery, but it is a mystery which carries within it the light of rebirth and new life, just as, in some of the goddess myths and paintings, the goddess of the underworld is shown carrying a torch.

While the earth goddesses represented the source of both life and death—the ongoing of life and the terror of chaos—the emphasis in their rites was upon birth, life generating from life, as comparative religionist, E. O. James pointed out. Only when a god becomes the central hero in a culture (as we shall see later on) does the central religious rite come to celebrate the mystery of life issuing through death.[18]

One of the striking features of the artifacts connected with goddess worship is their frank sensuality. The goddess is almost always naked, her breasts and pubic region openly and proudly displayed. The natural voluptuousness and symmetry of the female body is neither hidden, as if it were shameful, nor displayed beguilingly, as if to tease or seduce. The religious modality operating here was obviously bound up with the sensual, the physical. The sacred was not something which was above or beyond the earthy, but was to be approached in and through it.

After the male's role in procreation had been established, one of the central rites which came to be associated with the goddess cult was the *hieros gamos,* or sacred marriage, which took place in the temple between a representative of the goddess (usually one of the *hierodules* or "sacred prostitutes" who served as priestesses to the goddess) and a man who represented the fertilizing power of the male. Through this symbolic union of the male and female principles, the fruitfulness of the ground and of animals as well as human life was thought to be assured.

The concept of the sacred prostitute is a difficult one for us to understand today, so conditioned have we become to thinking of the sexual act as immoral and perhaps "dirty" unless performed in the service of love or procreation of children within a legal marriage. But for these ancient peoples, it was originally a sacred act which symbolized and made efficacious their most pressing preoccupation in life—that of the ongoing fruitfulness of the earth. It is interesting to note that the term "virgin" was used for these sacred prostitutes, virgin meaning unmarried rather than uninitiated sexually. Purity of mind and dedication to the goddess thus signified the state of virginity; and the body was not a cause of defilement, but a sacred vessel.

Such rites associated with the goddess must have had great meaning for those who engaged in them, for the Old Testament is filled with warnings against the worship of this goddess (in the Bible called Asherah) and her consort Baal, and the prophets were constantly calling the people away from idolatry (worship of the goddess in which statues were used) and were leveling imprecations against harlotry. It should be remembered that the Old Testament warnings against idolatry and harlotry were leveled, not primarily out of repugnance at the sexual nature of the religion, but because such practices represented the worship of a rival power to that of Yahweh. Only later, after the triumph of Hellenic Platonism, did the prostitute or harlot become associated with bodily defilement.

We have been concerned up to this point with exploring the

implications of the goddess as Mother Earth. In prepatriarchal times this is about the only way we know her, as a symbol of life and fertility. With the rise of city-states and the male's discovery of his role in the procreative process, however, the role of the goddess began to change.

While the primordial image of the goddess as Mother Earth, the matrix of all things, continued, we find feminine symbolism moving out in other directions as the needs and fears and conceptual apparatus of ancient society became more complex. Whenever a goddess took on another attribute, there was a change in name, so that eventually there were many goddesses with but one feminine principle lying behind them. Of course, there was much borrowing from culture to culture, so that it is not always easy to separate one goddess from another.

The first major change which took place in the religious life of the ancients was the entrance of the masculine element into the divine pantheon. Before the male's discovery of his role in procreation, the goddess was alone, one-in-herself, needing no other figure to complete her. Gradually, as males assumed a greater role in the life of clan or tribe, we find the appearance of a male god, who became the son of Mother Earth, the seed of grain which grew up and died each year and was rescued by his mother from the underworld. The mother was thus both the cause of death and the source of regeneration, rebirth—again, an analogy from the natural world in which the ground is both the womb and tomb of all living things; or perhaps this mother figure represented for the emergent male consciousness both the desire and fear of returning to the womb.

The annual death and resurrection of the young male god, known as Dummuzi-Tammuz in Babylonia, Adonis in Greece, Osiris in Egypt, was enacted ritually each year at an event known as the New Year's Festival. This occurred at a time when the fields were barren and it was thought to be efficacious in producing a fresh crop. But it must also have had a great spiritual meaning for the people, for the mysteries in which it was enacted lasted for several thousand years. Characteristic of this worship is the figure of the desolate mother, wandering in the barren fields, among the sheepfolds, or sitting in the temple waiting and mourning her lost son. (In the mysteries celebrated at Eleusis in Greece it was the myth of Demeter and her lost daughter Persephone, who had been kidnapped by Pluto of the underworld and there raped, which provided the occasion for an outpouring of grief.) From this pervasive myth and rite comes the connection of women with mourning and grief and the tender, passionate love of mother for children, which we see later in the figure of the Christian Madonna and her Son, the *Pieta*. But it was more than just the love of mother for child, for the goddess was still the central deity and the son (or daughter) represented both humanity and the fruits of the earth. It is, says one Near Eastern scholar, "the love of the goddess for perishing humanity" which was the dominant religious and theological motif of the ritual [19]—a love which was later to be usurped by the patriarchal Father-God. Some of the most beautiful and haunting lyrics of sorrow, love, and compassion in all of literature are those recited at the New Year's festivals of the ancient Near Eastern mother-goddesses.

The culmination of these festivals was the resurrection of the young god and a celebration of the return of life and fruitfulness. It is probable that resurrection in the early stages of such religious practices was not viewed as resurrection to an eternal life beyond the earthly domain but rather the cyclical return of life and health in this world. Later on, as civilization advanced toward the classical age and human activity was separated more and more from its connection with the earth, the New Year's festivals were transformed into esoteric mystery rites to secure the transformation of the initiate's soul and to secure eternal beatitude. Far from lacking any transformative power, as John Bright in his history of Israel insinuates, these "pagan cults" played a profound and meaningful part in the life of the ancient world. As Cicero wrote of the mysteries which were held at Eleusis:

> Nothing is higher than these mysteries. . . . They have not only shown us the way to live joyfully, but they have taught us how to die with a better hope. [20]

Throughout the period from about 5000 B.C. to 600 B.C. we see the gradual shift in religious understandings and constellations of images. From the all-powerful mother, self-generating and self-fecundating, we have seen introduced the element of the son, who at first remains subordinate in meaning and popular affection, but as time goes on increases in importance until he becomes the coequal lover or consort of his mother (or sometimes sister). As the male symbolization increases in importance, it becomes associated with the sky, the sun, and the heavens—that which is above and beyond the earth. For most of this time, feminine imagery, while associated with the earth, never fully loses its wholistic appeal and the mother goddess is often referred to as Queen of Heaven.

Elizabeth Janeway speculates that "it was pastoralists and herdsmen who brought the Father God of the Sky down to do battle" with the Earth Mother, after learning about the male role in procreation through their work with animals.[21] In any case, after the importance of the male is recognized in the fertilization process, it is the union of male and female in the sacred marriage which comes to symbolize renewal and regeneration.

THE PATRIARCHAL REVOLUTION

A study of the religious currents of the period between 5000 B.C. and about 600 B.C. leads one to the inescapable conclusion that a major psychosocial shift from a world view which was matriarchal and agrarian to one which was patriarchal and urban was taking place. This shift was to have sweeping ramifications in the religious arena. Before going on to review the manifestations of the feminine in Judaism and Christianity, it will be necessary to ask why and how this shift came about.

Rosemary Ruether offers both a psychological and a religio-sociological explanation. Taking a cue from Jung, she interprets the major role played by the feminine in history to be that of the undifferentiating unconscious, which had to be conquered by the self-conscious, transcending, patriarchal ego in order for civilization to advance in the way that it did. "The emphasis upon the transcendence of the mind over the body (the feminine, symbolized by the mother-goddess) has been literally the creator of the modern earth."[22] Ruether points out that some time during the first millennium B.C. the communal world view in which humanity's fate was bound up with nature (as enacted in the New Year's festivals) gave way under the alienations of civilization and imperial conquest to a vision of salvation which was no longer associated with seasonal renewal but was projected onto an otherworldly future, or in Israel's case, onto an historic future. In this process, men came to visualize their bodies as foreign to them and the earth as something which had to be subdued rather than lived with in harmony.

The unfortunate consequence of this apparently inevitable course of events was that it became too one-sided. In gaining ascendance over the eternal natural round, the dominating ego had to renounce its former link to the unconscious and to deny that unconscious any transforming spiritual value. Woman, who symbolized the unruly forces of nature which the transcendent will was seeking to dominate, thus became the victim of the onward thrust of civilization. As the incarnation of nature she was confined, her being reduced to mere "matter," and she and nature were stripped of any transcendent power of their own.

Marxists attribute the shift from a matriarchal to a patriarchal world view to the development of technology and the rise of private property, both of which gave males an advantage over females in the economic realm and led to women's enslavement in the social realm. The Marxian analysis is based fundamentally on a biological determinism, which saw women as bound to the home and the earth as a result of their reproductive capacity. As long as a kind of primitive agricultural situation pertained in which the male hunted while the woman remained the sustainer of home and family life and the developer of the domestic arts, the two sex roles remained somewhat reciprocal. Once paternity was discovered, however, and copper, tin, bronze, and iron changed the capacity of the male to respond to his environment, the balance was upset.

Simone de Beauvoir does not think the Marxian analysis penetrates deeply enough because it does not explain what she sees as the inevitable tendency—regardless of economic circumstances—for man to set himself over against woman whom he perceives as an alien Other. Basing her position on existentialist philosophy, she sees the human condition as one of inevitable ontological oneupmanship. Wherever two human systems or categories exist together, she points out, there is always the tendency for one to claim sovereignty over the other. Thus, man has always viewed woman with antagonism, and in the course of history, his biological and economic advantages have enabled him to dominate that Other successfully. Like the Marxists, de Beauvoir admits that early agricultural society did give women more power than they have had ever since, but she is unwilling to admit that there might have been anything like a true political matriarchate in which women determined the course of history. Women, she claims, have never made their own laws, nor determined which gods they would worship. Even the great mother-goddess was a projection of the male's fear and awe of nature! [23]

In contradistinction to de Beauvoir's thesis, Greek myths seem to suggest that the shift from goddesses to gods reflected an actual political struggle between two conflicting forces. Many passages from the Greek playwrights, indeed, the themes of several whole plays, seem to reflect such events. In Aeschylus's play, *The Eumenides,* the question of which is the greater crime, patricide or matricide, is played out between the forces of the patriarchate, represented by Apollo and Athena, and those of the matriarchate, represented by the Erineyes, or Furies. Apollo and the forces of patriarchy win out by denying that the mother is the true begetter of the child, in effect, by asserting that she is a mere vessel. The Furies' words upon hearing the verdict are revealing:

> I, I dishonoured in this earth to dwell,—
> Ancient of days and wisdom! I breathe
>   forth
> Poison and breath of frenzied ire. O
>   Earth,
> Woe, woe for thee, for me!
> From side to side what pains be these that
>   thrill?
> Hearken, O mother Night, my wrath, mine agony!
> whom from mine ancient rights
>   the gods have thrust
> And brought me to the dust—
> Woe, woe is me!— with craft invincible.[24]

One might almost read Euripides' play *Medea* as a plea for women's liberation—a plea which Euripides dooms to failure because of the dominance of the patriarchal system. Elizabeth Gould Davis speculates that Colchis, the land from which Medea was said to have come, was the seat of the same mother-goddess religion which was worshiped at Catal Hüyük which, like Colchis, was on the Anatolian plain. Medea, she asserts, was probably the historical queen of this ancient matriarchate.[25] Greek legend had it that Medea was a sorceress, a possessor of magical powers, which dovetails with her possible role as queen and chief priestess of a goddess cult. By the time we see her in Euripides' play, she is a woman lamenting her reduced status in a patriarchal land—or so the following lines could be read:

> Of all things that have life and sense we women are the most hapless creatures; first must we buy a husband at a great price, and o'er ourselves a tyrant set which is an evil worse than the first; and herein lies the most important issue, whether our choice be good or bad. For divorce is not honourable to women, nor can we disown our lords. Next must the wife, coming as she does to ways and customs new, since she hath not learnt the lesson in her home, have a diviner's eye to see how best to treat the partner of her life.[26]

That Euripides could even have put such a statement in Medea's mouth must have meant that the status of women vis-à-vis men was at least a topic of some concern and debate in the public mind of the time.

There are other indications of a battle between conflicting world views and systems. Apollo's insistence in the *Eumenides* that "the mother is no parent of that which is called her child" and that the only parent is "he who mounts" seems too headstrong, too arrogant; it is the voice of the insecure male. Bruno Bettelheim was struck by the same irony in some of Yahweh's speeches in the Old Testament:

> In reading, in the Old Testament, certain of the Lord's statements to the Israelites asserting His power and uniqueness, one seems to hear undertones of boastfulness and of overassertion, as if to drown out voices of doubt that exist because all this power is so new. If it were not sacrilegious one might be tempted to say: "Methinks the Lord doth protest too much." Several students of Jewish religion have remarked on this emphatic, defensive, almost querulous assertion of masculine superiority.[27]

In Yahweh's case we have a little more evidence to indicate that such insistent self-assertion was necessary than we do with regard to Greek culture, for we know that the establishment of Yahwism was won, in part, through a religio-political struggle against an opposing system—a system in which women had their own goddesses to which they clung with a fierce tenacity, as the story of Jezebel in the books of Kings indicates.

Thus, I think it possible, if not probable, that some kind of conscious struggle was going on in the ancient world between two contending religio-political systems in one of which women held a kind of power and prestige that men felt it necessary to revoke. Bachofen, Helen Diner, and Elizabeth Gould Davis all adhere to such a theory.

If the power that women held was not political and economic, it was at least a kind of psychological and religious power of which men were deeply envious. Although it has been played down in the literature (probably because psychiatrists and psychologists themselves, who were mostly male, could not admit their own feelings), the psychological profession has long known of the strong feelings of ambivalence men have for women. Such ambivalence, indicating both fear and fascination, is attested to in clinical work as well as in numerous anthropological studies of primitive tribes in which ambivalence is readily discernible in tribal rites and taboo. Traditionally, scholars have been content to interpret the male's antagonism toward women and the patterns of female exclusion from male rites as indicative of a negative evaluation of women. One might also assume that women's exclusion from the Christian ministry indicates solely a negative feeling about women! But the phenomenon runs deeper. Many feminists and several prominent male anthropologists and psychologists (for example, H. R. Hays, Theodor Reik, Wolfgang Lederer, Bruno Bettelheim, Joseph Campbell) are coming to the conclusion that the force of masculine ambivalence toward women indicates the presence of a "sacrality," the numinous. The truly sacred is always the focus of great fear and fascination.

But why should men react to women as to a sacred object? What sense does such an assertion make? A Freudian would explain that we are witnessing the never fully sublimated reaction of the infantile boy to the mother, who appears to him as the source of all beneficence and of sexual desire, a force so powerful that he knows he must conquer it if he is to mature. Woman thus symbolizes for man both a return to the all-encompassing womb and the source of his uncontrollable sexual impulses. Both terror and fascination are involved in his responses.

Joseph Campbell points out that fear of woman and the mystery of her motherhood have been, from primordial times, "impressive imprinting forces"—as impressive as those of nature itself—so that in the "mythologies and ritual traditions of our entire species" we find "innumerable instances of the unrelenting efforts of the male to relate himself effectively—in the way, so to say, of antagonistic cooperation—to these two alien yet intimately constraining forces: woman and the world." [28]

Theodor Reik believes that myths were originally produced by men as a way of explaining to themselves the origin of things—an origin which women from their own experience already know. [29] Margaret Mead has observed that in those primitive societies which have emphasized breast feeding and the closeness of young children to their mothers there occurs the greatest symbolic preoccupation with the differences between the sexes and the greatest envy, overcompensation, and ritual mimicry of women by the men in their rites. [30] Such an explanation might go far in explaining the patriarchal revolution which, in ancient times, strove to overcompensate for the extreme emphasis in the goddess religions on the female anatomy and functions.

Still another explanation may be that women represent for men that ultimate Other, the radical heterogeneity of the universe, which they are forever trying to deny. One woman has read the history of the relations between the sexes as evidence of the male's deep and continuing envy of the female's capacity to bear children. "If the maternal instinct is defined as an innate tendency to want children, and to love, cherish, nurture and protect children," then it is the men who have had more of this desire than the women, she avers.[31] The arguments she marshals to support her reversal of a familiar cliché are powerful.

The reasons for the always testy relationship between the sexes lie deep within the human psyche. They may even be an inheritance from our ancient evolutionary past.

Anthropologists have often noted that the men in primitive tribes will attribute the origin of their magico-religious rites to the women. They claim to have stolen the secrets away from the women who possessed them in an ancient time. Recent research in cytogenetics adds an even stranger dimension to the exploration of sexual differences, throwing Freud's theory of penis-envy in women to the winds. Research has led to the startling conclusion that "nature's first choice or primal impulse is to [produce] a female." Genetically speaking, the beginning of everyone's life is female! Only when a new substance, the male hormone, is added to the fetus does its gender change.[32]

Can this be the answer to the fear and fascination with which men regard women? Is their desire to return to the womb really their desire to possess the womb they lost?

The reason for man's ambivalence toward women will probably always remain elusive; but one conclusion is becoming inescapable: religious history is fraught with examples of the way in which men have sought either to degrade feminine religious meaning and power and to assert their own religious modalities in its place or to appropriate feminine meaning and power for themselves.

One of the ways to observe this male tendency both to degrade and appropriate feminine meaning is to study the changes in myth which occur throughout the ancient world during the last three millennium B.C. We have already observed the emergence of male symbolization, first in the figure of the subordinate son and then in the coequal consort or lover. We can trace this tendency still further in the dethroning of Mother Earth from the position as sole progenitor of the universe. In later myths, such as the Babylonian *Enuma Elish,* it is the warrior-god Marduk who fashions the world from the body of the chaos-mother Tiomat. In the Hebrew Scripture it is the decidedly masculine god Yahweh (in the Prophets) who creates the world out of nothing, while in Greek mythology Prometheus was said to have created man in the image of the gods. There are numerous examples of gods usurping not only the power of creation but also even that most feminine of traits—giving birth! Of course, since gods do not have wombs, there are some very remarkable births recorded, such as the birth of Athena, in full armor, from Zeus's head or the gestation of Dionysus within Zeus's thigh—or even Eve emerging from Adam's rib.

One of the theories which attempts to explain the functions of myth claims that they are stories told to explain why certain rites are performed. If this is the case, then myths such as these may be but the reflections of long-forgotten male initiation rites, in which a process of rebirth through the father takes place. Male initiation rites notoriously seek to emulate the naturally occurring rites of the female—namely menstruation and childbirth. They are an attempt by men both to downgrade or dissolve the power of the actual women over their young and to incorporate the seemingly magical power of women for themselves.

In the male initiation ritual, the pubescent boys are snatched abruptly from the care and life of the females with whom they have become deeply involved since infancy. They are then put through a series of rigorous and often terrifying experiences in which a death and rebirth through a womb are ritually enacted. Circumcision and sub-incision (the slitting of the penis right down the middle) are practiced in imitation of the female's menstrual flow, and the wound so made is often referred to as a vulva or penis-womb. Young boys are told that they have died and are born again. They are given a new name, are made to act like babies, and are often fed milk by the fathers. Another custom practiced by primitive men, the *couvade,* is an imitation of female labor and it occurs when the man's wife is in actual labor.

Theodor Reik, in a convincing study of the myth of Eve's birth from Adam, came to the conclusion that the myth is a remnant of an early Semitic puberty rite in which Adam is born anew from the father (Yahweh), while in a second reversal, Eve (who was perhaps a vestige of the mother goddess—in the biblical account she is called "the mother of all living things") is born from man.[33] Such reversals are common in mythology and no doubt reflect the changing status of the sexes.

Although it was originally probably performed at puberty, followers of the cult of Yahweh transferred the practice of circumcision to infancy where it became a mark of the covenant between Yahweh and his people which only males were privileged to bear. Concomitantly, woman's natural circumcision, her menstrual flow, was declared ritually unclean by that strict and very patriarchal band. Two mysterious accounts in the Bible: that of the visit of a dark, demonic god to Moses and his family who were on their way back to Egypt (Exodus 4:24-26) and the story of Jacob's nocturnal wrestling match with God (Genesis 32:24-33) may both be remnants of archaic puberty rites. The first account involves the circumcision of Moses' son, while in the second account the mysterious God is said to have touched the hollow of Jacob's thigh.

Like Apollo in the *Eumenides* the Hebrew male comes to believe that only he is the bearer of new seed, new life, and that woman is simply the repository—thus the emphasis throughout the Old Testament on the male seed, the prohibitions against spilling it, and on the male line. How far we have come from the mother goddess who was the self-fecundating progenitor of all life!

Before we leave our discussion of the patriarchal revolution, we should not forget to add that shamans and priests in all ages have appropriated female functions and even attire. The priests who served the mother goddess in the temples of the ancients were often castrated and were required to wear false breasts, feminine robes, and to be clean shaven. Emily Hewitt and Suzanne Hiatt, in their book *Women Priests: Yes or No?*, point out the male cleric's fondness for vestments and ceremony as well as the fact that the traditional functions of the ministry are simply the natural functions which women perform daily.[34]

THE FEMININE IN THE OLD TESTAMENT

One writer has remarked that biblical Judaism "stands midway between the worship of women and their total condemnation."[35] If this is the case, we have to probe rather carefully to find those images and symbols of the feminine which are not derogatory; for much of the Old Testament was compiled by editors who, in looking back upon Israel's history, tended to distort that history by filtering it through the lens of their own patriarchal biases.

As Christians, our history naturally began with the Yahwistic editor's interpretation of events; but as we have seen, our history as feminists begins much earlier. A long view of the ancient Near East greatly facilitates our ability to sift distortion from fact and to reinterpret certain events and symbolizations from a new perspective. What new insights can we learn from this point of view? What transvaluations of value perhaps need to be made from a broadened perspective?

In order to answer these questions, we must first assess the presuppositions concerning females and the feminine religious modality which lay behind the Yahwistic interpretation of history and which have passed over into popular culture.

1. The Yahwists interpreted the religious devotion shown to the goddesses of their neighbors as mere idol worship. Such religious expression was devalued as being illegitimate because it concerned "graven images"; and it was condemned as sin because it tempted the Israelites away from the one, true, omnipotent, and invisible God. In order to define himself as distinct from these other gods and goddesses, Yahweh had to impress upon his people his oneness, his invisibility, his transcendence.

2. The favorite image used by the prophets and other patriarchalists to symbolize Israel's devotion to false gods was the image of the harlot.

3. The image often used to describe Israel's faithful obedience to Yahweh's commands was that of the faithful wife.

4. The wife in ancient Israel was little more than a chattel to her husband. She was the bearer of his seed and the raiser of his children.

5. In a curious inconsistency, although woman was seen only as the bearer of the male seed, she was blamed for barrenness. It was thought that God was punishing her for some wrongdoing by not opening her womb.

6. Because of the command to "be fruitful and multiply," barrenness was seen as a great calamity, and husbands who remained childless often took concubines to produce children for them.

7. Religious experience and participation were denied to women. They were excluded from the priesthood, from worship in the inner courts of the temple, and even from saying certain prayers in the home.

8. The only feminine images for God which have come down to us in English translation are those few passages (such as the one in Isaiah 66:7-13) in which God is compared to a woman giving birth and, later in the passage, to a mother breast-feeding and comforting her child.

Taking the long view of history, one can read the Old Testament as yet another chapter in the story of the struggle for masculine predominance. Still further, one can read it as the struggle of the priests and legislators for the minds and hearts of the people, who appeared to want to hold on to the form of religious expression which was embodied in the worship of the mother-goddess.

Archaeological discoveries pointing to the extent of the goddess worship in the ancient Near East have changed our perceptions about the role played by these goddesses in the development of Israel, so that we are now able to reread the Old Testament with a different set of tools at our disposal. The names of goddesses in the Old Testament occur about forty-nine times, and it was the decided bias of the Hebrew editors to play down their importance. But archaeologists have been impressed with the number and ubiquity of goddess figurines, which have been found in every major excavation in Palestine dating from about 2000 B.C. down to about 600 B.C.—that is, down to the end of the divided Israelite monarchy.[36]

Yahweh's chief rival for the affections of the Israelites was the Canaanite goddess Asherah, sometimes known as Elath (an epithet meaning goddess), Astarte or Ashtoreth (which originally meant womb), or "The Queen of Heaven." The names of the goddesses in the ancient Near East were often interchangeable as they were but the various manifestations of a central theme. This goddess was worshiped both in the countrysides and even in the temple at Jerusalem from the time of the Israelites' entry into Canaan until the destruction of Jerusalem by Nebuchadnezzar in 586 B.C.

Through successive reigns we see her cult alternately set up in the temple (usually when one of the kings married a foreigner who brought her goddess with her) and burned or destroyed by Yahwist purists in the succeeding royal house. While the worship of the Baal, who was Asherah's male counterpart, eventually succumbed to the worship of Yahweh, the mother goddess continued to command the loyalty of the populace. Raphael Patai, who has studied the evolution of this goddess, concludes that Baal worship finally died out because it was too similar to the cult of Yahweh, while the worship of Asherah continued to offer psychic rewards which were not present in the strict and patriarchal Yahwistic cult.

The worship of Asherah, Astarte, or Anath was a thorn in the side of the Yahwist purists, especially the prophets, who were constantly predicting dire consequences for the people of Israel if they did not give up their idol worship. Even the very presence of an image of the goddess in his temple was enough to send Yahweh, through his prophet Ezekiel, into a fiery rage of jealousy. (It is generally admitted by biblical scholars that the image "which provokes to jealousy," shown by the Lord to Ezekiel in a vision of the Jerusalem temple, was the statue of Asherah set up by King Manasseh sometime between 698 and 642 B.C.)[37]

The vehemence of Yahweh's jealousy in the Prophets and elsewhere makes one wonder what went on with this worship of the goddess to provoke such rage, for often Yahweh's curse was out of all proportion to the crimes supposedly committed by the idolaters. We have only very limited ideas of what the rituals consisted in these rival religious systems, but we do know that women were much more involved in a direct way with the worship of the goddess than they were involved with the worship of Yahweh. The following passage in Jeremiah gives us some idea that the rituals involved the whole family including children. The Lord, here, is speaking to Jeremiah about his idolatrous people:

> Do you not see what they are doing in the cities of Judah and in the streets of Jerusalem? The children gather wood, the fathers kindle fire, the women knead dough, to make cakes for the queen of heaven; and they pour out drink offerings to other gods to provoke me to anger (Jeremiah 7:17-18).

In a later passage, covering the entirety of chapter 44 in Jeremiah, we get a better sense of the way in which women's religious expression was at odds with the cult of Yahweh. In this chapter Jeremiah is explaining to a group of Judeans who had fled to Egypt that the destruction of their land was brought by Yahweh as punishment for their sins of idolatry. Throughout the passage Yahweh seems expressly to include women as idolaters, perhaps even to emphasize them, in a way that stands out. The people refuse to accept Jeremiah's interpretation of the event, insisting instead that their downfall was caused by their failure to burn incense to the queen of heaven.

> Then all the men who knew that their wives had offered incense to other gods, and all the women who stood by, a great assembly, all the people who dwelt in Pathros in the land of Egypt, answered Jeremiah: "As for the word which you have spoken to us in

the name of the ᴸord, we will not listen to you. But we will do everything that we have vowed, burn incense to the queen of heaven and pour out libations to her, as we did, both we and our fathers, our kings and our princes, in the cities of Judah and in the streets of Jerusalem; for then we had plenty of food, and prospered, and saw no evil (Jeremiah 44:15-17).

The passage affords a rare glimpse of the kind of religious power with which Yahwism had to do battle.

The continuing worship of Asherah and her daughters by the Israelites throughout so much of the period of Israel's formation was bound to have some effect on the development of Yahwistic monotheism itself, for feminine imagery and symbolism and the meanings which lay behind them could not easily be erased. Some of this imagery is obvious, as in the rich and sensual love poem, the "Song of Solomon," which was probably borrowed from the Asherah-Baal cult where it was sung in the ceremonies of the *hieros gamos*. Most lay people lack the knowledge of Judaism's history and the familiarity with Hebrew to uncover the other symbolizations of the feminine, and much of it has been lost to us in translation. The full weight and substance of feminine imagery in the Old Testament has yet to be tested, but women are becoming increasingly interested in ferreting it out from the scholarly works hidden away in university and seminary library stacks.

One of the longest-lasting feminine symbolizations which has been explored by Raphael Patai is the female cherubim—graven images, in spite of the prohibition against idolatry—which guarded the ark in the Holy of Holies in both the desert tabernacle and later in the temple at Jerusalem.[38] Very little is known about the early meaning of these strange winged creatures, except that they seemed to be interpreted as the clouds upon which Yahweh rode. Later on, the idea slowly gained ground that this indivisible God was made up of two aspects, symbolized by male and female cherubim. Still later, in Talmudic times, the male cherub came to represent God while the female was the community of Israel in an erotic embrace with the male god.

The Hebrew word used for God by the priestly editors of the first creation story, "In the beginning God," was *Elohim*, which is also the most commonly used and most general term for God in the Old Testament. The word is made up of *Eloh*—the feminine singular term for goddess, a variant of which we saw was often used for Asherah, Astarte, or any of the other Near Eastern mother goddesses, and the masculine plural ending *im*. Thus, the word can be translated variously as god, goddess, gods, or goddesses. As Anne Bennett, a feminist theologian has pointed out, the word has always been translated as masculine singular, and scholars, in trying to account for the fact that it is a plural form, will speak about the majesty of God being plural.[39] Ms. Bennett's analysis seems more to the point. "Does it not seem likely," she asks, "that the plural word *Elohim* reflects the actual situation and feeling of the early Hebrews that God . . . included somehow both *El* and *Elath?*"[40] Ms. Bennett goes on to point out that scholars are aware of hundreds of examples throughout the Hebrew Bible in which deliberate changes from feminine to masculine terminology have been made for dogmatic reasons, usually to express reverence for the Holy, which strict Yahwists felt could not be expressed in feminine terms.

In later biblical times, God's overwhelmingly transcendent, patriarchal, otherworldly image, it seems, had to be mediated by some more comforting images, for we find the development of several personified attributes of God all expressed in the feminine gender.[41] The *Shekhina,* a word which never appears in the Bible but is developed in the Talmud, is the palpable presence of God among the people. At first a rather abstract concept, it became more and more personified as time went on—a kind of compassionate mediating presence between the people and the transcendent, unapproachable Father. In the Talmudic period the *Shekhina* and the "Holy Spirit" were interchangeable terms. The second feminine attribute of God, developed in later Judaism, was *Hokhma,* or wisdom, who was often said to be God's wife. *Hokhma* can be found in the Bible in the Book of Job, in Proverbs, and in the Apocrypha in the Wisdom of Solomon. In later Jewish mystical thought, *Hokhma* was thought to have existed before the creation of the world.

Other feminized attributes or numinous qualities of the godhead which at one time or other influenced the development of Jewish thought were the *Torah* or law of God, the *Adamah,* the "Earth," from which the name "Adam" comes, the "Word," which is similar to the Greek *Logos,* and the "Daughter Voice," through whom God's will was made audible on earth.[42]

This list has by no means exhausted the ways in which the feminine was embodied in Hebrew thought. It will be up to those women who find enough interest and meaning in searching for their own herstory in the wilderness of patriarchal scholarship to discover and elaborate upon these themes so briefly set out here.

While Judaism was struggling to free itself from the corrupting influence of the mother goddess, she continued to live on in the ripening classical world as the Magna Mater. In almost all of the centers of culture in the Mediterranean world and elsewhere (her influence even reached to Britain and the Americas) temples were built to her, and strong centers of worship grew up around them. Except in Phrygia in Asia Minor, where she was known as Cybele and her worship along with that of her son Attis took on orgiastic tendencies, the Magna Mater became a kind of mystic object of devotion, especially for women, not infrequently to the despair of husbands whose wives took to ascetic practices before taking part in the ceremonies, writes E. O. James.[43] The Magna Mater took on many appellations. In addition to being "Queen of Heaven," she was also "mother of the stars," "first-born of all ages," "patroness of sailors," "star of the sea," *"Mater dolorosa,* giving comfort and consolation to mourners and those in distress," and in Apuleius's *Metamorphoses* she is even referred to as "the saviour of the human race."[44] After a brief interlude, we shall see the Magna Mater next in her metamorphosis, as the Virgin Mary, Mother of God, of the early Christian church.

In the meantime, we have the appearance of Jesus, who appeared as the fulfillment of the ancient longing of the Hebrew people for a Messiah, yet radically broke with the ways of the past. One of the ways in which he scandalized tradition was his relationship with women. As we have seen, women under Jewish law and tradition were increasingly encumbered by taboos and prohibitions which kept them in virtual bondage to their husbands and treated them as nonpersons in the religious life of the community. In an article which has been widely used by feminists in the church, "Jesus Was a Feminist,"[45] Leonard Swidler shows the enormous extent to which Jesus broke established laws and conventions to treat women as human beings in the same way that men were to be treated. Not only did he break the prohibitions about talking with women in public, touching or otherwise being in close affinity with a woman who was bleeding (the old menstrual taboo), and consorting with prostitutes, but he seems actually to have had women followers—if not disciples—and he revealed the central message of all—the resurrection—to women, not only upon his appearance to women at the entrance to the tomb, but also in his words to Martha over the raising of her brother Lazarus (John 11:20-27). In addition, in one of the three parables in the Lucan Gospel (Luke 15:8 ff.) the figure of God is actually represented by a woman. Since the parable was told to the Pharisees who prayed each morning thanking God that they were not born women, the use of such imagery by Jesus must have been scandalous indeed.

Swidler also suggests that we might read Jesus' prohibitions against divorce (Mark 10:2-12 and Matthew 19:3-9) as an attempt to give equal rights and responsibilities to women in the marriage relationship; for in the society in which these words were spoken, a man could divorce his wife at will, but she had no reciprocal rights. It is interesting here, too, that Jesus interprets the creation story as one which gives equality to men and women: "But from the beginning of creation, 'God made them male and female'" (Mark 10:6), a revolutionary affirmation in the time in which it was pronounced.

In view of the fact that the Gospels must be seen through the lens of the first-century Christian communities which shared the anti-woman bias of the times, it is all the more extraordinary that the Gospels reveal no negative attitude toward women, for, as Swidler points out, "if there were no very special religious significance in a particular concept or custom we would expect that current concept or custom to be reflected by Jesus."[46] Jesus must, then, have attached great religious importance to his breaking of the taboos surrounding women.

Women throughout the ages have always responded to the simple humanity and dignity they felt Jesus offered them, in spite of official ecclesiastical and civil sanctions against their exercise of this humanity. In the first few years after Jesus' death this contagious freedom and dignity was taken up by women and in the atmosphere of impending apocalypse was probably allowed to flourish.

We know that in the early church, women were just as active as men in spreading the Good News, and it is probable that some of them left home and family in order to do so. Acts 18 records that Priscilla was as active as her husband Aquila in teaching the gospel. In Romans 16:3 she and her husband are mentioned by Paul as "fellow workers in Christ Jesus, who risked their necks for my life." In fact, both of them are said to be tentmakers, which sounds like the first recorded instance of a liberated family!

Phoebe, whom Paul mentions in Romans 16:1, was also an active worker for the early church; in fact, she was a minister, although her title, in Greek, *diakonos,* has always been translated as deaconess, connoting a subordinate class of church workers to that which we think of as the official "ministry" or priesthood. Paul also calls her a *prostatis,* which means "ruler" or "guardian," although, again, this word has always been translated as "helper" or "servant."[47]

Feminist theologizers point out that much of our history has been lost to us through such (deliberate? or unconscious?) mistranslations and obscurantisms. In fact, long before the current interest in our religious history the feminists of an earlier age (notably Lucy Stone, Elizabeth Cady Stanton, and her fellow-workers on *The Woman's Bible)* were learning their Greek, Hebrew, and Latin in order to correct the sins of several thousand years of patriarchal scholarship. Again, in 1924, a missionary doctor, Katherine Bushnell, published *God's Word to Women,* in which the distortions and misrepresentations were further elaborated. Most recently, Ruth Hoppin, in a delightfully witty paper entitled "Games Bible Translators Play," has continued the list of indictments.

But, alas, the Christian church could not long tolerate such untrammeled freedom for women! As soon as the threat of impending doom had passed, the men set about to reclaim that superordination they had so very nearly lost. The scenario has a familiar ring to it. In the midst of national emergency during both World Wars, women emerged from kitchen and nursery to take over the reins of the country while their men were off at war. Familiar clichés and roles were forgotten in the press of national unity. We all know what happened in the nation's story. That of the Christian church was similar.

Even Paul, it seems, had trouble with the consequences of the faith he so dearly loved, because his well-known admonition to the women to keep silent in the churches (1 Corinthians 14:34-35)—an admonition which was taken out of context by subsequent preachers and made an article of faith—indicates that women in the early church were becoming quite uppity, even to the point of prophesying and interpreting Scripture. There was probably a strong charismatic cast to their participation, as women have always seemed to gravitate toward this religious modality. Several scholars (Ruth Hoppin among them) believe that the anonymous Epistle to the Hebrews may have been written by Priscilla, who could not add her name to it for fear it would not be taken seriously if it were known it had been written by a woman. It may be that the Pauline passage cited above was not genuinely Paul's but the work of a later editor who added this gloss to the text at a time when the woman's role in the church was becoming problematical.[48]

Women's bold participation in the life of the early church and society must have scandalized Christian males, especially those of Jewish background. While Paul was at least contradictory in his opinion of woman's estate (we know that he had many genuine friendships with women whom he mentions without prejudice), later writers set about to topple the balance. Most of the glaring examples of anti-woman bias in the Epistles, for many years wrongly attributed to Paul, for example, Ephesians 5:21-27 and 1 Timothy 2:11-12, are believed to have been written in the post-apostolic period. If one considers that women took a prominent, active role in the leadership of the early church and were later debarred from such participation, the reason for assigning these letters to a later period becomes all the more valid.

What of the mother-goddess figure we seem to have lost track of with the incarnation and first flowering of the Christian faith? The truth is, she was there all along in the syncretistic Greco-Roman world, enormously popular, reigning over her mysteries, dispensing comfort and justice, and offering herself as the embodiment of feminine sensuality and beneficence. The Christian church could not ignore this pressing impulse, especially after it had demoted actual women almost to the role of onlookers in the life of faith. It seemed as though the popular will was crying out for that warmth and tenderness, that sense of mercy and firm comfort which was lacking in the strict patriarchal theology of the Church Fathers. Eventually, the church was forced to incorporate this persistent figure into its own doctrine.

At first, references to a female divine figure were very few, although she had become a symbol of mystical devotion in the many early Christian and Jewish Gnostic sects. It was especially among the Christian converts in Asia Minor (which was the home of the most intense goddess cult of all—that of Cybele) that the Christianized Gnostic image of the Magna Mater took hold. In these sects she was conceptualized as the Holy Ghost bringing forth the male principle, Sophia. There are grounds for regarding Gnosticism, claims E. O. James, as a cult of the Magna Mater.[49] Could one of the major reasons for the Church Fathers' insistence on doing away with Gnosticism be its elevation of feminine symbolism to the status of the divine?

The development of Mariology, which was to incorporate and transmute so much of the symbolism and iconography of the ancient mother goddess into Christian tradition, came about as a result of the church's struggle to find a balance between Gnosticism and Docetism—which denied the humanity of Christ and insisted on his supernaturalness—and Arianism, which denied Christ's unity with God. To meet this impasse (and probably also to weaken the influence of the pagan mother goddess), Mary was brought in as the *Theotokos,* the Mother of God, and "as the Second Eve, bringing forth [Christ] the Second Adam to reverse the judgment on fallen humanity."[50] Around the figure of the Madonna and her child were eventually assembled most of the symbols and deeply ingrained meanings which had adhered to the Magna Mater. Like Astarte, Mary was known as the Queen of Heaven; like Isis, her symbol was the Holy Dove; like so many of the ancient goddesses, she was often pictured with a crown of stars and with the moon under her feet; and with her infant son on her lap, regally crowned, she repeated the picture of another royal mother, the Egyptian Isis and her son Horus. Like all the great mother goddesses she was both a mother and a bride of her son, the Christ, for Mary was often confused with the symbol of *Mater Ecclesia,* the holy bride and body of Christ.

As the years passed, Mary's influence increased. By the end of the fourth century, churches dedicated to her honor were being built right on the sites formerly occupied by the pagan *Magna Mater!* Like her pagan counterparts, she came to be associated with certain cities, localities, or shrines. We know her as Our Lady of Fatima, the Virgin of Guadalupe, etc.

In the Middle Ages, Mary's role grew so strong that she often overshadowed completely both Father and Son. In traveling through Europe during the turn of the century, Henry Adams was struck by the enormous influence she must have had on the hearts and minds of people. In his book about the great European cathedrals, *Mont-Saint-Michel and Chartres,* he details the work, devotion, money, and art that went into the veneration of the Virgin and asks himself why this came to be, for in most instances she is the overpowering figure, while her Son remains a mere baby and God is not even mentioned. Indeed, in a sixteenth-century French statue entitled the *Vierge Ouvrante,* studied by Erich Neumann, the scope of her meaning is graphically represented. The statue is of a seated Madonna, holding in her one hand a small world and in her other a baby. But the body of the statue is also a door which, when opened, reveals the Father God holding up the crucified Christ, while all the saints look on—all within the womb of the Great Mother![51]

With the following words, Adams answers his question, "Why did the Middle Ages turn to woman instead of man for their devotion?"

> . . . their attachment to Mary rested on an instinct of self-preservation. They knew their own peril. If there was to be a future life, Mary was their only hope. She alone represented love.[52]

> God could not be Love. God was Justice, Order, Unity, Perfection; He could not be human and imperfect, nor could the Son or the Holy Ghost be other than the Father. The Mother alone was human, imperfect, and could love; she alone was Favour, Duality, Diversity. Under any conceivable form of religion, this duality must find embodiment somewhere, and the Middle Ages logically insisted that, as it could not be in the Trinity, either separately or together, it must be in the Mother.[53]

The Mother, then, was human, imperfect, a figure the masses could identify with and from whom they could obtain comfort, a mediatrix between the stern patriarchal and transcendent Lord and King and the people. E. O. James echoes Adams' conclusion when he points out that the interpretation of Christ as the divine Logos by the Church Fathers "had the effect of making the Saviour of mankind somewhat remote. Therefore, the need of some more intimate and truly human intermediary" developed.[54] But the church removed even this function of the goddess with its promulgation in 1854 of the doctrine of Mary's immaculate conception, which left her without any taint or tarnish of sin with which people could identify!

While Mary took on many of the functions and meanings formerly supplied by the pagan goddesses, she differed from them in one important respect, and it is a fairly crucial one, I believe, for our understanding of what we do with this herstory. For the Church Fathers, and in official doctrine, Mary was a virgin, but a very different kind of virgin than Ishtar or Isis or Demeter or Astarte; for Mary was completely asexual. The only way in which the Church Fathers could allow her to enter their pantheon was if she renounced all thought of sexual pleasure or the pleasures of a natural childbirth. Gone from her image was the sensuous, robust sexuality of the pagan mother-goddesses, whose virginity did not rest in their remaining intact genitally but in their remaining intact in their personhood, who could take lovers as they wished and not be constrained by doctrine, legislation, taboo, or guilt, or who could refuse lovers, if that was their pleasure, and not be thought the less for it.

As the delight in things bodily was lost from the godhead and thus from religion and pushed farther and farther toward the edges of culture, the center became stiff and austere. Women who wished for a life of service and fulfillment outside the home were shut up in convents and hemmed in with the most cruel and absurd restrictions and paraphernalia, lest they even catch sight of their bodies. Their sexuality, as well as that of their male counterparts, was sublimated into some of the most beautifully sensuous but hauntingly pathetic spiritual exercises, when one realizes with what a price it had been bought.

The Protestant Reformation, which promised so much and gave so little to women, may represent a step backward for the female of the species. At least the Romans had Mary to console them, when times were unbearable, and a tradition of independent, albeit ascetic, service and intellectual activity.

But even these judgments may be distortions of the facts. There have always been women who have responded to the call of their inner light, ignoring, circumventing, or defying religious law and taboo to assert their own sense of that which brings depth and transcendence to life. One thinks of Theresa of Avila who, though she remained cloistered, sang with the beauty of a nightingale in knowing that Jesus, when he was on earth, would never have treated women as they were treated in her day; or Ursula of Münsterberg, who fled the convent in the sixteenth century because the "prescribed readings in medieval works of piety and theology were to her entirely unedifying";[55] or Joan of Arc, who was burned at the stake for listening to voices and for, among other things, wearing male attire;[56] or Ann Hutchinson and her friend Mary Dyer, the first of whom was sent into banishment, and the second of whom was hung for challenging the doctrine that God could be mediated only through a duly appointed, male clergyman. Or one could think of Barbara Heck who, though she is rarely mentioned in Methodism while the names of Wesley and Asbury appear over many Methodist churches and colleges in the country, was the first to bring this new evangelical spirit to America. Then there are the Grimké sisters, who challenged male ecclesiastical arrogance to fight for the rights of the slave and their own sex, or Elizabeth Cady Stanton, who took on the higher criticism of European theology and read the Bible according to her own lights, which included some good, plain common sense.

And lest we forget, as most historians do, there were those

thousands upon thousands of nameless women who were slaughtered as witches during the Middle Ages and later by many of the luminaries of the Christian church. They, too, have their religious heritage which it might be enlightening for Christians to discover. The interlude of the witch-hunts is a chapter in the church's history which it would like conveniently to forget; and it has, until now. But women, who are concerned about their own history as women, are beginning to dig out the information and to make an assessment of its meaning which is independent of the bias given in official ecclesiastical documents.

What women are discovering is that the "witch-cult," as it was commonly called, was actually a form of the "Old Religion" which dates far back into antiquity and which we saw in its Near Eastern manifestations as the cult of the mother goddess. Some believe that the religion was actually that of the peasant masses of Europe. Sybil Leck, the noted British witch, claims that the proportion of witch cultists "to those of other religions" during those times was about one to one.[57] We know they represented a tremendous threat to the church, for they were hunted with a vengeance. Often entire towns came under the scourge of the inquisitor, and people were wiped out by the hundreds. We have evidence from the accusers themselves that witches were much involved with healing of disease. They were, in fact, the Middle Ages' true doctors: lay women abortionists, midwives, healers of abscesses, internists, pathologists, and pharmacologists. Indeed, many of the substances now used in medical practice were well known by these lay healers. At that time when the "official" physicians of the universities and theological schools were relying on bloodletting and pious incantations, the witches, with their knowledge of herbal medicines and a long history of empirical research, were actually curing people!

Some of the most persecuted witches were those who could claim cures; as a leading English witch-hunter put it:

> . . . and in the same number we reckon all good Witches, which do no hurt but good, which do not spoil and destroy, but save and deliver. . . . It were a thousand times better for the land if all Witches, but especially the blessing Witch, might suffer death.[58]

The principal accusations leveled at Jacoba Felicie, who was brought to trial in Paris, were that she had cured her patients and assiduously visited the sick, examining them in the manner of a physician! Professional jealousy has had a long history.

No doubt the healing ability of people who remained outside the Christian faith was a mortal threat to the church. But when it was performed by women, it was even more of an abomination.

There is also evidence to suggest that the followers of the Old Religion and their women leaders presented a formidable threat to ecclesiastical and political authority. They may even have been behind the several peasant revolts which occurred during that time.

You will remember that one of the aspects of the mother-goddess religion which was mentioned earlier was its lack of prohibitions around sex and the body. According to modern practitioners of the "craft," as they call it, the same frankness and naturalness about the human body prevails. To the ecclesiastics of the Middle Ages, for whom the body was the very locus of the devil, the frankness with which these women treated it must have been intolerable. The ecclesiastical literature of the time is filled with allusions to the sexuality of the witches.

A definitive history of the story of the Old Religion has never been written; but we know that for caring for illness, dealing openly with sexuality, and organizing peasants, thousands of women (and men, but fewer) were put to death by the Christian church, and an entire chapter of our herstory, spanning some three centuries or more, was distorted and eventually ignored.

The story of woman's unfolding religious consciousness and the place she played in religious movements is an ancient one, and yet it has hardly begun.

4 Reflections on the Meaning of Herstory

"History, therefore, is nothing but a compilation of the depositions made by assassins with respect to their victims and themselves."

Simone Weil[1]

History, Simone Weil pointed out in *The Need for Roots,* has always been written by the conquerors. To the extent that history represents the world view and value system of those who have "won," it is to that extent a distortion of the totality of reality-systems which could be extant at any period of time.

Judeo-Christian history, for the most part, has perpetuated a hierarchical, patriarchal world view characterized, as Mary Daly has pointed out, by "social and psychic models of dominance and submission."[2] By projecting this world view onto the heavens and claiming it as divine revelation from "without," breaking in upon human experience, the Judeo-Christian churches have sought to legitimize their own particular world view and authority systems. In doing so, they rejected and devalued the reality system of the ancient world—a system in which the sacred was found, not above, beyond, or in spite of the carnal, but in and through it—a system in which the organic processes of the natural world were found to be conjoint with human activity and relationships—and a system in which woman's natural functions were not demeaned but were actually understood as paradigms of salvation.

It is indeed ironic that a movement which would eventually destroy

139

this reality system and for the next five thousand years would extend its hierarchical and generally imperialistic world view across the globe should have entered the historical drama with an image of itself as victim. Still more ironic is it that its chief salvific model was seen as a victim. But perhaps there is nothing so unusual in all that. The image of oneself as victim, if it does not debilitate, leads almost inevitably to the need for scapegoats; and there has been no lack of scapegoats to which the Christian church has rallied.

As our herstory indicated, the first scapegoat to fall sway to the drive of patriarchal monotheism for predominance in the ancient world was the organic interrelationship of humanity with nature and, concomitantly, the role and importance of woman. As we have seen, the natural world was demeaned. It was no longer the locus of the numinous, the sacred, but an inferior "order" of creation which man was to dominate and subdue. Later on, it became not only inferior, but also the very seat of evil. Woman, as the human equivalent of the natural world, was likewise demeaned and subjugated. Her natural processes—menstruation, childbirth, lactation, and the beauty and symmetry of her body—which were formerly understood as channels of the divine and as resonant with symbolic, salvific meaning, were now viewed as dirty, unclean, contaminated, and evil.

The gods and goddesses which had symbolized for the ancients the depth of their experience of the mystery of life and death were castigated by the monotheists as "false" or "pagan" gods, and the rites surrounding them as mere idolatry. What was happening in the transition from a polytheistic, matriarchal world view to a monotheistic patriarchal system was a reversal in values, or rather, a supererogation by one side of the human equation of the values of the good and a projection of evil onto the other side.

Women's herstory seeks to open up to purview the vast panorama of human experience, so that reality systems may be seen in their relationship to one another. Just as colors assume differing hues depending on the colors they are surrounded by, so Judeo-Christian history and its authority systems take on a different gestalt when juxtaposed with the world view they sought to extinguish.

The development of herstory involves the ability to see through the cracks of the present reality system or "world construction," to use Peter Berger's term, to distinguish the outlines of another. During the course of his apprenticeship to Don Juan, Carlos Castaneda (in *The Teachings of Don Juan, A Separate Reality*) is asked by the old

Indian sorcerer to concentrate on the interstices between the leaves of a tree, rather than on the leaves. When he does this, the spaces themselves assume an objectivity, a reality they hadn't had for him previously. Herstory is somewhat like the space between the leaves; it is the forest which could not be seen by patriarchal historians because they had been concentrating so hard on the trees.

What happens when we begin to crack the prevailing reality system to discover new layers beneath and around it? Based on the rather limited treatment given to herstory in the last chapter, I believe there are certain affirmations which can be made and certain inferences which can be drawn.

The first affirmation is that the imperialism of the historical event as the authority for faith has been broken. Herstory relativizes history as it points to the fallibility of men and institutions to report accurately and fully on the events in which they are immersed. Herstory focuses light on the hidden assumptions and agreements, the disguised structure of language and emotion, and the cultural biases and accretions which determine the telling of patriarchal history. By the same token, herstory realizes its own agreements and assumptions but declares these at the outset, so that at least it cannot be accused of being devious.

In relativizing history, herstory undermines the authority of biblical revelation to be the exclusive channel of truth. It shows that the rise of monotheism and the development of what has been lauded as the "ethical impulse" in religious history were not won without great sacrifice: namely, the rejection of the body as a vehicle for the sacred, the subjugation of women and like "others" whose experience did not fit the right categories, and the rape of the earth.

The herstorian recognizes and affirms the noble impulse, the thrust of promise and fulfillment which lies behind the biblical epic, but laments some of the ways in which this impulse was translated. She is therefore not likely to find in particular biblical passages, events, or people that completeness of intent that the tradition claims for itself, but looks before, behind, beyond, and even outside the tradition as well as at it for her affirmation.

Thus, the feminist herstorian must reject the biblical literalist viewpoint as being unworthy of the true dimensions of the faith she is seeking. Patriarchalism and fundamentalism go hand in hand. It is no accident that researchers have found strong patterns of sexism in the fundamentalist Jesus communes,[3] nor that The Lutheran Church—

Missouri Synod and the newly splintered fundamentalist Southern Presbyterian Churches have strongly denied women the right to leadership positions in the church.

Once the imperialism of the historical event has been relativized, the feminist herstorian is free to choose from the tradition those points of insight and affirmation which speak most forcefully to her own experience and that of her sisters. She is also freed to explore the rich heritage of myth and symbol—both biblical and extra-biblical— and to allow it to speak to her, rather than accepting an interpretation of it as given by Scripture or authority.

The Christian church professes to believe that God is at work in the world. Yet, by locking God into formulations and symbols which may at one time have had meaning for a particular group of people but which since have become formal and static, it has prevented the numinous from breaking through the practical, rational barriers with which most of us surround ourselves.

As the herstory of women relativizes the imperialism of history as fact, event, or narrative, it also widens the historical lens. That is, it establishes a more inclusive range and depth of meanings which human societies have elaborated and which can have transforming power for us. In order to develop a comprehensive anthropology of *homo religiosus,* we cannot simply begin with the revelation of Yahweh to the Israelites because that "revelation" was predicated on the debasement of woman and of the natural world. As Christian and Jewish women, we have participated in that definition of ourselves at the expense of our *selves.* We have become our own oppressors.

We must begin, then, as far back as artifact, myth, legend, and unconscious memory will take us in order to understand ourselves fully as religious beings; and we must look seriously at those religious impulses which lay outside the boundaries defined by the Judeo-Christian tradition.

Some exciting things begin to happen when we dare to go beyond the stated boundaries in order to discover more of ourselves. First, the exclusivity of the linear view of history dissolves, and other paradigms begin to assume an ontological and existential importance for us: for example, the cyclical view of history becomes once again a possibility. When the historical lens is widened, we realize how fallible the Western linear view of history has been. No longer can history be conceived as a progressively upward movement from savagery and ignorance toward civilization and enlightenment. We see it as a much more complex and convoluted process. Whether or not one assigns one age to a higher rank than another depends upon the particular world view one holds. In questioning the value assumptions undergirding the Western theological/historical tradition, women also question the place assigned to certain events and movements on the scale of historical justice.

Who can say, for example, that the "pagans" were more ignorant or more savage than the Israelites? Yet it is precisely this assumption which forms the silent agreements upon which Christian theology rests. When the role, condition, and freedom of women is weighed in the balance, we would probably have to assign the pagans a more enlightened position than the postexilic Hebrews or the medieval Christian church. Likewise, on what basis do we assign the "Old Religion"—the witch cults of the peasant masses of medieval times— to a place of ignominy in the pageant of history while exonerating the efforts of the Christian church to stamp out this aberrant movement? Some claim that the attitude toward the natural world which is expressed in Genesis 1 (man is to "subdue" the earth) is "better" than the reverence for life which was expressed in the lamentations of Ishtar or in the Mysteries at Eleusis. Idolatry, then, exists in the eyes of the critical beholder, rather than in the eyes of the worshiper. Were the images constructed by the Judeo-Christian church—"God, the Father," the untainted virgin, the all-sacrificing mother, Jesus, the "Logos"—any less subject to idolatrous use than the figures of Astarte, Ishtar, and Demeter through whom the forces of mystery, transcendence, and the organic unity of life were mediated for the pagans?

Without being fully conscious of it, women today are recovering or rediscovering the pre-Judeo-Christian understanding of themselves as women. The interest in exploring our own bodies and our sexuality frankly and openly, the decision by many women to have children regardless of whether they are married, the fierce insistence on defining ourselves in ourselves and not simply in relation to men, and the deep empathy for the organic world which I see among many feminists today all have their echoes in the ancient matriarchal world view. In addition, there is a self-conscious exploration into ancient myth, symbol, and archetype going on among feminist artists, writers, psychologists, and theologians. In their experience the ancient mother-goddesses are being resurrected and are demonstrating that their transformative and integrative powers are equal to that of the Christian Christ.

There is at work among women today a powerful religious force which cannot be fully explained in Christian terminology. It is inadequate to say that women want to return to the ancient world view. Such a desire would be both stupid and impractical. But there is a sense in which we are beginning to understand and incorporate the deep psychic meanings which that world view expressed, and which have been continually suppressed in Western culture, in order to go on to a new synthesis. Women today are able to incorporate these meanings with a self-consciousness which the ancients did not possess, immersed as they were in a struggle for survival.

Thus, we are involved in a kind of cyclical return to our origins and are going beyond them to a new understanding of future possibility. The paradigm which expresses this process is more like that of a sprung spring than an enclosed circle, for we never simply return to the beginning as it was. We incorporate that beginning from the vantage point of greater understanding, which then allows us to go on to incorporate ever larger meanings. A diagram of the paradigm might look something like this:

eeeee

Each intersection of lines is thus the beginning and end of one circle or loop and the beginning of still another. This experiencing of life as a continuing spiral is expressed in the comment of a woman who was in a course given by Mary Daly at Union Theological Seminary. "Since being in the women's movement," she stated excitedly, "I am ten years younger and I have more of a future than I did ten years ago."

My own experience reflects the same paradigmatic schema. The more I allow myself to be open to life in the present, the more I discover myself anew in the past, and the greater my future possibilities. I am, as it were, plunged back into my past only to be catapulted into my future. For example, many of my present concerns and many of the insights I thought I had only recently discovered were present in my thoughts as a teenager, although never fully articulated or understood then. I realized this after rereading a diary and several poems I had written during my teenage years and then forgotten.

In a similar way, as women discover themselves in the present, they also discover the sisterhood of souls in the past, who asked some of the same kinds of questions and began to articulate the same kinds of answers. It was surprising to a group of us at a conference on women exploring theology in the summer of 1973 to discover that what we thought were new questions we were raising about certain biblical figures had been raised three-quarters of a century earlier by the authors of *The Woman's Bible!*

Another paradigm for the historical process, which is made possible by a consideration of herstory, is that of radical discontinuity. This paradigm presents more problems for us in light of the evidence pointing to the efficacy of the cyclic or sprung-spring paradigm, but there is some justification for being open to this possibility. Elizabeth Gould Davis's speculations lead to a consideration of this possibility. Based on the assumptions of Immanuel Velikovsky that somewhere around the tenth millennium B.C. a worldwide shifting of the poles occurred, Mo. Davis speculates that the mythical kingdom of Atlantis, the race of Amazons, the mysterious knowledge of the Druids, the inexplicable existence of stone monoliths around the world, and the early evidence of belief in a mother-goddess all point to the preexistence of an advanced technological civilization ruled by women—a civilization which was eventually destroyed by the world cataclysms which myth and recent archaeological discoveries record.[4] There is also a sense in which the technological breakthroughs in the biomedical field which have been made in the last few years present us with the possibility of a truly radical future, as radical as the patriarchal age must have been from the matriarchal. The development of cloning, test-tube babies, genetic manipulation, and the like presages a totally different kind of human animal and community. Radical discontinuity is indeed a possibility.

Since feminist women have least to lose from a break with the old system, we are more open to a radically discontinuous future. The question we must ask ourselves is: Will we allow this future to overtake us, as we allowed the patriarchal revolution, or will we have some voice in its direction?

The herstory of women relativizes the historical event; it widens the historical lens and brings into consideration paradigms other than the linear to explain the historical process. As it does this, it also brings into focus the cellular substructure of the religious enterprise, the life force which determines the genetic character of the system. It focuses on what Christian theologians and historians have consistently ignored in their analyses of the development and function of religious systems: namely, the part played by sexual fears, myths, fantasies, and necessities in the elaboration of religious convictions.

Christian theologians have sought to define God above and apart from the basic sexual duality of the universe; yet each of their formulations has been based on sexually determined assumptions. Our herstory has revealed that the mystery of life and death was originally understood in explicitly sexual, morphological terms. The mother-goddesses were powerfully sensual and sexual. Intercourse was a paradigm for creation and regeneration.

With the rise of monotheism, the explicitly sexual imagery eventually went underground, but it continued to inform the determination of doctrine, even though that doctrine was now spiritualized and abstracted. God the Father was above and beyond the contingency of human sexuality, or so the tradition taught us. Nevertheless, he was a very masculine figure. And while Jesus was the incarnate Logos, the "man for others," the "second person of the Trinity," the scandal of his particularity did not extend to interpreting what he was about in feminine terms.

Circumcision, originally the primitive male's imitation of menstruation, became a mark of the Covenant. In the Christian era, Jesus' blood and body—the wine and bread—took on the symbolic resonances formerly associated with the great goddess, while birth from the womb became rebirth through immersion in the baptismal waters (amniotic fluid). Male priests eventually assumed in a professional capacity the nonprofessional roles naturally assigned to women—nurturance, care, maintenance, education.

A look at herstory reveals the extent to which Jewish and Christian doctrine has been determined by the sexual fears and fantasies of men about women. In denying to themselves the psychic origins of these doctrines, Christian theologians have at best been dishonest and at worst tyrannical. Not only have they denied women a proper role in the practice of religion, but also they have denied all of us the chance to explore the fullest dimensions of the sacred.

One further insight which a look at herstory affords us is a broader understanding of the dimensions of human evil and of the longing for human liberation and fulfillment which are expressed in the doctrine of the Fall and in the experiences of the Exodus, the incarnation, and the resurrection.

Herstory provides us with several different ways of reinterpreting the notion of the Fall, paradigms which seek to make broader and deeper sense of the alienation which lies at the heart of creation. These paradigms will be explored more fully in the following chapter. Herstory also points out that we can no longer limit God's work in history to the deliverance of the Hebrews from bondage nor to the incarnation in Jesus Christ. That lens is just too narrow. Rather, what we see when we look at woman's role in the history of patriarchal religions is that in various eras there is a pattern of the rising of women toward full personhood and transcendence of their culturally defined roles and a concomitant suppression of this force by the patriarchal authority system.

Such a rising, it would seem, was occurring even as the patriarchal Yahwist cult was struggling for supremacy in ancient Palestine. The Yahwistic tirades against idolaters are really a backhanded compliment to the force of feminine expectations. The earliest Christian church, again, witnessed a rising of women and then a suppression of this movement by the post-apostolic Church Fathers. Similarly, the witches of the Middle Ages, and perhaps those who were persecuted in New England, can be seen as examples of the striving of women toward liberation and humanity. The cruelty with which the Christian church exterminated this movement speaks poignantly of the power which must have been alive among those women. The nineteenth-century women's movement is yet another example of the attempt of one-half of creation to be free. Who is to say that a powerful, numinous force is not at work now in the current women's movement? Perhaps only those who have failed to understand herstory will deny the power of the present reality.

5 The Personal Is Political: Toward a Wholistic Ethics

Our dissection of the patriarchal world view and our penetration through the cracks of that reality system into another have indicated that the values one holds, the particular ethical systems that social groups construct, are largely dependent upon the reality paradigm held by a particular person or group. The way in which one perceives the world determines the relative values that person assigns to persons, acts, and events.

Reality systems, especially as they are legitimized by "sacred" authority and solidified in the very language one uses, tend to change very slowly. So it has been with the reality system operative in traditional Christianity and in Western culture. There have been, of course, many modifications in this reality system, but they have been modifications which did not penetrate to the essentials.

Thus, for example, the Copernican revolution shook man out of his complacency in the bull's-eye of the universe, but it did not undermine or reverse the ancient hierarchical order of the created world in which manliness was next to godliness. The "great chain of being," as it was defined by philosophers, or the "order of creation," as Christian theology conceived it, was a secure, rational system in which each form of existence had its appointed place and was valued in relation to its approximation to the ultimate good, order, or God. The Copernican revolution did nothing to disturb the order in which man stood as God's proxy and in this capacity had the right to own woman and animals and to manipulate and subdue the earth. The seeds of the desacralization of nature and the body, which reached its apotheosis in the industrial revolution, were planted in the soil of postexilic Judaism and watered by the springs of Christian Neoplatonism.

Nor did Darwin's "revolutionary" theory of the evolution of the species disturb in any essential way the paradigm expressed in Genesis 1 that the last created was the best—the culmination of God's work. (In citing man as the culmination of God's handiwork and woman as a secondary helpmate, the Church Fathers displayed a bit of masculine inconsistency. For if they had been consistent, they would have recognized that Eve, in the second biblical account, was created last and therefore should have been preferred over Adam. Phyllis Trible, in an article entitled "Depatriarchalizing in Biblical Interpretation," postulates, through an examination of the ring structure of Hebrew literature, that Eve was intended by the biblical writers to be seen as equal to Adam.)[1] The paradigm that the lower precedes the higher has undergirded the Western idea of progress, with its will toward transcendent power; it has provided Christians with an excuse for feeling superior to the Jews and for civilized man to feel superior to primitive man; and it has eliminated all but a self-righteous reading of history.

The scientific era, ushered in by Galileo, Descartes, and Newton, with its emphasis on what Theodore Roszak has called "single vision"—on objectivity, differentiation, and measurement—did not signify a radical break from the theocentric world view of the past.[2] Rather, Newton's mechanistic universe was merely the secularization of the impulse which was operating in the development of Yahwism and came to full expression in Hellenistic mind/body dualism. This was the impulse of the transcendent consciousness which sought to separate God from nature, mind from matter, and to locate salvation either in a flight from the contingencies of the world or in a capitulation of the world to the rational intellect of man, i.e., the "technical fix." If, in the old physics, God molded his creation according to his divine will, in the Newtonian physics, man through his transcendent will was able to mold and reprogram the world according to his own wishes. Coercion and manipulation, outside purposeful force operating on unintelligible matter, remained the operant world view. Even the entire controversy between science and religion and the uneasy truce which was negotiated between them reflect the dichotomizing world view.[3] Science and religion are two different spheres: the one deals with the soul, the other with matter, and never the twain shall be integrated.

The secularization of popular consciousness which began in the late nineteenth century was not accomplished through any radical change in world views. Rather, the throne, formerly occupied by God and his delegated ecclesiastical authorities, was now taken over by secular "expert elites." These scientists, educators, philosophers, psychiatrists, and politicians of the modern age exercise a similar kind of coercive power to define reality and to punish deviations from their world view as that formerly exercised by Christian ecclesiastical authority. Both Thomas Szasz *(The Manufacture of Madness)* and Phyllis Chesler *(Women and Madness)* point out that the modern psychiatric profession has taken over the functions formerly assumed by church authorities. Witches were burned by the medieval church; today such persons are declared insane by the psychiatric profession and are shut up in mental institutions.

The nature of the authority exercised by ecclesiastical elites in former times or by modern elites of "experts" today is similar. It is authority based on concrete power—economic, political, social— and the power which comes from possession of or access to expertise or specialized bodies of "knowledge." In terms of operant world views or reality systems, there is very little difference between Moses' receiving the law from God and "handing it down" to the Israelites (even the mountain upon which he is supposed to have received the tablets participates in the symbolic overtones of high authority, power, judgment, coerciveness) and the situation which exists in most American classrooms, foreign aid programs, business establishments, law courts, doctors' offices, the legislative process, or churches on a Sunday morning. The communication is usually one-way: it is knowledge, reality defining, handed down from expert elite to uninitiated recipient, and it fosters in the recipient feelings of dependency, inferiority, and apathy. The familiar phrase of the "man in the street" who says, "I don't know that much about it; I think the president (substitute for president, 'doctor,' 'teacher,' 'minister') knows best; he has more information" indicates the depth to which this world view has been accepted in our culture.

If we may summarize thus far, it is reality paradigms, or the set of interlocking, precognitive assumptions about the world held by particular societies which determine the ethical and moral values that society holds. Paradigms thus author, and authorize, the way we think, the way we act, the way we communicate, and the way we judge.[4]

Generally speaking, there has been a fairly consistent world view or reality paradigm operating throughout the long course of Judeo-Christian history and even down into the secular age. This world view, for want of a better term, I have called patriarchalism, because it was developed in the age of the patriarchy and has been maintained ever since by a male-dominated culture. The patriarchal world view has been challenged at many points along the way—by the antique pagan mystery cults, possibly by the early Christian community, by the witches and alchemists of medieval Europe, by the Eastern experience, by the nineteenth-century feminist movement, by modern physics—but each time it has managed to maintain its control because of its belief in and willingness to use coercive power. Today, this world view faces its most crucial and far-ranging challenge both from the women's movement and from Third-World liberation movements.

Traditional Christian ethicists, working as they have within the overarching canopy of the patriarchal world view, have never been able to question the validity of their most basic assumptions. What, then, are the assumptions, the value judgments upon which Christian ethics has been based? What is the moral stance which proceeds from a patriarchal world view?

The most fundamental assumption from which Christian ethics proceeds is that human nature is predicated upon a fall from a state of grace—a fall which occurred outside time and space and which therefore is never fully capable of being corrected in this life. This fall from grace, moreover, was defined in terms of willful disobedience, a refusal to accept one's divinely ordered limitations, a reaching for too much. Pride was, and in many cases still is, the essential sin in the Christian ethicist's lexicon.

Humanity, through its own efforts, is never able to overcome the alienation brought about through such a fall. Only through divine intervention, in the act of atonement, was the possibility of reconciliation indicated. But even that act of atonement was only a sign of things to come, an indication of possibility rather than a demonstration of complete fulfillment. The human condition, then, is fundamentally pessimistic.

Human beings can approximate the fulfillment and reconciliation hoped for only through an imitation of that divine intervention. Only through radical conversion, death to the old self and rebirth to the new in Jesus Christ can humans begin to overcome the fundamental error in their existence. Only by *negating* the prideful in oneself, by *surrendering* the self, by *submission* and *obedience* can humans hope to recover that state of wholeness and bliss which was promised in the beginning. Evil = pride; good = self-abnegation; change = willingness to die in order to be reborn, or radical discontinuity with the old self. Such is the framework upon which Christian ethical systems have been built.

A corollary to the assumption that pride is evil is the assumption that anger is evil, for anger represents insolence against one's ordained place, against the Divine. Anger is the outward manifestation of the inward condition of pride. Love, then, is equated with a lack of anger, with sweetness and humility.

As we have seen, such an ethical posture proceeded out of a vision of the world as a hierarchically ordered plenitude in which each living entity had its own place and function. Whatever tended to disturb that order was seen as evil, and what could not be controlled by the rational mind (which was close to the top of the hierarchy) was construed as dangerous. Thus, women who aspired to more than their just rank had assigned them were viewed with suspicion; and because anger, strong emotions, and sexual urges often were not controllable by the rational mind, they, too, were considered powerful and to be feared and avoided.

The ethical posture of the Christian churches has led to many acts of true compassion and altruism, but it has also provided the rationale for the suppression of freedom and for acts of cruelty and coercion. Some of the woes attributable to the Christian patriarchal world view and its value assumptions have already been catalogued: the denegration of women, the destruction of the natural environment, the extermination of witches, the holy wars fought in the name of Christian righteousness, the colonialist and imperialist policies of white "Christian" countries, etc.

The most serious failure of Christian ethics has been its inability to provide a theoretical foundation for the establishment of wide-ranging social justice. It has failed in this endeavor because it has refused to look at the underlying reality paradigm upon which it has been built. The hierarchical world view which determined that evil was to be equated with pride and self-transcendence while salvation was found in submission to the divine will is a world view which leaves intact the political status quo; in fact, to upset that status quo, to overstep the divinely sanctioned boundaries, is to commit sin. Such a set of values speaks not to the dynamics of systems nor to the way in which persons interact with systems, but only to individual motivations and aspirations. It suggests that corporate evil is overcome only through a multitude of individual conversions, and it leaves the Christian bewildered in the face of political power. It provides no way of understanding or of influencing social change.

Thus, most Christian ethics have been individual or social ethics. The personal and the political have been separated in the Christian's mind, and indeed, in his or her actions. This separation of the personal from the political has led to an excessive preoccupation in the Christian church with matters of personal morality, often based on a set of distorting and cruel legalisms, again, a residue from the hierarchically ordered paradigm which continued to inform the Christian conscience.

A case in point is the example of a young, unmarried Methodist minister who was recently removed from his church and refused another appointment in that same conference because he announced to the senior pastor with whom he worked that he was planning to take a canoeing vacation with a woman friend. For the young minister, the decision to take such a vacation was a carefully thought-out one and represented the culmination of a deepening and mature relationship with the young woman. Moreover, his decision to tell the senior pastor about it was based on his desire to be completely honest about his life. Instead of understanding the entire gestalt in which this decision had been made, the church hierarchy focused on the breach of conventional sexual morality which the decision to take that vacation represented. At the same time that the Christian church becomes upset over a breach of conventional sex morality like this, it often ignores or even condones the real crimes being committed by the body politic—the bombing of Cambodia, the deceit and ruthless arrogance of the administration revealed in the Watergate affair, the murders and the eclipse of freedom in Chile, the racism and sexism which exist within its own domain.

Sadly, as the case of the young minister indicates, even though the church has tended to ignore corporate ethics and to be overly preoccupied with personal morality, it has not even done a very good job with the personal. Its continuing resort to legalistic categories (especially where sexuality is involved) often creates sin where none existed before.

In *Moral Man and Immoral Society,* Reinhold Niebuhr attempted to right the lopsided balance between personal and political ethics by exposing the ways in which human collectives operate, often in defiance of one's personal ethical convictions. In unmasking the self-seeking pretension in much of Christian idealism and in advocating the application of a critical sensibility to the study of political and economic systems, Niebuhr's contribution to Christian ethics was enormous.

But even Niebuhr's critical sensibility did not carry him far enough. The failure of Christian realism, the school of thought which he espoused, is written in the history of the 1960s. So many of the "best and the brightest" pragmatists who got us into the quagmire of Vietnam were tutored in the ethos of Christian realism. The Watergate hearings have more than anything else exposed the inability of "realists" to comprehend either the reasons for their actions or the results of their decisions. The incredulity and surprise expressed by the senators conducting the hearings represented a kind of naiveté about the very system in which they, too, were immersed. The Watergate hearings did not reveal some kind of ontological venality in the hearts of these men who sought power as much as they exposed the entire hierarchical world view in which these men were immersed—a world view based on social and psychic models of dominance and submission. Such a world view or reality paradigm may actually create a *need* or *drive* for power which may not "naturally" (i.e., in other circumstances) be at the heart of the "human condition."

Niebuhr's realism failed to penetrate to the edges of the reality system in which it was immersed. Christian realism is still very much a product of the patriarchal mentality. It continues to define sin as pride—renamed "egoism" or "self-interest" by Niebuhr; it is essentially pessimistic about the ability of human beings to shape creatively a more humane destiny; and its solution to the human dilemma is to accept and work within the limits of the status quo, that is, to accept the presence of competing political power blocs and the definition of collective self-interest as evil but necessary.

Thus, realism positing a kind of ontological determinism offers no new vision by which to understand reality and therefore no new hope for the oppressed. The result is that Christian realism tends to become the ideology of the establishment masquerading as a universally valid world view, as Rubem Alves, the Latin American liberation theologian, pointed out in a reply to Thomas Sanders's defense of Christian realism in *Christianity and Crisis:*

> Realism and pragmatism are words dear to American ears, hearts and brains. If this is so, anyone who is involved in social analysis should suspect at once that realism is functional to the system, contributes to its preservation and gives it ideological and theological justification. This is the source of my irritation. Realism has not yet recognized that it is an American ideology and yet proceeds to pass universal judgment over the other "regional" theologies.[5]

The Christian realists' stance, as revealed in the title *Moral Man and Immoral Society,* perpetuates the traditional Christian ethicists' assumption that there is a qualitative difference between group and individual behavior. Yet if, as Niebuhr assumed, group self-interest was simply individual egoism exponentially multiplied, then how could a person be moral and still participate in the immoral activities of society? "Moral man" and "immoral society" is a contradiction in terms. One of Niebuhr's young friends came closer to the truth in suggesting that the book should have been entitled "The Not So Moral Man in His Less Moral Communities."[6]

Rosemary Ruether suggests that Niebuhr merely gave voice to a tendency which was developing with the industrial revolution and the rise of bourgeois society. This was the tendency to split the consumer home off from the alienated world of work and to make the home the locus of morality, while decisions based on "rationality" and a balance between conflicting power forces operated in the world of work. Women who were confined to the home thus became the upholders of morality, while men made "rational" decisions out in the "real world" of the marketplace. Morality, Ruether points out, became "privatized, sentimentalized and identified as 'feminine.'"[7]

The effect that this privatization of morality had on women of the bourgeois class is reflected in countless diaries kept by Christian women in the nineteenth century; into these mute witnesses were poured pages of guilt and anguish over sins which were often "too terrible to record"—sins such as not feeling content with their duties or feelings of anger directed toward husband or children. Modern women are often heard to record the commission of similar "sins" in consciousness-raising groups and in chatter which occurs while watching children in a playground or while meeting "over the garden fence."

The guilt which is generated over the commission of such sins is both false and neurotic—false because the sin is caused, not by any volition on the woman's part, but by the social system in which she is immersed, and neurotic because it leads to no genuine repentance, no personal growth or understanding.

The dichotomization of the public and private spheres—which came to its apotheosis with the industrial revolution but was endemic to the structure of the patriarchy—has led to an attitude today which derides any attempt to apply moral standards to public life. We saw this happen in the last presidential campaign when McGovern attempted to call the country back to some sense of moral values in the public realm and was made a laughingstock because of it. It is seen in a recent United Nations Secretarial publication which states that "the United Nations deals in the realm of what is possible, not of what is right or wrong,"—this statement in seeming contradiction to the moral obligations laid on the U.N. by its Charter and Declaration of Human Rights.[8]

Many men in our culture today believe they are being good, i.e., "moral," if they consider themselves "good family men." But these same men think nothing of taking kickbacks, cheating on their income tax, or exploiting others through the kinds of business they are engaged in. Morality, for them, simply doesn't enter into the world of business or finance or politics. Christian realism, I am afraid, has to take some kind of responsibility for giving "sacred" legitimation to this kind of psychic dichotomy. All too many persons in our Christian churches believe that their faith has nothing to say to them about the kinds of decisions they have to make out in the "real world."

In believing that there was a qualitative difference between individual and collective behavior, Niebuhr and other "realists" reveal their immersion in the patriarchal reality system. The feminist experience has taught us that there is no difference in kind between the personal and the political attitudes and behavior of men in patriarchal societies, but that, in fact, they are beholden to the same reality paradigm with its psychic model of a hierarchically ordered world, its view of the relationship between things as governed by a superordinate-subordinate pattern, its distrust of the nonrational and its heavy emphasis on reason and will, its mind/body dualism, its linear view of history, and its tendency to exclusivity and definition through differentiation.

Scratch the surface of any marriage in which the man of the house insists on a dichotomy between private morality and public rational decision making and you will find the same patterns operative in the home as on the job. The man may consider himself a "good family man" because he provides all the necessary conveniences for his family. The family relationships may even, on the surface, appear to be smooth. But underneath it all runs the same thread of dominance and submission. There is probably little mutuality in the male-female relationship. The woman is usually "kept" by her husband, placated by more and more consumer products as a way of keeping her submissive and in her place. The "separate but equal doctrine" (which blacks have learned means separate and unequal) operates in the home. The wife is in charge of the home, but not of herself; and should she want to broaden her interests, expand her education, become involved in a cause outside the home, she finds that it can be done only in the extra time left over from keeping the family and home together. The man identifies himself as a man through his more valued (by both himself and society) involvement in the world of work and through differentiating himself from his less valued (by himself and society) wife. His advancement up the corporate or political ladder is made possible by his wife's ability to keep home and family intact and by his dependence on a low-paid and often exploited female labor force—secretaries and clerks.

Women have come to an understanding that the personal is political through the consciousness-raising process. In the course of this process we came to learn that the problems we thought were purely personal—that we thought were due to our own peculiar upbringing or to our own inabilities or neuroses—were, in fact, shared by every other woman. We began to see that our relationships with our mothers, our fathers, our male and female peers, our bosses, our husbands, and our children followed similar patterns and met with similar resistances. We realized that while each woman's life follows a distinctive course, there is a general pattern that unites us all. We realized that women inhabit a different culture from that inhabited by men. We realized that our relationships with men, no matter how intimate, were governed by certain unequal distributions of power—educational, economic, social, political, and physical.

As we moved out from the family unit to analyze our role as women in the larger society and in the world, we began to see the same kinds of general patterns emerging, the same kinds of resistances to our growth displayed, the same kinds of power games operating. Through the consciousness-raising process women have come to see that our position in the home or in the larger society is not so different (paradigmatically speaking) from the position of the Latin American peasant vis-à-vis the ruling elite or the black welfare mother in relation to the affluent white. We have come to see that the football games so enjoyed by the men in power in this country are but a mirror image of the war-games played in the Pentagon, and that the white European or American male theologian's claim to "scholarly objectivity" and "academic excellence" is but a weapon in the arsenal by which they protect their privileged position of power against the threatening incursions of Third-World liberation theology or feminist theology. We understand now that those in positions of ecclesiastical, political, or economic power who still insist that the worst sin is egoism, pride, or self-interest are not applying those categories to themselves but to those whom they would keep subordinate.

Racism, sexism, class exploitation, and ecological destruction are four interlocking pillars upon which the structure of the patriarchy rests. The structures of oppression are everywhere the same, although the particular forms in which oppression is manifested may at first glance look different. The democracy of the Athenian *polis,* to which the Western world has always looked as its ideal, was made possible only through the restricted domestic labors of the slaves and wives of the Athenian property owners. Western "freedom" and affluence depend on the domestication of women and the exploitation of a low-paid labor base made up of minorities and women as well as unlimited access to foreign sources of natural resources which are taken from the ground without regard for the rights of the earth or the people who live on the land.

The feminist experience has thus enabled us to penetrate the superficial differences to see the systemic and psychic links between the various forms of injustice. Feminists hold that the alienation of woman from man—because it was the first and still is the longest lasting form of human alienation—can be seen as a primordial paradigm from which all other unjust relationships derive.

Modern women, however, were not the first to understand the

sources of injustice. Imagine our surprise to find John Stuart Mill, writing one hundred years ago to the very same point:

> All the selfish propensities, the self-worship, the unjust self-preference, which exist among mankind, have their source and root in, and derive their principal nourishment from, the present constitution of the relation between men and women. Think what it is to a boy, to grow up to manhood in the belief that without any merit or any exertion of his own, though he may be the most frivolous and empty or the most ignorant and stolid of mankind, by the mere fact of being born a male he is by right the superior of all and every one of an entire half of the human race; including probably some whose real superiority to himself he has daily or hourly occasion to feel.[10]

Mill again echoes the modern feminists' complaint that the Christian church attempts to heal the very diseases it has created:

> The example afforded, and the education given to the sentiments, by laying the foundation of domestic existence upon a relation contradictory to the first principles of social justice, must, from the very nature of man, have a perverting influence of such magnitude, that it is hardly possible with our present experience to raise our imaginations to the conception of so great a change for the better as would be made by its removal. All that education and civilisation are doing to efface the influences on character of the law of force, and replace them by those of justice, remains merely on the surface, as long as the citadel of the enemy is not attacked. . . . If no authority, not in its nature temporary, were allowed to one human being over another, society would not be employed in building up propensities with one hand which it has to curb with the other.[11]

Because we are aware of our own subjugation and objectification by men, feminists are particularly sensitive to the way in which others are objectified and oppressed. It is no accident that the feminist movement in this country from its very inception was linked with the abolitionist movement, that the modern feminist movement grew out of the civil rights movement of the 1960s, and that groups like the YWCA and the National Women's Political Caucus, which have been strongly influenced by the feminist perspective, have taken strong stands against racism as well as sex inequality and have been working for the rights of welfare and working-class women as well as equal rights for the middle class.

The feminist experience and its understanding of history, then, provide us with a handle on the human condition, with a way of understanding and explaining the fact of human evil. Because it is able to see the connections between the various forms of human evil, it is able to offer a vision of the health and wholeness to which the entire biblical experience points but which has never been adequately delineated before, either by Christian idealism or by Christian realism.

A similar vision of health and wholeness, an assertion of the integration of all moral perception, is being offered by the oppressed of the Third World. Colin Winter, the exiled Anglican Bishop of Namibia and a firm supporter of the black liberation movements in Southern Africa, recently pointed out to a group of us that while representatives of the Western super-powers at the United Nations and other international gatherings continue to talk about "balances of power," "expediencies," "economic stability," etc., representatives of the oppressed insist on talking about morality and values.

What we see when we look at the history of the human condition through feminist eyes—through the eyes of those who have inhabited a culture of silence—is a basic alienation at the heart of life. This alienation or estrangement occurs within the individual human psyche as well as between men and women, humans and the earth, between group and group, race and race, nation and nation.

Whence developed this alienation, and why? Orthodox Christianity asserted that human evil came about as a result of the Fall. Eve's reaching for knowledge, her disobedience of God's command brought about the expulsion from the Garden—from that wholeness, unity, and bliss which humanity has been searching for ever since. But orthodoxy's simplistic explanation of human evil as caused by overweening pride, disobedience, egoism, or self-interest will no longer do. We have seen how this very doctrine served to perpetuate the structure of alienation and injustice which it sought to explain and correct.

Paul Tillich's explanation of the Fall as the moment of passage from essence to existence, from dreaming innocence to self-actualization, is a little more palatable, but it does not go very far in explaining why alienation occurs as it does. Moreover, Tillich's analysis is essentially pessimistic, offering little hope that the human condition can be other than it is. To assert that human self-actualization must of necessity (ontologically) be accompanied by guilt and anxiety is not to provide much motivation for persons to want to become self-actualized. Though he demythologizes the myth, Tillich accepts its basic reality paradigm: that human self-transcendence is basically tragic and dangerous. Again, it is an argument for the status quo. The only way out of this tragic human dilemma for Tillich and other Christian apologists is the positing of a divine intervention into human affairs in the person of the Christ. Humanity's acceptance of and participation in the "New Being" brought about by Christ constitutes its salvation. In spite of his existential posture, Tillich cannot help resorting to a *deus ex machina* as the solution to the dilemma he posits. Moreover, his God is still the patriarchal figure who molds and manipulates his creatures and who demands obedience from them. Tillich's language eventually gives him away, as when he describes the relationship of the "New Being" of Christ to people as a "grasping and drawing into itself." The characteristics of this "New Being" again are described in the old terminology: "faith instead of unbelief, surrender instead of *hubris,* love instead of concupiscence." [12]

Unlike Tillich and most other theologians who locate alienation in the ontological structure of things, a feminist reading of history and the feminist experience suggest that this alienation may actually have been a function of certain historical processes. The Fall may have occurred *in* history, not outside of it!

We know from our own experience, and from psychological, sociological, and anthropological studies, that the alienation between males and females may not be a "natural" alienation (that is, an ontological necessity) but to a large extent has been created through cultural pressures exerted on us from the time we are born, first by our parents and then by the host of other cultural influences which impinge upon us as we mature. We also know that we are taught from an early age that our bodies are dangerous and dirty (especially our genitals), that our feelings and senses must be kept under control by our rational faculty, and that dirt and decay, ooze and slime, and all of the messy, smelly organic processes of nature are to be avoided or cleaned up. We know, also, that in certain other cultures these prohibitions, inhibitions, and fears do not exist. The equatorial woman goes about her work bare-breasted; the primitive man's rituals involve painting himself with mud; the women and men in the Mozambiquan liberation movement, *Frelimo,* share everything equally.

We also know that in premonotheistic religions women played a greater role than they do in ours, that for premonotheistic society and for American Indian tribes the earth was not merely a repository of natural resources for human use but a divinity, "Mother Earth," Demeter, Ceres; and for the ancients, sexual intercourse was a holy symbol rather than a dangerous practice.

Our reading of history suggests that the beginnings of the alienation of woman from man and humans from the earth (from which all other alienations derive) occurred with the patriarchal revolution sometime between 5000 and 600 B.C. With the discovery of paternity came the rise of primogeniture and private property, the subjugation of women, the desacralization of nature, the development of city-states and political life, and the beginning of war. Somewhere in all that mix monotheism arose to legitimate these various forms of alienation. Arnold Toynbee lays the genesis of pollution at the feet of monotheism:

> My observation of the living religion of eastern Asia, and my book knowledge of the extinguished Greek and Roman religion, have made me aware of a startling and disturbing truth: that monotheism, as enunciated in the Book of Genesis, has removed the age-old restraint that was once placed on man's greed by his awe. Man's greedy impulse to exploit nature used to be held in check by his pious worship of nature. This primitive inhibition has been removed by the rise and spread of monotheism.[13]

After all, the injunction of the Scripture was that man was created in God's image in order that he might have dominion over every living thing. Plants and animals were made *for* man; they did not exist in their own right, but only as they could serve man's needs. From the Yahwist's perspective, anyone who thought that a grove of trees or a piece of stone was holy was castigated as an idolater, a whorer after false gods, an evil one. The development of the priestly version of the creation story in Genesis 1 came rather late in Israel's history. No doubt prior to this, Hebrew society had already been moving to separate itself from nature. But the development of this theological position with its clear enunciation that *this is the way life was meant to be* gave "sacred" legitimation to what had probably been at best a tendency which was fraught with ambivalence. Paradigms both *author* and *authorize* thought and action.

Why man lost his awe of nature, why he felt it necessary to subordinate woman, why the idea of private property arose, we can only speculate. Did it have to do with the biological nature of the two sexes—that as man the hunter discovered his role in procreation, he was able physically to subdue woman and claim her and her children as his property? Did the subordination of woman have anything to do with the necessity to curb woman's insatiable sexuality in order that civilization might advance, as Mary Jane Sherfey *(The Nature and Evolution of Female Sexuality)* has suggested? Was the emergence of the individualized, self-conscious, male-dominated ego functional to the development of civilization as we know it, as Rosemary Ruether postulates? Did the first form of alienation hinge, as Engels thought, on the development of bronze and iron tools, which suddenly gave man an advantage over nature? Or was the patriarchal world view with its succession of alienations the product of the political force which happened to *win,* to conquer in a concrete sense over another people who possessed a different world view which eventually passed into oblivion?

The paucity of records as to what early life was like can only mean that such questions will be rhetorical. By positing a Fall within human history, I am not pointing to the existence of a Golden Age in some ancient time, so much as to the connections between human systems and human evil, to the effect which particular human reality paradigms or world constructions have on human behavior. In this sense a feminist ethic is likely to be labeled utopian, for it believes that human nature can be changed. However, positing a belief that it can be changed and believing that it is likely to happen are two different things. Feminist ethics looks not simply to a change in political systems, as Marx did, but to the breakthrough of a radical new world view in which thought and feeling, response and behavior, in both the private and public realms, will be transformed. We are not sanguine that such a transformation will occur. The engines of patriarchy are powerful indeed and may well engulf the world in ruins before a more humane dawn has a chance to shine.

Our utopianism, however, is not simply idealistic. We do have some evidence that a purposeful perceptual and behavioral transformation is at least partially possible. We see it happening within the women's movement itself, in the transformation in Communist China and in the Frelimo liberation movement in Mozambique. If we cannot affirm that a perfect society will come about, we can posit, with Third-World liberation theologians, the nonnecessity of this imperfect order.

We can also offer a more penetrating critique of the present order than that offered either by Christian idealism or by Christian realism and in so doing hope to show the nonnecessity of the present order. By locating the source of human sinfulness in the patriarchal world view, we are able to find metaphors which help to explain and to connect the various manifestations of sin, both personal and corporate, in a way that was not possible before.

Such metaphors are summed up in a series of dualisms, the two halves of which are related to each other as superior to inferior, superordinate to subordinate. Male/female, mind/body, subject/object, man/nature, inner/outer, white/black, rational/irrational, civilized/primitive—all serve to explain the way in which the patriarchy has ordered reality. As we have seen, the left-hand side of each equation has assumed a kind of right of ownership over the right. The relationship is one of owner to owned, oppressor to oppressed rather than one of mutuality.

The links between the various forms of alienation and oppression are clear when we begin to analyze and then compare the psychic relationship that exists between each of the pairs listed above. For example, in Western culture and in the Judeo-Christian tradition, male and female have been related to each other as mind to body. The male owns or subordinates the female just as the mind controls and manipulates the body. In the Western theological mind, woman was body, while man was mind or the spiritual, rational will. The divine *Logos* which was carried over from Greek philosophy into Christianity was distinctly male. It was thought by the Church Fathers to represent the essence, or the original archetype of life, while bodiliness, femaleness, and sexuality occurred as a result of the Fall.[14] In the early church tradition it was man who represented the subject of creation, while woman was a distinctly subhuman object. She was irrational nature, rampant sexuality, the primitive dark, bestial side of life, while man represented the light, civilizing, rational superego. Salvation was located in an otherwordly return to the spiritual essence and in a repudiation of nature and the body.

In the same way that man subordinated and stereotyped woman, so each dominant group has subordinated and stereotyped those whom they have conquered or whom they wish to conquer. To the Israelites and their modern equivalents the Baal and Astarte worshipers represented all that was irrational, sexual, bodily, primitive, and dangerous. In the eyes of the Yahwistic writers they were not real people with a mixture of traits, but idolaters, objects of scorn and derision. Jezebel became a symbol of female infamy through this objectification process. It was not until the nineteenth century when women, realizing the way in which they had been stereotyped and objectified by male culture, could begin to make anything like a realistic assessment of Jezebel's character. Here is what one commentator in *The Woman's Bible* wrote about Jezebel:

All we know about Jezebel is told us by a rival religionist, who hated her as the Pope of Rome hated Martin Luther, or as an American A.P.A. now hates a Roman Catholic. Nevertheless, even the Jewish historian, evidently biassed *(sic)* against

Jezebel by his theological prejudices as he is, does not give any facts whatever which warrant the assertion that Jezebel was any more satanic than the ancient Israelitish gentleman, to whom her theological views were opposed. . . .

I submit, that if Jezebel is a disgrace to womankind, our dear brethren at any rate have not much cause to be proud of Elijah, so, possibly, we might strike a truce over the character of these two long-buried worthies.[15]

The social and psychic models of dominance and submission which operated for men against women and for the Israelites against the pagans continue to operate today wherever one group oppresses another. For the white racist, the black takes on all the characteristics which we have seen attributed to women. He is bestial, irrational, sexually dangerous, dumb, yet also passive, slow, emotional, and shiftless. In essence, the black is objectified, made into a subhuman species. The peasant, the Oriental, and the African have been similarly labeled. Countless Vietnam veterans have spoken of the fact that they were able to kill the Vietnamese because they thought of them as "gooks," as a mindless subhuman species, rather than as people like themselves. Indeed, they have testified that the army taught them to think of the "enemy" in this way. As the song from *South Pacific* goes, "You have to be taught to hate." Much of man's aggression, his impulse to murder and exploit, has been taught him by his culture and by the world view which dictates the values he assigns to objects and persons. Contrary to popularizers of the notion that man is inherently aggressive and bellicose (such as Robert Ardrey and Desmond Morris), most reputable biologists, psychologists, and anthropologists conclude that war is a learned or conditioned behavior—a product of human culture. Psychologists at the Canadian Peace Research Institute find the person involved in war doesn't even have to be especially aggressive. Their research indicates a high correlation between militarism and conformity or obedience to orders. In order to teach our children to be peacemakers, they contend, we should teach them to be nonconformist as well as nonaggressive.

It is a well-known observation that Fascist regimes combine an authoritarian world view with a hierarchical social system, an appeal to puritanical "personal morals" and strict sex-role differentiation. War, ecological disaster, the subordination of women, slavery, racism, and colonialism can all be seen as extensions of the deep-seated psychic dualism which arose with patriarchal culture. To say that such sinfulness stems from humanity's inherent selfishness, pride, or egoism is to mistake a symptom for the disease itself.

Indeed, pride and egoism may even be good. The oppressed inevitably internalize the dehumanizing traits projected upon them by the oppressor. Their own inadequate self-image—that is, their *lack* of pride and egoism—coupled with their deliberate exclusion from avenues to growth and self-actualization, contribute to the oppressor's myth of fixed and inherited natures.[16] For the oppressed, the development of pride and a healthy self-esteem is a necessary prerequisite to overcoming their condition as oppressed and for liberating both themselves and their oppressors from an unhealthy dualism. Thus, the development of pride among the oppressed can be an act of love which frees not only themselves but also their oppressors.

Recent scientific discoveries about the brain, mentioned briefly in chapter 3, shed even more light on the strange nature of the psychic and social dualism we have been talking about. These discoveries have confirmed that among the mammals human beings alone have developed different uses for each half of the brain. Curiously enough, the left side of the brain, which controls the right side of the body, has developed the functions which Western culture has traditionally associated more closely with the male. This half of the brain controls language, the ability to read, logic, the analytic or dissective abilities, and sequential knowledge, while the right half of the brain, about which we know less, seems to be involved with the kind of knowing traditionally associated with musical and artistic talent and with feminine imagery: spatial ability, intuition, emotion and feeling, the ability to grasp the total *gestalt* of a scene, and recognition of faces. This half of the brain appears to scientists to be mute and illiterate, and it has generally been neglected by our culture; yet scientists believe that it actually perceives, feels, and thinks in ways all its own, which in some cases may be superior to the other half.[17] Indeed, Einstein's theory of relativity may have been generated in the right half of his brain. When he was asked how he arrived at some of his most original ideas, he explained that he almost never thought in terms of words at all. His concepts appeared first through "physical entities"—certain signs and images that he could reproduce and combine. "Conventional words or other signs have to be sought for laboriously only in a secondary stage," he is reported to have said.[18]

Such research on the brain, developed only within the last decade, throws some astonishing light on the nature of the human condition and should be of keen interest to philosophers and theologians. Let me speculate a bit about the implications of these discoveries for the development of a new theological anthropology.

It would seem that the dualism which arose with patriarchal culture amounted to an excessive reliance upon and valuation of the left half of the brain (the rational, logical, verbal half) over the right half and a consequent devaluation of and projection onto an outward "object" of the kind of knowledge and understanding of life assumed by the right half of the brain. Men began to claim for themselves the exclusive rights to logical thinking, verbal ability, reading and writing, the storage of and passing on of communicable knowledge while prohibiting women from this sphere of activity. As women and other objectified groups, such as slaves, were relegated to the home and to activities which did not call for logical thought, for verbal or literate abilities, they consequently did not develop the left side of their brains and were left with the culturally devalued functions of feeling, intuition, emotion, and relationships. Women have long been associated with prophecy, psychic powers, and magic—all functions of the right half of the brain.

Does this mean that women, because of their biology, are less rational and verbal than men? The evidence indicates that culture plays a large part in determining which half of the brain gets more fully developed. According to Dr. Robert Ornstein, early in life many of us become shaped either as "'left-hemisphere types' who function in a largely verbal world, or as 'right-hemisphere types,' who rely more on non-verbal means of expression." He points out that

> children from poor black neighborhoods generally learn to use their right hemisphere more than the left—they outscore whites on tests of pattern recognition from incomplete figures, for instance, but tend to do badly at verbal tasks. Other children, who have learned to verbalize everything, find this approach a hindrance when it comes to copying a tennis serve or learning a dance step.[19]

Premonotheistic religion must have favored the functions of the right hemisphere of the brain, for it would seem that mystical knowledge, the apprehension of divinity in the natural world, sexual and emotional abandonment, and an intuition of the oneness of the universe are all part of the ancient, and in many cases primitive, apprehension of reality. They may correspond to what Rollo May in *Love and Will* describes as the *daimonic,* which lies at the heart of all passion and creativity. No wonder, then, that the stern Yahwists felt that they had to stamp out Baal and Astarte worship with a vengeance. The irrational, the intuitive, the daimonic has always been a frightening force to the rationalist. Such activity does not lend itself to control very easily; it tends to undermine efficiency and "progress." Here, again, modern scientific research throws some light on history. In observations of persons whose two hemispheres have been separated either through surgery or accident, scientists discovered that the verbal, logical hemisphere does not trust the other hemisphere and will tend either to ignore it or put it down.[20]

Theodore Roszak points out that the Jews' insistence on a God who was to be heard but not seen or touched, which was at first an attempt to purify the faith by focusing on the "spiritually potent symbolism of sound," ended up by literalizing and desacralizing the symbol.[21] It was the first step in the long process by which a vibrant religious world view became fossilized, compressed into laws, teachings, creeds, and dogmas. It represented the transference of religious knowledge from the right to the left side of the brain.

With the first blush of nascent Christianity there occurred a resurgence of religious enthusiasm and a partial return to the way of knowing engaged in by the right hemisphere of the brain. In the excitement of Pentecost and in the fervor of apocalyptic times the normal order of society became upset. Forgetting their duty to be submissive, chucking the veil of modesty and seclusion, women began to prophesy, pray, preach, and minister. The new enthusiasm probably stimulated more reciprocal social intercourse between the sexes than had been seen in Jewish culture for hundreds of years. But it was soon to come to an end. Paul's insistent warnings against idolatry (e.g., Acts 17:16 ff.; 1 Corinthians 8; 1 Corinthians 10:6 ff.; etc.) are reminiscent of the earlier warnings of the Hebrew prophets. Paul's God would not be mediated by sight, by touch, or by any of the senses but the specialized Word, spoken by the apostles in consonance with certain prophetic pronouncements found in the ancient Scriptures. In 1 Corinthians 10:6 ff. he even warns against dancing, as a sign of pagan immorality. The body, then, with its sensual, nonrational, nonverbal understanding could not be an avenue to the sacred.

When one considers that Christianity was spreading in a world in which the pagan mystery cults were again raising their ecstatic heads, one can understand (although not necessarily sympathize with) Paul's insistence on defining and delimiting his God apart from the manifestations of these other "gods." It was a situation somewhat similar to that in which Yahwism fought for predominance in Canaan centuries before. At the same time Paul was claiming a universality for Christianity, he was also cutting it off from avenues of correlation and consonance with the other religions of his day. The Christian God could not be understood through dance or visual imagery, through totalistic participation in the deep mystery of rite and symbol, but only through the interpreted Word. Paul's influence on the early church meant a return to that singleness of vision which Roszak believes has plagued the development of the Western world ever since.

Visual symbolism and, as we have seen, the feminine began to creep back into the Christian church in the post-apostolic age but only in a denatured, spiritualized form and always mediated by the authoritatively delivered word. Consider, for example, what became of the symbol of the mother goddess in the Christian church. For the ancients, the mother goddess was a symbol pregnant with a multitude of meanings which could never be fully contained in rational discourse about her. In fact, except for myths and "stories" in which she is featured, there has been very little written about her. We know that she symbolized for her devotees the deepest mystery of life and death, that she reflected the organic relationship between human and animal and vegetable life, that she summed up the meaning of sexual and parental love, that she incarnated the "feminine" as one of the basic polarities of life, and that she represented and transformed for humanity the painful knowledge of its own mortality. But such *talk* about the symbol of the mother goddess does not begin to encompass her meaning. As a symbol she had to be *lived into* and participated in through rite and mystery. Only through such nonverbal, nonrational participation could her mystery be grasped.

When the Christian church took over this symbol of the great goddess in the form of Mary, she became deflated, emptied of most of her visionary and transcendent meaning. Gone was her function of unifying the spiritual with the sensual and with the earth, life with death, heaven with earth. Gone was her overarching meaning as the mother of all of life. Henceforth she was only to be known as the "Mother of God." Mary could only be a mediatrix between humans and the mystery which is God by denying her humaneness, her sexuality, her taint of human mortality and limitation. She became the ethereal, saccarine, spiritualized *essence* of womanhood, to which women could aspire only by denying the fullness of their own humanity. The Church Fathers *taught* people to see the mother goddess in only one dimension. They *legislated* out the multidimensional aspect of the symbol through the various doctrines of the annunciation, the virgin birth, etc. It was as if the brain's left hemisphere had said to the right: "I will allow you to speak only when you are called upon and only under the conditions I set down."

With the Protestant Reformation came the final triumph of the rational over the nonrational, the left over the right hemisphere. The Reformers' insistence on the Word as the center of worship and authority spelled doom for any wholistic understanding of or participation in the mystery which is God. Even the sacraments, which in Catholicism had maintained a glimmer of their participation in the mystery which cannot be contained in rational thought, were reduced to ciphers, mere signs which *stood for* but did not become that to which they pointed. The coldness, sterility, lack of depth, and unfriendliness which one sometimes feels in white Western Protestant churches today represents the fossilized remains of the course on which the patriarchy set itself—a course which increasingly denied the right hemisphere of the brain, the mute and illiterate but passionate and creative side of human beings, equal time with the volitional, rational side.

Thus, the alienation, the dualism which arose with patriarchal culture we find to be not simply a split between the rational ego and the outside world, between men and women, race and race, nation and nation but a split within the very mind of humanity itself—a valuation and dominance of one part of the mind over the other, which is then projected outward onto the world forming patterns of dominance and submission.

Understanding the source of human evil in this way enables us not only to see the psychic and systemic connections between various forms of evil and to understand why the personal cannot be dissociated from the political, but it also presents us with a clearer vision of the wholeness to which the Hebrew term, *Shalom,* points or the salvation and reconciliation which is offered by the Christian gospel.

To give flesh to a vision of wholeness is to close the gap between the polarities which have been separated and alienated from one another, to right the lopsided balance which has occurred where one side of the psychic or social dualism has predominated at the expense of the other. A vision of wholeness suggests patterns of reciprocity, mutuality, equality, and intermingling. The Chinese symbol used for this concept serves as a good illustration of the way in which such reciprocity, in the rhythmical balancing of forces, is to operate. Unfortunately, because the symbol has conceptualized darkness, receptivity, passiveness, and death in feminine terms and creativity, light, and active assertion in masculine terms, it has tended to be misinterpreted by Western scholars who saw in it a confirmation of their own sexual stereotypes. The concept of *yin* and *yang* is much more complex than that. *Yin* and *Yang* do not represent male and female but the primal forms of life energy from whose interaction—somewhat like the interaction of the positive and negative poles of the magnet—all of the variety of life is thought to spring. Behind the symbols of *yin* and *yang* lies the concept of the T'ai'chi, or the undivided One, the Eternal, the Absolute, of which *yin* and *yang* are but the tangible or phenomenal manifestations.

We do not have to go to Chinese culture, however, to find the concepts and symbols which point to wholeness. They are there in the cosmic myths of every people—in the great cosmic egg from which the heavens and earth were thought to have sprung. The seeds of liberation and wholeness, as feminist theologian Nelle Morton has often pointed out, are found even in the very traditions with which we are familiar. They have simply been translated out of the texts or ignored by the male-dominated culture.

Nelle Morton and others point to the fact that the *'adham* in the Hebrew creation myth, the Hebrew word for the creature which was formed before the female was taken from it, incorporated the notion of *both* male and female, although in English it is translated as "man," thus obscuring the original intention of the passage, which was the creation by God of an androgyne, a male/female. Only after Eve is formed from the *'adham's* rib (Genesis 2:23) is the androgynous noun *'adham* replaced by the term, *ish,* meaning man the male, and *'ishshah,* meaning woman. Of course, the priestly version of the creation account in Genesis 1 states quite simply that man (i.e., human beings) was made in the image of God, male and female.

In further support of the contention that the biblical creation account intended to convey the idea of the equality of the sexes and their union in an androgynous whole which preceded the fall into duality, Christian feminists (that is, those who still uphold the sacred canopy of the Judeo-Christian revelation) cite other biblical evidence. Phyllis Trible, associate professor at Andover Newton

Theological School, asserts that the "intentionality" of biblical faith functions as salvation for both men and women. She finds this intentionality through a rereading of the Bible "without the blinders of Israelite men or of Paul, Barth, Bonhoeffer, and a host of others."[22]

Ms. Trible points not only to the mistranslation of the word *'adham,* but also to the mistaken interpretation of the Hebrew word *'ezer* for helpmate or helper, used in reference to Eve as the helpmate of Adam. The word *'ezer* connotes not an inferior status, as we have come to think of it, but one of perfect equality. The same word has often been used in reference to God in the Old Testament.[23]

Ms. Trible also points to the fact that "feminine imagery for God is more prevalent in the Old Testament than we usually acknowledge," occurring frequently "in traditions of the Exodus and wanderings." She reminds us that women figured prominently in the revolutionary movement by which the Israelites escaped from Egyptian bondage, and she sees in the Song of Solomon, a resolution, in the imagery of mutual sexual love, of the alienation between man and woman which occurred with the Fall.[24]

Other Christian feminists see in the figure of Christ that androgynous way of life to which they assert the gospel calls men and women. They point to the fact that Jesus treated each person uniquely and as an individual, rather than categorizing them in sexual or class terms. Jesus, it will be remembered, contravened law and custom to treat women as human beings equal in status, faith, and knowledge to men. Not only did he disregard the laws which sustained woman's inferiority and uncleanness, but he seems in certain passages even to have advocated the dissolution of socially fixed roles, as when he commended Mary for "choosing the better part" by listening to his teachings rather than helping her sister Martha in the kitchen (Luke 10:39-41) or when he asserted in Luke 8:19-21 that his "mother and brothers" were not necessarily those who were linked to him by blood but all "those who hear the word of God and do it."

These and all the other instances in which Jesus relates to sinners, rich men, prostitutes, tax collectors, the sick, and demon-possessed, not on the basis of their socially defined roles or status, but on the basis of their common humanity, convince Christian feminists that the seeds of liberation and wholeness are there in the Gospels waiting to be nurtured by a society which sees through the patriarchal biases of later ecclesiastics and theologians. How absurd, then, that men and women who claim to be Christian still insist on making patriarchal distinctions between people, which set one group in a position of superiority to another. From the feminist perspective, the Catholic and Episcopalian hierarchies and the fundamentalist sects which continue to insist on woman's exclusion from the priesthood or on her subordination to man are not truly Christian, if to be Christian means to accept the life and teachings of the Christ of the Gospels rather than the Pauline, Augustinian, or Lutheran Christ.

The ethic of wholeness—that androgynous vision to which the Old Testament creation stories, the Christian Gospels, and the feminist movement point—is not solely contained within these movements but runs like translucent thread throughout the garment of the patriarchy. It is found in myth, in literature, in art, in song, in movements such as the medieval peasant revolts, in utopian thought, and, yes, even in the dreams of Marxism. To limit the longing for wholeness to the Judeo-Christian tradition or simply to the feminist movement would be to deny the cosmic scope and existential depth of the desire for human freedom and wholeness. The vision represents the yearning to be fully human and to be fully in touch with the ground of one's being. It is rooted in existentiality and tethered to transcendence. It is the yearning to be a self-actualized subject rather than an other-defined object. It is the legacy women everywhere share with the oppressed and exploited of the earth, and it is even that which we share with our sister, the earth, which has been exploited by patriarchal man.

The ethic of wholeness points to the need to dissolve both personally and corporately the culturally fixed categories by which human beings are defined and too often delimited. It means breaking down the stereotypes of masculinity and femininity which are prevalent throughout our culture, in our churches, schools, business establishments, laws, media, etc. It means finding ways to dissolve the categories by which one group of persons is subordinated to another—whether it be categories of race, class, age, caste, "developed" or "underdeveloped," manager or worker, ruling white or peasant.

The androgynous ideal to which a liberation from sex roles points does not mean that male and female will suddenly disappear and become absorbed into some kind of neuter or unisexed creature, as many seem to fear. Rather, it means an openness to the tremendous natural variety which exists within each person and a structuring of society in such a way that each person can develop to the fullness of his or her own individual potential. If no other evidence were needed to show that we are all potentially more androgynous than we believe, the conclusions being reached by scientists about the functions of both hemispheres of the brain indicate quite clearly that what have traditionally been considered male and female ways of knowing and thinking are present in each of us. Males could learn to be more intuitive, emotional, and creative, and females could learn to be more rational, logical. and verbal if the social sanctions for such exploration into "forbidden territory" were present. By denying males the access to their "femaleness" and females the access to their "maleness," the patriarchy has kept each of us from developing into whole persons—into that androgynous ideal to which the creation stories point. If there is any way in which being "made in the image of God" has meaning, it is surely in such a concept of wholeness.

The intermingling of sexual characteristics, within one person and between persons, then, constitutes the androgyny of creation. Men will continue to be males by virtue of having a different set of genitals from females, but their masculinity will no longer be dependent on their conforming to some culturally defined set of goals or characteristics, such as their ability to beat up other boys, to "make it with a girl," to have large muscles, to be the "provider" of the house, to be superior to women, to make it to the top of the business ladder. Rather, what was formerly the pressure to define their false "masculinity" will be transformed into an effort to define their humanity—that unique combination of interests, talents, and skills which is theirs by virtue of heredity, environment, and that mysterious quirk of fate which lies at the heart of our individuality. Similarly, women will remain women by virtue of their genetic construction but will no longer be bound and limited by that heredity. They, too, will define themselves in terms of their interests, skills, and talents.

Interestingly enough, in the process of redefining ourselves, women are rediscovering what it means to be a woman, that is, to be possessed of breasts and a vagina rather than a penis, and to see and feel the world through our female bodies. The question of biological heritage has taken some interesting turns since the feminist movement began. It may be that our biological heritage as male and female has more to say about how we respond to the world than we, at first, thought; but the true roots of our masculinity and femininity will never be discovered unless we first get rid of the cultural baggage which has confined and constricted us for so long.

The shedding of culturally defined sex roles promises the release of real love between men and women, women and women, and men and men. Categories which previously determined that our responses to and behavior toward one another would be held in check through limits have restricted our ability to love one another fully. Contrary to the fears of many that a loss of sexual distinctions means a loss of attraction and therefore of love, feminists have found just the opposite. Where persons are open to accepting and rejoicing in the full humanity of another, whether it be a man who can rejoice in his wife's election to public office, or a woman who can rejoice in her husband's newfound delight in a creative art or craft, there true love flourishes. As long as men perceive women as an inferior Other, as long as they fail to notice that some of the same human qualities exist in women as exist in men, they will fail to love. What passes and has passed for love in the long history of patriarchal culture is but a caricature of the real thing.

As soon as women begin to experience the freedom to become fully human, self-actualized subjects, they find that they no longer need to find their identity through their children. This frees them to accept their children's full humanity and uniqueness rather than to see them as objects to be molded or as vehicles for their own unfulfilled desires. Possessive love (which is not love at all) is stopped at the door of androgyny.

Perhaps one of the most significant flowerings of love to have come out of the feminist movement has been the discovery by women of their love for each other. Under the patriarchal system, woman was set against woman in the unending competition for favor with superior men. Through the consciousness-raising process, women have discovered their common humanity, and in the discovery they have experienced a kind of love for each other which is so deep and profound that it can only be described as transcendent. It is that love which we uncover when we discover the common links of feeling, ambition, fear, hurt, and desire which we all share because we are all human or because we are all women. It must be the kind of love which, in Jesus, was so contagious—that love which enabled him to accept and to *be with* a variety of people, no matter what their station in life.

Another way to conceive of the wholeness to which we were born and for which we yearn is to consider the split between mind and body which occurred with patriarchy. An ethic of wholeness would posit an integration or rhythmical balance between the logic of the mind and that of the body. Sam Keen in *To a Dancing God* points out that the body has a logic and a way of knowing all of its own, which may in some cases be more attuned to the law of cosmic justice than the rational mind. He cites as evidence that the body's first reaction to the sight of carnage is to rebel, to scream, to retch, to protest this violation of another's flesh as if it were a violation of one's own.[25] The mind, however, is able to abstract the experience and to rationalize it away with excuses that "terrible things happen in war," "they weren't real people, anyway, they were gooks or 'the enemy,'" and so on. Murder, war, and genocide are thus possible because we are able to objectify the enemy, separate him from ourselves by an act of logic and will. It is the old self-definition through differentiating ourselves from a subordinate Other, which is at the heart of the patriarchal world view with its valuation of the mind over the body, the rational will over the irrational affections.

The abortion debate offers us another explicit example of the way in which patriarchal thought separates mind (or person) from body and objectifies an Other. I am always amazed and incensed to read articles on abortion written by men (most of the debate is also carried on by men) who have so little understanding of the woman's experience of her body.

The rigid Catholic or "Right to Life" viewpoint is well known and needs little denunciation here. What disturbs me most is the attitude displayed by supposedly "liberal" theologians and theoreticians as they discuss abortion. Two articles on abortion which have appeared in religious publications illustrate my point. Both articles, one by Amitai Etzioni, a prominent sociologist at Columbia University, and the other by C. Eric Lincoln, a renowned theologian, recognize that abortion may be a necessary evil but speak to the need for the law to give the husband and the state some voice in any decision on whether to abort. In effect, both men argue against the policy which leaves a decision on abortion up to a woman and her doctor.

Both authors reduce the woman's argument that the fetus is a part of her own body—an argument which is derived from the complex, wholistic way in which a woman experiences her body and the fetus within her—to a simplistic abstraction. Here is Etzioni's argument:

Some women activists argue that the fetus grows in the woman's body; the husband's contribution is miniscule; the woman invested her energy, time and resources in the fetus. But by this logic most lawn mowers will be the husband's property, and dishwashers—that of the wife. And, above all, it does not recognize that a pure biological approach will not do in these matters. Socially and culturally the evolving child should be viewed as a product of both parents, although one can readily agree that the woman's contribution is much greater at this stage.[26]

For Etzioni, the abortion decision becomes one of arguing over the relative rights of husband and wife to control a piece of property. Indeed, his article is entitled "The Fetus: Whose Property?" The woman, he implies, stands in the same relation to the fetus as she does to a dishwasher in which she has invested time, energy, and resources. Dr. Etzioni distorts completely the feminist argument that a woman should have a right to her own body. The body is not a piece of property!

Dr. Lincoln in his argument trivializes the experience of an unwanted pregnancy by reducing that experience to a mechanistic operation. Here is Dr. Lincoln's argument for changing his stand on laissez-faire abortion (itself a loaded term):

Stress is put on the fact that the woman must carry the child in her body, to her possible inconvenience in one way or another. But "incubation" is in some sense only the counterpart of "procreation." Both require the instrumentation of the body and its processes and resources. One of these processes requires more time. But society evens out the responsibilities by placing the subsequent burden of primary liability upon the male.[27]

(Aside from the remainder of the argument, Dr. Lincoln's assumption that society places the burden of primary liability for the growing child on the male is utterly false. In patriarchal societies it is the woman who has the primary responsibility for children.)

But there is something even more disturbing about Lincoln's argument. Pregnancy, he assumes, is a "possible inconvenience." Moreover, he labels it "incubation," as if the woman's body were merely a repository in which the baby is stored until gestation. Here is a modern male theologian appropriating the ancient male argument (used by the Hebrews and Greeks, as Apollo did in the *Eumenides*) that the woman is only a nurse, an incubator of the live seed which is delivered into her body by the male. This period of incubation, Lincoln claims, is only the counterpart to procreation—both require the "instrumentation of the body and its processes and resources." Incubation just takes a little more time. Dr. Lincoln's terminology is revealing. Pregnancy is "incubation" requiring the "instrumentation" of the body. With these words he reduces the body to a machine or tool and the person to a manipulator of that machine. Both the father and the state, he goes on to say, have some claim over that body/machine—the father because the child "belongs equally to its progenitors," and the state because in other instances the state "requires the conversion of some (male) bodies to military tasks; it confines some bodies in jails or other institutions, thereby drastically reducing the options for personal decisions regarding those bodies."[28]

The horror of such a reductionist rationale for conscription and incarceration seems to have escaped Dr. Lincoln. He is able to use that analogy himself, because as a male in a patriarchal culture, he has been taught to view his body as something alien to him, as an instrument or tool which can be worked on or "converted" or "confined" by some outside force. As we have seen, such an attitude reflects the mechanistic world view of patriarchy in which the mind (i.e., person) is separated from the body. Such a psychic dichotomy results in the ability either to turn one's own body into an object or to view others as objects. Women then become "incubators," sexual playthings, bodies, pieces of property, and *people* are seen as "gooks," "niggers," "criminals," or "communists" who can easily be liquidated.

That false dichotomy between person and body is alien to the female experience, although we, too, have been taught to objectivize our bodies. But it is especially alien in pregnancy. When we are pregnant, *we are pregnant.* We do not experience the fetus as a separate being within us which might have rights which are in conflict with ours. It does not become a human being—in our experience—until the umbilical cord has been cut and we can have a reciprocal relationship with it. It is only by a monumental effort of abstraction and a wrenching distancing of our minds from our bodies and our affections that we can convince ourselves that we are harboring an Other within us. Thus it is a violation of our *total being*—it is a falsification of our experience of life for men to suggest that pregnancy is "incubation," that it is merely a nine-month "inconvenience," or that the time, energy, and resources which go into that process are comparable to those which go into dishwashing or mowing the lawn. During pregnancy it is *our* bloodstream which is made to do double duty, often resulting in broken capillaries, varicose veins, embolism, and toxemia; it is *our* legs which swell, *our* stomachs which produce nausea, gas, and heartburn, *our* backs which ache, *our* breath which becomes short, our total person which feels fat and ungainly, *our* energy which is sapped. The male does not bear this same relationship to the fetus. Pregnancy can be a wonderful experience if freely chosen, but a disastrous one if not. As women, we experience our bodies as *ourselves*. The question then becomes: Do we have a right to our *selves?*

Perhaps another way to look at the mind/body split is to look at the predominance of the left hemisphere of the brain over the right, for it appears that the body's responses are somehow linked to that mute and inarticulate but emotional and creative side of the brain—the side which has consistently been devalued in Western Judeo-Christian culture.

An ethic of wholeness would call for ways, in both the personal and corporate spheres, for people to get in touch with their bodies again and to learn their special rhythm and message. One of the chief messages of the body, Sam Keen points out, is the message of our own mortality. Perhaps if we could hear that message at a more elemental level, we would have no more need for ethics based on the negative, on the "thou shalt not," but on the positive, on the knowledge that life and time are precious. We know that persons who are facing a terminal illness find life so much more meaningful and full in the present than those of us who can forget about our own deaths. Body knowledge keeps us humble.

Body knowledge is also our window on the world. Through an understanding of and participation in the ecology of the body we can gain a better understanding of the ecology of the natural world and our place in it. The premonotheistic peoples understood this relationship better than we do, as do American Indians—at least those who have not been corrupted by the white man's culture. We have come to a point in the history of civilization where, if we do not begin to understand these relationships, we may very well end by destroying everything. What we need, states Rosemary Ruether, is a "new ethic of reconciliation with the earth."[29]

An ethic in which humans are reconciled with their bodies and with the earth does not mean a return to the primitives' complete immersion in nature. Such a feat would be both impractical and absurd in the light of history. If wholeness means anything in this context, it means a balancing of the needs for the survival and comfort of the total human community with the inherent rights and ecological balance of the natural world. Clearly, an ethic of wholeness would condemn the arms race, the rush to explore outer space, and the standard of living which most Americans enjoy. A reconciliation with the earth could mean a great deal of living in harmony with it, without being at its mercy. Rene Dubos has seen such a model at work in the Benedictine order with its management of nature in compatibility with the maintenance of environmental quality.

Instead of sending rockets to the moon in a patriarchal effort to transcend the limits of our humanness—as the Christian apocalyptic salvation myth sought to deny mortality by looking to an angelic new creation—we must learn to cultivate our earthly garden, which is at once our beginning and our destiny as human beings. We need, says Ruether, a new "salvation myth of *humanization.*"[30]

It is rather frightening to realize how deeply ingrained in our consciousness—through the patriarchal world view with its transcendent, omnipotent Father God on whom we are patterned—is the need to believe that there are frontiers out there to be conquered and subdued if we should destroy our planet. I remember arguing with a group of clergymen about this. All of them felt that it was man's destiny to use every bit of technology he invented, to explore every piece of outer space to which his technology would take him. When I pointed out that the money and energy spent on exploring outer space could better be spent on the poor and the hungry and in making this planet livable, they declared that the earth would burn out in the sun in so many million years anyway, so that it was a waste of time to spend all our money and energy on it. The frontier mentality with its aggressive, manipulative impulses was so powerful in these clergymen that I might have been talking to a stone wall.

The wholeness which we have been discussing in these pages is a wholeness based on a multidimensional vision of the world, rather than on the single vision which has dominated Western culture and most theological thought. Such a multidimensional vision means the ability to grasp complexity, to live with ambiguity, and to enjoy the great variety that exists in the world. Wholeness does not imply the eradication of differences as the old assimilationist model did or as the fear of a monotonous unisexual creature implies. On the contrary, wholeness of vision may lead to a multiplication of differences, as people are able to choose freely the person they want to be rather than following a pattern of one they are *expected* to be. Only through an affirmation and celebration of our differences can we come to an understanding of the ties that bind the total creation together.

Not until the white Westerner comes to an appreciation and affirmation of the physical characteristics, spiritual qualities, life-style, and culture of those whom he has formerly looked down upon as "primitive" or "underdeveloped" or "savage," can he discover the common humanity which binds them together. Only after males can appreciate and affirm women and women's culture, only after males realize that they might yet learn something about life from females, can true reconciliation be achieved between them. A wholistic ethic affirms singleness within community, diversity within unity, the validity of *both and,* rather than *either or.* It is the only kind of ethic worthy of a pluralistic world.

Well, you may say, the vision sounds fine, but how do we get from here to there? The path from alienating dualism to integrating wholeness is here for the taking, most especially in the liberation movements of women and the oppressed, which are swelling with the leaven of freedom below the crust of the patriarchy. The mute and inarticulate hemisphere of the brain cannot be suppressed for very long before it has its say in reckless and frightening ways. Sometimes it appears as ulcers, at other times as fits of rage, or as madness. The mute and inarticulate ones of the earth are now clamoring to be heard. Will the world heed their angry voices, or will it suppress them with destructive consequences?

There can be no essentially just (wholistic) ethical decisions made if the voices, the feelings, and the life conditions of the formerly mute and inarticulate ones go unheeded. For example, solutions to the abortion dilemma, family planning, day care, and the like, must be made with regard to the total condition of woman's position in society and with full regard for her own feelings and the way in which she experiences her body. No just solution to the abortion dilemma can be made until woman's role has been equalized with man's. Just decisions in this realm, therefore, will never be made by men who do not share the same kinds of conditions and liabilities as women do who, up to now, have been among the mute and inarticulate. Similarly, Western powers cannot make just decisions as to how development money is to be spent for the so-called underdeveloped nations, unless the voices of the peasants, the oppressed, and the poor are considered of equal value to those of the ruling elite.

Mary Daly has suggested that the feminist movement

transvaluates the values of patriarchal society; that is, it calls for going beyond good and evil as they have been defined in the Christian tradition and in Christian culture toward a new understanding of the nature of values. We have already seen how the dichotomy between private morality and corporate "realism" were transvalued as they were swept up into a broader vision of the nature and source of human evil.

One of the emotions most consistently rejected by the Christian tradition as negative is the emotion of anger. Anger, it was assumed, was in some way the antithesis of love and kindness. Christian women were ever exhorted to be sweet, gentle, and kind, that is, loving. Feminism rejects the totally negative valuation of anger. A wholistic ethic sees anger as a legitimate part of the human constitution alongside the more gentle virtues. If anger is not seen as a legitimate partner in the human struggle for growth and fulfillment and is not allowed to speak, it becomes very angry. It may even take over.

Through consciousness-raising, women came to discover their anger; they discovered that it had been there all along, but it had been turned in against the self, erupting through frequent feelings of illness, ill-temperedness, nagging, and depression. Once released, however, this anger became the driving force for overcoming the situation of dependency and subjection in which women found themselves. It is thus with any oppressed group. Without anger, love becomes dull and powerless, unable to effect a change for the better. Whoever cannot become angry over injustice, inhumanity, oppression, cruelty, and terror is incapable of loving. Anger is the body's resounding "no!" to its violation; it is love's answer to the question left by human evil.

During the terrible Christmas bombing of Cambodia, I remember walking through the halls of Congress with a friend of mine, an old radical who has fought and marched and picketed and been arrested for just about every cause in which man's inhumanity to man has been protested. I remember asking him, "Lee, what has kept you going these many years; what sustains you in the fight?" Without a moment's hesitation, he replied, "Anger—just plain anger!" Jesus knew what anger was. There was anger in his tears for Jerusalem, as there was anger in his throwing the money changers out of the temple. How strange that his disciples should have forgotten so quickly!

As anger gives force and impetus to love in overcoming the structures of oppression and dehumanization, so love without power, that is, without the means to achieve its goals, is useless. Pride, anger, and power have been three of the hardest concepts for Christians to deal with, chiefly, I believe, because they have been seen through the eyes of single vision rather than as concepts which have a legitimate place in the human struggle if balanced by their counterparts— humility, kindness, and the willingness to surrender. Tillich rightly saw that love, power, and justice cannot be separated. Without power, love is an empty shell, a useless sentiment, and justice separated from love becomes calcified and rigid. Power separated from love and justice becomes ruthless. To these three I would add pride and anger, for without anger, love lacks impetus; and without pride, there is no anger.

Mary Daly has suggested that the central ethic for feminists is the existential *courage to be* in the face of the experience of their own nothingness. Since women have never before (at least in recorded history) defined themselves, their future is essentially open, and thus their courage to be and to become is a pushing forward into the unknown. Paulo Freire has suggested that it is necessary to have a vision of where one wants to go; otherwise actions become confused. He points out, however, that this vision should be provisional, always subject to revisioning and change. This chapter has been an attempt to summon up a vision of where we might be headed as we face the unknown, excited and unafraid.

6 "For Those Who Have Ears to Hear": The Language of Feminist Theologizing

Linguists have pointed out that the limits of one's language are the limits of one's thought. We might also say that language limits and defines perception. What we cannot name or communicate tends to remain unseen, just as the ball remains an inchoate blob for the infant until she can name it and thus locate it in her developing world view.

If we are to move from this imperfect order to a better one, if we are to enable others to see through the cracks of the present reality system into a more wholistic one, we will have to begin to change our language. Feminists perceive the new reality and are able to communicate with each other because through our shared experience old words either begin to take on new constellations of meaning or new words or forms of communication are developed in the communal context.

At first it was enough for feminists to communicate among ourselves. Now we realize that if we do not begin to communicate with others about what we have found, if we do not begin to find ways for others to enter our experience and to discover there the power and excitement of the new reality, the vision in which we place our hopes will die a quick death. We are empowered with a sense of the importance of what we have experienced and by the knowledge that if a better way is not found, the present patriarchal system may end by destroying all of us. Perhaps we are living in times not unlike those inhabited by the first-century apostles, except that now the evidence of an eschatological age is clearly palpable. Overkill systems, the increasing devastation of earth, sky, and water, the depletion of natural resources, and the growth of what has recently been called the techno-totalitarian state [1] give urgency to our voice and conviction to our message.

What women are attempting to communicate today is the good news of our own liberation and self-actualization, the good news of our newfound sense of community, and the good news of our vision of the possibilities for a better world. It is a gospel whose promise of fulfillment is not located in some future time or in some apocalyptic vision of God bringing forth a new age, but in the struggle of people here and now to win their liberation, to redefine themselves, and to create a truly humane world.

In many ways, the good news which feminists have to share is a sequel to, or perhaps a parallel of, that good news which Jesus brought forth two thousand years ago. Christian feminists, at least, understand Jesus as the archetype which stands behind their present experience, or, as James Cone puts it for the black experience, "Jesus is the eternal event of liberation." [2]

For the feminist experience, however, there are some important differences in the telling of the present story from the way in which the previous story was told, or at least the way it came through its patriarchal interpreters. First of all, the feminist gospel is a communal gospel. It cannot be traced to one person who gave it articulation and concreteness. Certainly there are spokeswomen who at points explain, interpret, and lift up what is happening, as this book attempts to do. But the real gospel is being lived among the thousands of women who every day are breaking through into liberation in their own way and time and who are working together in countless quiet and often unseen ways on the boundaries of patriarchal culture to bring into existence a new order.

The good news of women's liberation, therefore, will never be tied down to a person or single event, nor can it be canonized in a set of propositions or doctrines. Rather, it must be lived into and experienced anew by each person who would seek to understand its meaning. Nor will this good news be the property of any one group, in the way that God's revelation was for the Israelites. Assuredly, women's liberation is for women, and so far it has largely been a white Western middle-class women's movement. But we recognize that our experience is but a part of the total picture of liberation and fulfillment which is taking place in the world. We recognize that the black woman will experience her liberation in somewhat different terms from the way we experience ours because she faces the double jeopardy of being female and black. We recognize that the liberation of black South Africans or of brown Latin Americans will be experienced through their own cultural and historical categories. We know that white men, who have been the oppressors, will have to find their own way to this experience. Women cannot hand it to them.

What, then, can we communicate, so that others may receive the spark, or at least understand what we are about? Sam Keen has suggested that the starting point for any theology in the post-Christian age should be individual biography and history. "Is there anything," he asks, "on the native ground of my own experience—my biography, my history—which testifies to the reality of the holy?"[3] Harvey Cox in his latest book, *The Seduction of the Spirit*, has taken up Keen's suggestion by telling his own story. I would suggest that the telling of our own stories is precisely what women have been doing since consciousness-raising began a number of years ago. In the very telling of our stories, in the painful act of remembering and reliving, and in the active listening and responding which goes on in the consciousness-raising process, we find our revelation. It is a revelation of depth and density, of closeness and intensity, of love and power, and it commits us to permanent change. It is in this sense that Mary Daly calls sisterhood "revelatory."[4]

Although most women do not experience this revelation in ecclesiastical or religious terms, I believe that it has all the hallmarks of what we used to think of as religious revelation, although the impulse is felt to grow from within, to burgeon up and out rather than, in the old terms, to break in upon the human person or community from without. Perhaps this is what divine incarnation really means for today: that God is that force, that energizing and life-generating spirit which is present in the painful struggles of people for liberation and self-actualization. It can easily be said that where two or three women who have been through the struggle and who have experienced that liberating revelation are gathered together, there that spirit or life-force which we may choose to call God is present.

There have been enough stories told so far that we can begin to discern the shape of a new language in which the good news of women's liberation is being communicated. While our stories bear many parallels to the stories which were put together to make up the sacred books of Judaism and Christianity, they cannot simply be correlated term for term, image for image, symbol for symbol, concept for concept with those used in the earlier sacred stories. The old language will not suffice to communicate the new reality system in which feminists operate. As One who sought to express a new system of reality himself has said: "Neither is new wine put into old wineskins; if it is, the skins burst, and the wine is spilled, and the skins are destroyed; but new wine is put into fresh wineskins, and so both are preserved."

It should be obvious why we cannot use the old wineskins. The language preserved in most of Scripture and in all of ecclesiology is male language. It is language expressive of the patriarchal, hierarchical world view. Such language not only fails to express the modern experience of the world as a pluralistic, multidimensional, ever-changing process (as the "Death of God" theologians and process thinkers have pointed out), but by omitting female nouns and pronouns and the female experience, it also denies the very existence of women, and in doing so, functions to falsify our own self-image and experience.[5] It is because the female experience of oppression is left out of most modern theologies—even the theologies of being, of hope, etc.—that women find even these expressions wanting.

Women are engaged in a process of naming themselves, the world, and God, Mary Daly has asserted,[6] but it is not a naming in the old sense in which Adam was said to have named the creatures which God had created for him. This latter naming of the world is analogous to the way in which the child begins to name its world. The child receives a word from the parent which the parent connects with an object. The child, then, magically creates the object in naming it. The object takes on the properties of the received name, as my four-year-old daughter, Megan, revealed to me recently:

> It's good that Jennifer [her sister] is named Jennifer, 'cause she looks like a Jennifer; and it's good that your name is Sheila, 'cause you look like a Sheila; and it's good that Daddy is named John 'cause he looks like John; and my teacher's name is Greg, and he looks just like Greg!

The name has been given to the object apart from the child's interactions with it. There is no dialogue between namer and that which is named.

Women's naming of ourselves, the world, and God is an emergent process wrung out of the dialogue with our own past and present and with other women in community, as well as out of the dialogue with our sisters of the past. The older method of naming was very simple. You received a word or set of relationships and propositions to describe something from an authority, from the Scriptures, from a teacher, from a clergyman, or from your parent. Receiving these words, you, in turn, named yourself and the world and passed them on to the younger generation.

The naming which women have been engaged in is not so simple. It has taken a long time to discover our own forms of language, and the discovery has involved struggle, pain, work, and growth. Perhaps this is why it has taken so long for writers and theologians to come out with books on the subject. The dialogical process of naming (which is similar to the process Paulo Freire describes in his work with Brazilian peasants in *Pedagogy of the Oppressed)* does not lend itself to immediate baptism and canonization. In fact, its efforts should never be canonized, for that immediately turns the continuing process into a product, the dialogue into dogma. That was the mistake of the Judeo-Christian church.

The language with which we are concerned here is to be seen in its dialogical context and accepted as a part of the process of women's becoming. It should not be, indeed cannot be, considered the final word on the subject. Its time and culture-bound limitations must also be recognized, as one woman who has struggled to hear the emergent language so eloquently put it:

Of the as yet unspoken language that we prophesy we observe: . . . .

That it shares meanings and forms with the as yet unspoken language of other oppressed peoples; but it is not in a Black or Third World voice that white women speak. The abyss of despair that couches our emerging cry has at its depths the same earth that murmurs at the base of other people's agony, but our emptiness is not their emptiness, our experience has not been their experience. The language that is to be born will be spoken by us all in multi-colored voices.[7]

For purposes of clarification and context, and in order to indicate the sense of women's liberation as *Heilsgeschichte,* the following remarks will be considered in the light of a pilgrimage or journey, with distinct transitional points. The reader may draw his or her own parallels.

THE LANGUAGE OF SILENCE

As in all the churches of the saints, the women should keep silence in the churches. For they are not permitted to speak, but should be subordinate, even as the law says.

(1 Corinthians 14:34-35)

Where are the women in the Church? I hear of Church "Fathers" but not of Church "Mothers"! God is called "Father" and "Son." (From a YWCA-sponsored rap group on "Why am I not as 'Religious' as I used to be?")

Some men tell us we must be patient and persuasive; that we must be womanly. My friends, what is man's idea of womanliness? It is to have a manner which pleases him—quiet, deferential, submissive, approaching him as a subject does a master.[8]
(Elizabeth Cady Stanton)

Our knowledge of Anne Hutchinson is scant and one-sided: she left no letters, no journal; no one in her family or among her followers set down a portrait of her or a description of her famous "conversations" that has come down to us. Most of our knowledge comes from the pen of the man who hated her most—John Winthrop, governor of the Massachusetts Bay Colony.[9]   (Eleanor Flexner)

Men who discuss human affairs frequently do so with an ambiguity amounting to double talk or half talk or talk so vague that one cannot be sure in every case whether they are referring to men only or to both men and women. This gives them a peculiar advantage of self-defense if the charge is made that they are not remembering women at all when they speak of "man" or "men," for they can claim they are using these words in their generic sense.[10]   (Mary Beard)

One of the gravest obstacles to the achievement of liberation is that oppressive reality absorbs those within it and thereby acts to submerge men's consciousness. Functionally, oppression is domesticating.[11]   (Paulo Freire)

A LETTER TO MY SISTERS:
ON THE LANGUAGE OF SILENCE

We first learned the delicate art of silence at our mother's, or more often, father's knee. "Nice little girls don't scream and carry on like that," we were told. Then we went to school where we were taught to be quiet and obedient. "Why can't you be as quiet as the girls?" the boys were asked. Since we didn't want to go to the principal's office, we kept quiet. We got good grades that way, too, and plenty of praise from our teachers. Silence, we were beginning to learn, was golden.

Then we went to church, and there, we were taught to be very, very silent. "You mustn't talk in church," we were told. "If you have to say something, make it a whisper." But the hard benches were uncomfortable, and the sermon was rather boring. Besides, the minister didn't even mention the word "girl" once. We might have pricked up our ears, had we heard it. Sometimes in church we felt as if we wanted to scream. Or sometimes we felt like doing something silly—something which would wake up those stiff, cold adults. Sometimes, perhaps, we just wanted to let out an audible yawn, or maybe even say "hi" to our friends. One time I can remember doing just that. I had run into my friend, Sherrin, as we entered church and the two of us decided to sit together in the front row. Naturally, we started talking. Girls, you understand, are supposed to be gabby. Well, you can imagine how shocked we were when, right in the middle of the sermon, the minister stopped and, glowering down at us and calling us by name, read us the riot act for talking in church!

I didn't talk in church again, except when called upon. That was when the minister asked all of us to come to the altar rail for a "Children's Story." I could never understand why the children had to have a separate story from the adults when it didn't make any more sense to me than the story he told to the adults; but march up to the front we did. After telling the story, the minister would ask us some questions, and we would raise our hands if we knew the right answer—that is, if we were smart enough to figure out the answer he wanted to hear. Just like in school.

The one time I do remember having a big part in the church service was in the Christmas pageant. I was chosen to be Mary. It was an important moment in my life. Only trouble was, Mary didn't have any speaking parts. The angel Gabriel had a speaking part; the three wise men speaking parts; and the boy chosen to read the story from the Bible had a speaking part, the biggest of all. But Mary's role, I came to learn, was to sit quietly on the stage, head bowed, and stare at her doll in the crib. No one ever told me that Mary had quite a large speaking part in the Bible. In fact, her speech covers almost half of an entire page!

By the time I was twelve, I had learned quite effectively to silence my voice in public. My friend Vivien's mother always used to say, "Why can't you be as nice and quiet as Sheila?"

Do you remember, as teenagers, the hours we spent talking among ourselves? Sex was a favorite subject, and boys, but so were our parents, our futures, and the meaning of life. How fragile our egos were then! But we were learning, through each other, to trust life and, more importantly, to trust our own feelings and ideas. We needed each other in order to hear what our own voices sounded like. We could not hear our voices in too many other places—not with the boys, not at home, not at school, and not in church.

Recently, I shared an afternoon with a young woman. She is fifteen years old and has no such group of friends with whom she can be open and vulnerable and among whom she can hear the sound of her own voice. She is very confused about her emerging sexuality, about her need for affection and identity, about how she is to understand God and the meaning of her life. And there is NO ONE in the little town in the Catskills where she lives who will listen to her without judging her, or preaching at her, or turning her off because she is an adolescent. So she has taken to becoming involved in a fundamentalist religious revival movement where she finds excitement and a chance to talk—except that her body and its awakening sexuality are considered dirty and dangerous by this group. Her voice is divided against itself.

As a teenager I remember spending many afternoons in silence, either pouring myself out to my diary or sitting on the wooded hillside by my home silently conversing with my mother, the Earth. I didn't understand, then, that she was my Mother, that deep and marvelous matrix of all that flows with the juices of life. I had been schooled in the idea that she was an alien force and that to find solace in her was to be "sentimental" and "romantic," pejorative terms in a time of "cold wars" and "realpolitik." But deep down, I knew better. For me, the woods were a haven from a world filled with words but little wisdom.

There was a fine communion between Mother Earth and me, and I always came away from an afternoon spent with trees and sunlight and dirt feeling a bit more whole and exhilarated. My first experience of falling in love was also permeated with the feel of nature. It occurred just after a spring rain when the air was heavy with moisture, the lilacs were pungent, and the trees were still dripping. The young man has gone out of my life, but I shall never forget that experience. I grieve for all of my sisters and brothers who are denied this form of communion/communication. I grieve for those who from morning to night see no sign of Mother Earth except for a few, spindly, smog-eaten plane trees which seem, by some miraculous force, to survive among the concrete jungles which have become our cities. I grieve also for those for whom Mother Earth is never a comforting Demeter, but only an avenging ogress, a Medusa, or Kali who must be fought against.

I wonder. If we women could have spoken in the councils of government and high finance, would we have paved over Manhattan, requested that almost 50% of our nation's budget be spent for military purposes, channeled foreign aid into the hands of those who spend it on weapons of death and on high-rise luxury apartment buildings?

Do you remember how in college we silenced our voices in class, so as not to appear smarter than the boys? Do you remember how on dates we refrained from talking about the intellectual ideas that excited us for fear we would lose our sex appeal?

Do you remember how in graduate school our tentatively voiced hypotheses were considered "mushy," "unscholarly," "sentimental"? Do you remember how many times you heard a female professor's voice in graduate school?

Do you remember how in seminary we poured over the ideas of the "Divine Logos," the "Triune God," the "Second Adam," the "Doctrine of the Atonement," trying for the life of us to find some thread, some link between the theological jargon and the content of our own experiences, our lives? Do you remember how we read and reread and reread paragraph after paragraph like the following?

> The dialectical interrelation between the referential and the phenomenological aspects of theological reflection correspond with the dialectical interrelation between word, faith (church), and spirit. A contextual way of doing theology presupposes and responds to a dynamic authority which in the catholic tradition, particularly in its Roman form, succumbed to heteronomy.[12]

And then when we couldn't make out the meaning of the paragraph, we thought ourselves too dumb to understand theology.

But the real silence settled in when we reached adulthood. For those of us who became housewives and mothers, silence became a precious reprieve stolen at odd moments during the day, either from our baby's incessant crying and chatter, or, later on, from our own voices which, by the second child had become shrill and redundant:

> "Brian, I have told you for the fifth time to pick up your toys!"

"Amy, if you do that one more time, I am going to give you a spanking!"

Eventually, we grew tired of the monotony of our own voices. Sometimes, we longed to share our frustrations with those closest to us; but often those closest to us could not hear us.

"My husband has this habit of not listening to me when I talk. I get angry at him, but I don't tell him."

"Whenever I would question his actions or attitudes, he would become furious and would say: 'If you can't take it, let's call it quits. I have too many important responsibilities at the office to have to deal with problems at home.'"

Meanwhile, in the offices and factories, in the welfare lines and in the doctor's examining rooms we were learning to quell our speech:

"I was the first woman to hold a position like this, and the men didn't know what to do with me. I began to notice that every time I made a suggestion, it would be greeted with a large silence. IT WAS AS IF I HAD NOT EVEN SPOKEN!"

"But, doctor, can you tell me why I could have developed such a problem?"

"Don't worry your pretty head about it, my dear; it's too technical to explain. What's the matter, now? Don't you trust me?"

It seemed as if the only people who were interested in our opinions were the market researchers, or those who wanted us to tell them that a war fought in Southeast Asia was as palatable and as American as our own apple pie.

Do you remember how we bit our tongues as, achingly, we watched our sons march off to a war we neither planned nor had a voice in? And then do you remember how bitter was our silence when those sons whom we had born in pain, diapered, and toilet-trained, comforted while sick, and placed our own best hopes in came home on crutches, or in wheelchairs, or in boxes?

Gradually, we came to enjoy our own silence. It was safer that way. No need to stick one's neck out and get shot down for it. No need to be thought of as "aggressive," "castrating," or "unfeminine." No need to sound ignorant because we had not had enough "experience in the world" to know what we were talking about—especially at those church finance meetings or in political discussions where the "world's business" was handled. Yes, it was safer that way.

Sometimes we didn't feel like talking because the subject had no relevance for our lives, or because we sensed that what was passing for communication was coercion. Sometimes we sensed that the chatter we heard about us lacked real conviction and humane feeling. Sometimes there just didn't seem any appropriate moment when we could interject ourselves into the conversation. After all, it was impolite to interrupt.

Eventually, some of us got so used to the silence that we decided to enter it entirely: the silence of the asylum, the silence of suicide.
UNTIL WE REALIZED THAT, NOT ONLY WAS OUR SILENCE KILLING US, BUT ALSO IT WAS BEGINNING TO KILL ALL THAT WE LOVED!

> Silently,
> Your sister (Eve), Sheila

This space is for you. What is happening in the silent garden of your mind?

THE AWAKENING

Liberation is thus a childbirth, and a painful one. (Paulo Freire)[13]

Now the serpent was more subtle than any other wild creature that the Lord God had made. He said to the woman, "Did God say 'You shall not eat of any tree of the garden'?" and the woman said to the serpent, "We may eat of the fruit of the trees of the garden; but God said, 'You shall not eat of the fruit of the tree which is in the midst of the garden, neither shall you touch it, lest you die.'" But the serpent said to the woman, "You will not die. For God knows that when you eat of it your eyes will be opened, and you will be like God, knowing good and evil" (Genesis 3:1-5).

For centuries we women were blamed for enticing poor Adam to bite into the apple, that succulent taste treat that blew the naive world of garden-type sanctity into the stridently evil market-places of our blasphemous cities. For centuries we women bore our censure. Our brows knitted in unremitted shame, we were on our knees in the confession booths of our churches, confessing to the MAN that we had sinned against God (him) and Man (him) and were not worthy to be called His own. We were "no longer worthy," burrowing our selfhood and flagellating the flesh that dared to tempt man away from His inherent goodness. (Susan Eenigenburg)[14]

The emergent, dialogical quality of women's naming of themselves, the world, and God is revealed in the way in which Nelle Morton, the woman who perhaps has done the most to try to interpret the language, first discovered it.[15] During the year 1970–1971, she traveled across the country under the sponsorship of Church Women United to lead and participate in a series of workshop-retreats for women. Out of these workshops she kept extensive notes, diaries, evaluations, findings, minutes, tapes, correspondence, and interviews.

Upon returning from the tour, she played and replayed the tapes several times and poured over her notes and diaries. It was not until she had achieved some distance from the events themselves that the special forms, content, and patterns of women's experience and languaging began to emerge. Nelle Morton is convinced, as I am also, that the core of what is taking place in the women's movement and the special kind of language which is emerging from it is revealed in the small-group setting, known as the rap group or consciousness-raising group.

In the small group such defensive claims as "I've always been liberated" or "I think women's liberation is for neurotics" begin to be translated into expressions of vague hurt and finally real pain running almost to despair as concrete examples of their own humiliation, dehumanization, and objectification are brought to the surface of consciousness. At some point, usually after many, many hours of talking and listening to one another, each woman reaches a turning point, a moment of truth in which her situation as a woman in her total environment achieves a clarity it had not before. Nelle Morton has recorded some of the images used by women as they come to this moment of awareness just short of despair:

> One woman referred to her moment as a "volcano erupting," another to a "dam breaking loose." Visible and audible gestures have been anything from choking, holding the stomach "as if touching the bottom of a pit," or "the very center of one's being." Pounding on the floor or table, shaking fists at the heavens, holding the sides of the chair, and shaking one's head all signified that something cataclysmic was taking place. Sometimes nothing was more visible than a face drawn and contorted. Other times no change was visible at all. Sometimes incoherent and inarticulate sounds became audible. Once I saw a woman's throat open with a cry so great the cry could not come to sound—as in an old person who dies.[16]

It is clear to us that women have been getting in touch with something that is so deep in them that words alone—conceptual language—cannot express it. Only gutteral body language, verbal and nonverbal metaphor are adequate to describe the experience. It represents a return to the elemental, to the primitive, to the time before language achieved a distancing from life. And curious to say, such language, within the communal context of the group, was heard. It was heard in a way that was never possible before. *Without the use of propositions, we were communicating more clearly than we had ever communicated before!* A new kind of hearing which was both a hearing and a seeing was taking place, as Nelle Morton describes it:

> Once they [women] recognized in themselves a common oppression they could hear from one another that which many, more astute and intellectual than they, could not hear. They could hear that which men, particularly, find it difficult to hear—not because men are incapable of hearing. But because the kind of thing that has been going on in and among women has been so long programmed out of the male experience little or no equipment is left with which to receive it.[17]

Nelle Morton describes this new way of seeing and hearing as a form of grace. She points out that the hearing involves not only an intellectual understanding of what is being said and an emotional acceptance of the tone and meaning, but also a wholistic acceptance of the *total person*. The person and the word are one. It is about as far from the classical definition of rhetoric as one can get, and no wonder, since the art of rhetoric arose in classical patriarchal Greece! The inseparability of women from their speech is also precisely the antithesis of the way in which words are increasingly coming to be used in our patriarchal culture: as weapons, as tools of manipulation, as smokescreens to hide real intentions, or as signs of superiority and eruditeness. Nelle Morton finds a clue to the meaning of *Jesus, as the Word,* in the experience of women as they see and hear one another clearly for the first time. Jesus, she points out, was inseparable from his words. "And since Jesus and his words were not separated we can indeed say with assurance that he is present in his word." [18]

If Jesus and the Word were one, the church has certainly destroyed that fusion. Every time the Word that we are all created in the image of God is spoken in a church which excludes women from the priesthood, the Word is wrenched from its original intention. Every time the Word about loving one's neighbor as oneself is preached in a church which excludes the black, brown, and poor, the Word is corrupted; every time the Word that Christ came that we may have life is preached or sung in a perfunctory manner and with no chance for the congregation to respond to that Word of life with a dance, a clap, or a shout, the Word is rendered meaningless. It is no wonder, then, that words today have become tools of manipulation and oppression, that we can speak of bringing peace to Southeast Asia while bombing it, or that we can speak of a "Free World" made up of several military dictatorships.

The totalistic fusion of word, speaker, and hearer, which leads spontaneously to new ways of seeing reality, might be likened by some to a conversion experience. Yet the terms "consciousness-raising" and "conversion" cannot and should not be interchanged. There is a world of difference between them. The latter involves a recognition of a sense of sinfulness and uncleanness, which is supposed to lead to repentance, followed by a symbolic death and rebirth through Christ. Conversion is based on the Pauline myth of original sin and on Paul's Christology, as this passage from Romans indicates:

> Do you not know that all of us who have been baptized into Christ Jesus were baptized into his death? We were buried therefore with him by baptism into death, so that as Christ was raised from the dead by the glory of the Father, we too might walk in newness of life. For if we have been united with him in a death like his, we shall certainly be united with him in a resurrection like his. We know that our old self was crucified with him so that the sinful body might be destroyed, and we might no longer be enslaved to sin (Romans 6:3-7).

This passage reminds one strikingly of the archetypal pattern of male initiation rites, in which adolescent boys undergo a symbolic death and rebirth through the father. One is also reminded of E. O. James's statement that the theme of life generating from death is uppermost in a culture in which a male god predominates. One is tempted to conclude that the idea of conversion and its underlying archetypes is born out of the "masculine" experience of life and has its roots in the ancient need of men to break the bond with the mother and to assert their identity as men by being reborn through a father-figure. Paul's insistence, later on in Romans 8, of the dichotomy between sinful flesh and pure Spirit and our knowledge of patriarchal religion's identification of woman with sin and flesh and man with spirit make this conclusion even more plausible.

> For God has done what the law, weakened by the flesh, could not do: sending his own Son in the likeness of sinful flesh and for sin, he condemned sin in the flesh, in order that the just requirement of the law might be fulfilled in us, who walk not according to the flesh but according to the Spirit (Romans 8:3-4).

Not only is the imagery of conversion a product of the patriarchal mentality, but also it may be a function of the oppressor mentality as well. Paulo Freire has pointed out that one of the characteristics of the oppressor consciousness is a necrophilic view of the world which issues in sadism. The oppressor is obsessed with death and in order to dominate "tries to deter the drive to search, the restlessness, and the creative power which characterizes life. . . ."[19]

One is struck by the obsession with death in so much Christian liturgy. Consider, for example, the following "Act of Thanksgiving" used at a recent Christian conference-retreat:

> Minister: All glory be to you, O Father, who sent your only Son into the world to be a man, born of a woman's womb, to die for us on a cross that was made by us.
>
> People: He came to us. Help us to accept his coming.
>
> Minister: He walked among us, a man on our earth, in our world of conflict and commanded us to remember his death, his death which gives us life; and to wait for him until he comes again in glory.

We are asked here to give thanks for our having killed Christ, so that through his death we might have life. It is indeed a strange perversion of love!

This concept of conversion with its adherence to a paradigm of life generating through death and sacrifice has functioned to preserve the oppressor status of patriarchal religion and institutions by inhibiting the "drive to search, the restlessness and creative power" which characterizes the life force. With this understanding of conversion, one gives up one's autonomy, one's restless drive for life and self-actualization, and becomes obedient to an image of God which demands constant self-denial. Self-denial then becomes the mark of the converted, a sign that one has "made it." Such concepts of obedience to an outside authority (God) and self-denial are easily used by authoritarian systems and institutions to suppress any form of rebellion and to maintain an oppressed class. In the process, the nature of love is perverted.

When secularized in Western culture, obedience and self-denial formed the psychic undergirding of the capitalist system. Richard Sennett and Jonathan Cobb, two sociologists who have studied the mind set and value system of one hundred white working-class families in Boston, indicate how this works. What they found among these families was a "fascination with and a strong and complicated belief in sacrifice" as a mark of self-esteem. Working-class fathers believed that "only sacrifice makes a person 'worth' something to those he loves." "Those who refuse to sacrifice" (code words for the poor and people on welfare) "must therefore be the reincarnation of evil, the denial of *anything* a decent man does." In this way the capitalist system, undergirded by the myth of the self-sacrificing, hard-working individual, does pit the oppressed against themselves. This kind of self-denial which is extolled by the capitalist system "makes possible the ultimate perversion of love."[20]

In contrast to conversion, with its imagery of life through death, consciousness-raising operates on the principle of life generating through life. Women do not see themselves as having given up or sacrificed anything in the process but rather as having taken on ever new responsibility, as having grown, blossomed, matured. It is a biophilic rather than necrophilic concept, perhaps more explanative of the matriarchal experience of life. Where a mother-goddess predominated, life generating from life was the theme.

Consciousness-raising's most appropriate imagery is the organic. The seed contains the germ of the mature flower or vegetable. It needs a fertile place in which to develop, to discover its potential. In just such a way have women in the loose, elemental soil of the small group begun to discover the potential for growth, understanding, maturity, creativity, and productivity which was there in us all along, but which lay hidden beneath the layers of false guilt, self-denial, and insecurity which the patriarchal system had laid on us.

It is a matter of deep significance, I believe, that, as women, we have gone through the consciousness-raising process; we have first shed the accoutrements of logical, conceptual thought and language and have gone back to the roots of the life-force that is in us through elemental sound and gesture. Nelle Morton has pointed out that this was precisely what Antonin Artaud and Samuel Beckett attempted to do in their dramatic works. She points out that Artaud became convinced that elemental sound and gesture were ritual closely allied with worship.[21]

If we accept Jane Ellen Harrison's definition of the religious impulse as that which directs us toward the conservation and promotion of life, then what women have been doing, without being fully aware of it, is going back to the primordial forms of worship in the consciousness-raising group process. We might even say that the consciousness-raising group is the primordial ritual in which life is affirmed. It is the new, emerging church, seeking its forms and symbols, its rituals and sacraments in the experience of women.

Harrison pointed out that there are two basic forms of religious rites: *expulsion,* or getting rid of evil, and *impulsion,* securing and conserving the good. It would seem that as Judeo-Christianity advanced, the expulsive rite began to dominate the impulsive rite. Christianity ofttimes sought to shut out evil at the expense of securing and uplifting the good. Religion became a series of "thou shalt nots"; women and the body were expelled as evil; and Christians were increasingly defined not by the life and spirit which they all shared, but by their adherence to a set of beliefs and a rigid and inhibiting code of conduct. Those who could not accept these beliefs and codes as defined by the church and its authorities were therefore expelled as evil. As a result, Christianity, as practiced by the official church, became a death-loving rather than a life-affirming religion, as attested to by its heavy emphasis on the crucifixion and the atonement rather than on Jesus' life and ministry and the concrete, time-realized hope and courage he gave to those with whom he came in contact.

Consciousness-raising is a rite of *impulsion.* It seeks to secure and conserve the good, the potential for growth and change, for happiness and fulfillment which is in everyone. Instead of focusing on what differentiates us from others, women, through consciousness-raising, focus on that which unites us, on that which we have in common. Masculine culture, having lived so long with expulsion and unable to grasp the meaning of impulsion, looks at consciousness-raising with suspicion and sees women's need to meet with other women in the absence of men as a categorical rejection or expulsion of men. Masculine culture, thus, can only appropriate reality through its own cognitive and emotional categories. The truth of the matter is that women have found it impossible to discover their common humanity when males are present, or when women who think in masculine categories are present, because of the overwhelming tendency of the masculine-oriented world view to categorize, objectify, and subordinate an Other. Through long experience, women have found that groups operating out of a patriarchal world view tend inevitably to create hierarchies and competition between the members. This happens even in groups of men who are struggling self-consciously to come to grips with the implications of the women's liberation movement for themselves. Such groups almost automatically tend to structure themselves with "leaders," thus setting up the hierarchy again, or they create situations in which the men become competitive and thus fail to meet each other on a common elemental level. Whereas the language of consciousness-raising is primordial, bodily, making use of organic images and symbols, and rooted in concrete life experience, the language of men in groups tends to be non-bodily, logical, abstract, and removed from the concrete and personal by generalization. The language, itself, tends to distance one man from another. The language shapes the reality.

LIBERATION, EXODUS,
or
EVE'S REVOLUTIONARY APPLE

So when the woman saw that the tree was good for food, and that it was a delight to the eyes, and that the tree was to be desired to make one wise, she took of its fruit and ate . . . (Genesis 3:6).

Picture us women gathered around the table for a celebrative sabbath meal—sixty of us, church women from around the country. We rise to a toast. Red juicy apples are lifted in unison as a sister proposes a toast to Eve: "She opened to us the knowledge of Good and Evil, and she's never been allowed to forget it." We laugh in ironic glee as we picture Eve, not shamed but a strong, inquiring woman who dared to take risks, to actively test herself, while Adam swallowed doctrine whole and waited in a garden corner until Eve gave him the apple; when challenged, he blamed it all on her. Suddenly the knowledge of good and evil seemed so appropriate to acquire, so healthy to seek. We crunched into the apple—twentieth-century Eves who are willing to take risks to regain and affirm full identity. (Susan Eenigenburg)[22]

"Exodus," too, we are beginning to hear with new ears. It means going *away* from the land of our fathers. We are going away because of a promise. The promise is not something handed down by a hypostasized God-Father, but rather something that we recognize—that we *hear*—in ourselves and in each other. It is the unfulfilled potentiality of our *foremothers* whose largely unrecorded history we are now assuming into our present/future. (Mary Daly)[23]

As women become more aware of what has been happening among us, we are beginning to explore both the content and form of that experience in a self-conscious and deliberate way and are then beginning to appropriate the new language which has arisen from our depths in the service of a wider constituency. We are also connecting the form and content of our own experience with the form and content of those women from the past who have left us some legacy as to what their experience was like. Not surprisingly we are finding deep connections.

NOTES ON CONTENT

The content of women's theology is the personal life history, the concrete, daily experiences, dreams, frustrations, hopes, fears, and feelings of women who live in a culture in which these experiences are devalued and in which our own personhood is that of a subordinate Other. The theme which recurs throughout these shared experiences is the struggle for life and for self-actualization, for freedom from constricting bonds which seek to deny the potential of the life-force. It is this thematic content which unites women with the oppressed everywhere who, like us, struggle for life, freedom, and self-actualization.

It has been a recurring theme for women, as Barbara Deming discovered recently when she reread several of the classic novels and poetry written by women in the nineteenth and early twentieth centuries. In the works of the Brontë sisters, George Eliot, Colette, Willa Cather, Emily Dickinson, and others, Ms. Deming found a common concern for a "Self that has been lost, or that stands in danger of being lost" and a working out of a struggle for self-assertion and life on the part of that self, usually in the form of the heroine.[24] It is precisely that desire for fullness of life which Eve was reaching for in the apple and for which she was condemmed ever after by patriarchal religion.

The theme of liberation and self-actualization which is found in the concrete experiences of women thus forms the content of feminist theology. There are many ways in which we are using it. Women's stories—reflections on our concrete life experiences—are being told in church services as an integral part of the liturgy. St. Clement's Episcopal Church in New York City was one of the first to experiment with this new kind of liturgy. Since then, feminists in many other congregations have picked up on the idea. The content of the stories themselves, apart from any literary or traditionally theological merit, speak powerfully to those who have ears to hear. They are a means of getting in touch with the holy.

In addition to contemporary stories, women are beginning to tell the stories of women from the past which have never been allowed to be told before. These stories, too, have become a part of many church services. One of the most powerful of these storytellers is Suzanne Benton, a feminist metal sculptor, who has developed a series of stories which she tells in dramatic form through the use of her ritual masks. The story of Sarah and Hagar from Genesis is told from a woman's point of view, which sheds a strikingly different light on the interpretation of that story from that which has been offered by the patriarchal biblical editors and male theologians. She also combines the story of Mary, the mother of Jesus, with the contemporary story of a friend of hers who became pregnant at the age of fourteen. The two stories in juxtaposition are explosive and shed an entirely new light on the meaning of the incarnation, different from that given to us by the male-dominated church.

NOTES ON FORM

I have been struggling mightily in this chapter with the problem presented by form, for the form in which the old theology was presented can never again be used to contain the richness and power which we women have discovered among us. The printed word, the expository sentence, though it must be used, cannot be the only form of communication of the new theology. Having tapped that luxurious potential of the right hemisphere of the brain with its nonverbal, nonrational ways of understanding, we can only appropriate and communicate the fullness of our theological understanding through a variety of forms, each of which has its own kind of value.

As I have already noted, storytelling, personal biography, is one of the forms in which a feminist theological understanding is being communicated. To this form must also be added poetry, song, dance, art, nonverbal body drama, elemental sounds and gestures, graffiti, visual diagrams, myths, parables, and sometimes simple lists of images, concepts, and symbols which emerge out of a communal theologizing process.

Obviously, the feminist understanding of theology cannot be

communicated thirdhand or even secondhand, but must be lived into and appropriated by each person in her own way. Thus, it is saved from becoming fossilized as traditional Judeo-Christianity tended to become imbedded in the granite of conceptual language, tradition, and the canonized Word.

One of the most important contributions to religious symbolization to arise out of the feminist movement has been a recovery of the organic vision—a vision which the ancients possessed in full measure but which was later replaced by a mechanistic vision of the world as, under the influence of Hellenic dualism, the Church Fathers excluded the body and the earth from the realm of the sacred. Mechanistic symbolization has dominated Christian thought since the time of Paul. As language shapes thought, so it also shapes action and determines human relationships.

A theology built upon a mechanistic vision inevitably led to mechanistic actions and relationships. One of the most startling ways in which the mechanistic vision is revealed is in the diagrams conceived by institutional planning committees to describe the functions of and relationships between various units of the institution. The diagrams used by church-planning committees often vary little from those conceived in the board rooms of large corporations. Both resemble machines! With this kind of symbolization operating subliminally to determine the very way in which we *perceive* reality, it is no wonder that we have begun to complain that ours is a dehumanizing culture.

Recently, I was asked to lead a group of almost one hundred clergy and laity in nonverbal group-interaction at a conference called to train church people in new ways of looking at the educational ministry of the church. During the course of the conference I was struck by how deeply imbedded in our consciousness is the mechanistic vision of reality. One of the conference trainers had asked the participants to diagram what they thought the church should look like if it were really performing its ministry and mission. As I glanced at the drawings of the various participants, I was overwhelmed by the mechanistic imagery which was displayed. One person had drawn the church as a giant power generator, the source of the energy coming from a God up in the sky, flowing into the church generator (which was a large square box) and flowing out through a tube to a few stick-figures who represented the world. Another had drawn what looked like some kind of food-processing machine. Again and again, the square and rectangular boxes, 90° angles, and straight lines displayed in these drawings spoke loudly of a view of the church and the world as machines.

My husband and I, in separate groups, had worked on our own diagrams. I had attempted to diagram the church and its interaction with the world. I knew rationally that I wanted a diagram which would indicate fluidity, flexibility, a great deal of interaction between church and world, and a picture which would show the church as an enabler, an energizer, and a coalescer. What I drew was very different from what those around me had drawn. It was a busy picture filled with amoeba shapes floating in a sea of smaller round shapes. Arrows were going and coming all over the page. It was not until someone else looked at the diagram and said immediately, "That looks like a microscopic picture of a living cell!" that I realized what I had done. My diagram was indeed different from the others—as different as the organic vision is from the mechanistic.

My husband had a similar experience. He had been attempting to diagram the impact of the Board of Church and Society on the church as a whole. The board he had conceived of as a large, fat arrow filled with many seeds. The church was an open-mouthed circular structure which the arrow was just about to penetrate. Inside the circular structure were symbols representing power, liberation, peace, creativity, inspiration, bread for the hungry, and love. The impression was that the arrow was somehow feeding or fertilizing those symbols. Consciously, my husband had been drawing a diagram of one unit of the church impacting the rest. Subconsciously, he had drawn the process of impregnation and conception! The arrow was a penis, the church a womb. The symbol was rich with meaning and vitality.

Recently, at an ecumenical meeting called to discuss the results of an Episcopalian study of congregational renewal, the local congregation was compared by the director of the study to an automobile factory, in which people, Scripture, traditions, dollars, and buildings were poured in to "produce" "nurtured and witnessing people," in much the same fashion that cars are "produced" out of steel, rubber, etc. The results of the study did not seem to offer, as far as I could tell, much hope for congregational renewal or revitalization. Could it be that the presuppositions upon which the study were based were all wrong? Perhaps, if we perceive of churches as factories and people as products, that is exactly what we get.

The organic vision is beginning to well up from the unconscious as more and more of us get in touch with ourselves, our bodies, and with our mother, the Earth. It is a vision pregnant with depth and meaning. It is our link back to the sacralizing of nature and the body which were subjugated and objectified during the rise of monotheism and the incorporation of Hellenic dualism into Christianity. A cultivation of the organic vision may be the only way in which we can begin to recapture a sense of the interrelatedness of all of life and a feeling for its fragility and preciousness. It is certainly the means to overcoming Christianity's long fear of the body and of sexuality—a fear which has ruined many lives and relationships. A cultivation of the organic vision may be the only way in which we can begin to curb the destruction of our natural world which came about because we were able to objectify that world as mere "matter" to be manipulated.

Feminists are rediscovering the natural world and our own bodies as a vast dictionary whose lexicon is endless. Poets and artists have always known this. Even Jesus understood the natural world as a potent reservoir of symbols and analogies for the human condition. In all of the theological treatises which have been written since, there has been nothing to equal the symbolization of the mustard seed, the "salt of the earth," the lily of the field, or the seed sown in fertile ground.

With women beginning to do theology, we find not only general symbols drawn from nature being put to use to describe the human condition, but also symbolizations which are unique to the feminine experience—the symbol of childbirth, for example. Many women have begun to describe their awakening to life, love, power, and liberation as an experience of giving birth to themselves. Others have discovered that the Old Testament God is often described as a mother, nurturing and feeding her children. Such an image is not only apt but is also needed to counterbalance the excessively masculine images of God with which we have become embued. Still others symbolize God as a midwife—as the one who calls forth from us new life and evokes the gifts within us.

Here are just a few of the ways in which the wealth of organic imagery and symbolism is being used by feminists who do theology:

The following poem was written by Susan Ross Clewell, a student at the St. Paul School of Theology, Kansas City, Missouri.

> I am life in life
> swollen with a beginning,

newness
hope.

And my sister is waste,
    unjust ending
    too soon
    despair.

I am blood and breath
    and muscle and bone and being.

She is ceasing of flow, coming
    to rest of motion.

To have seen these few years
    for me is birth,
    joy, anticipation.

And for her it is waiting
    and knowing death.

Spring's body aches for her,
    ache of creation for slaughter.
    And learns from her pain—
        green turned to ashes—
        fragility.

The following "Litany for Movement" was written by the Reverend Davida Foy Crabtree for her service of ordination to the ministry of the United Church of Christ. Here a symbol long familiar to Christians is given depth and freshness through a consideration of bread's elemental qualities.

"we insist on being fresh
    in the human race there is a long tradition of freshness
in a way things are always new and always the same
    we eat every day, fix fresh food and break new bread"[25]

HELP US BE FRESH, LORD

"we knead new bread
    and we need new bread
and this can be said
    of the bread and of the word"[26]

HELP US KNEAD, LORD

We need good bread
                flour
water   s
                milk   e
    salt   s
            yeast   i
        good bread r

HELP US RISE, LORD, AND GO INTO ALL THE WORLD.

At a conference on "Women Doing Theology," held in the summer of 1973 at the Grailville Community in Loveland, Ohio, a service of celebration and thanksgiving was held. Each woman was asked to bring to the service something which she could offer to the rest as a symbol of life and as a gift of love. The ability of each woman to see in her gift a depth and range of symbolic resonance provided for the rest an experience of the holy. Below are examples of the kinds of offerings which were made.

—I light these candles as a symbol of the new life and light which has come into our lives and to celebrate a kind of sisterhood and brotherhood in which we will each see the light of potentiality in others.

—I am bringing this candelabra down into our midst and I ask that you form a circle around it. These candles symbolize the fact that new life is welling up from our center rather than coming in from "out there" or "up there."

—I offer you this interpretive dance to symbolize my growing experience of the potentialities of my own body, which formerly I had considered awkward and inexpressive.

—I offer this Tampax to celebrate that part of me which is uniquely woman, but which I had been taught by masculine culture to consider unclean, taboo, or embarrassing.

—I offer this simple stone, hard, solid, uncolorful, as a symbol of women's history which has been one of steadfastness and unsung courage. This rock has been broken off from a stratum of earth of unknown origins and unknown endings.

—I offer this long onion-like weed, which has a bulb on one end and an ugly, but seed-producing pod on the other end. This weed symbolizes my life—the bulb my own unique smell which has been hidden underground until now, the seed-producing pod is also me. I may not be beautiful, but I can give life.

—I offer this Queen Anne's lace, which is beautiful and delicate but is called a weed by most people. This plant is prettiest when it is seen growing in a field with others. When it is plucked and separated from its sisters, it withers.

—I offer this dance which I do with my hands. I have always been a verbal person. Now I am discovering my physical nature.

—Two songs about liberation and womanhood which had been written by the singers were offered.

In addition to rediscovering, or rather, recovering the organic vision, feminists are reclaiming the use of myth as one of the nonrational ways in which truth is appropriated. We are reexamining many of the myths which have served to keep us divided against ourselves—such as the Garden of Eden myth—and we are reappropriating these myths in new ways. Eve, we have discovered, is not to be censured for tasting of the fruit of knowledge but rather is to be commended for taking such a bold step. Without her we would not be human. Feminists have also rediscovered the figure of Lilith, a night demon who, in Rabbinic tradition, was said to have been Adam's first wife but who flew away because she could not live with him. Here is the way in which a group of women who attended one of the "Women Doing Theology" conferences at Grailville remythologized the figures of Eve and Lilith to express a truth about their own lives.

APPLESOURCE: THE COMING OF LILITH

In the beginning, the Lord God formed Adam and Lilith from the dust of the ground and breathed into their nostrils the breath of life. Created from the same source, they were equal in all ways. Adam, being a man, didn't like this situation, and he looked for ways to change it. He said, "I'll have my figs now, Lilith," ordering her to wait on him, and he tried to leave to her the daily tasks of life in the garden. But Lilith wasn't one to take any nonsense; she picked herself up, uttered God's holy name, and flew away. "Well now, Lord," complained Adam, "that uppity woman you sent me has gone and deserted me." The Lord, inclined to be sympathetic, sent his messengers after Lilith, telling her to shape up and return to Adam or face dire punishment. She, however, preferring anything to living with Adam, decided to stay right where she was. And so God, after more careful consideration this time, caused a deep sleep to fall upon Adam and out of one of his ribs created for him a second companion, Eve.

For a time, Eve and Adam had quite a good thing going. Adam was happy now, and Eve, though she occasionally sensed capacities within herself which remained undeveloped, was basically satisfied with the role of Adam's wife and helper. The only thing that really disturbed her was the excluding closeness of the relationship between Adam and God. Adam and God just seemed to have more in common, both being men, and Adam came to identify with God more and more. After a while, that made God a bit uncomfortable too, and he started going over in his mind whether he may not have made a mistake letting Adam talk him into banishing Lilith and creating Eve, seeing the power that gave Adam.

Meanwhile Lilith, all alone, attempted from time to time to rejoin the human community in the garden. After her first fruitless attempt to breach its walls, Adam worked hard to build them stronger, even getting Eve to help him. He told her fearsome stories of the demon Lilith who threatens women in childbirth and steals children from their cradles in the middle of the night. The second time Lilith came, she stormed the garden's main gate, and a great battle ensued between her and Adam in which she was finally defeated. This time, however, before Lilith got away, Eve got a glimpse of her and saw she was a woman like herself.

After this encounter. seeds of curiosity and doubt began to grow in Eve's mind. Was Lilith indeed just another woman? Adam had said she was a demon. Another woman! The very idea attracted Eve. She had never seen another creature like herself before. And how beautiful and strong Lilith had looked! How bravely she had fought! Slowly, slowly, Eve began to think about the limits of her own life within the garden.

One day, after many months of strange and disturbing thoughts, Eve, wandering around the edge of the garden, noticed a young apple tree she and Adam had planted, and saw that one of its branches stretched over the garden wall. Spontaneously, she tried to climb it, and struggling to the top, swung herself over the wall.

She did not wander long on the other side before she met the one she had come to find, for Lilith was waiting. At first sight of her, Eve remembered the tales of Adam and was frightened, but Lilith understood and greeted her kindly. "Who are you?" they asked each other, "What is your story?" And they sat and spoke together, of the past and then of the future. They talked for many hours, not once, but many times. They taught each other many things, and told each other stories, and laughed together, and cried, over and over, till the bond of sisterhood grew between them.

Meanwhile, back in the garden, Adam was puzzled by Eve's comings and goings, and disturbed by what he sensed to be her new attitude toward him. He talked to God about it, and God, having his own problems with Adam and a somewhat broader perspective, was able to help him out a little—but he was confused too. Something had failed to go according to plan. As in the days of Abraham, he needed counsel from his children. "I am who I am," thought God, "but I must become who I will become."

And God and Adam were expectant and afraid the day Eve and Lilith returned to the garden, bursting with possibilities, ready to rebuild it together.[27]

Finding new wineskins in which to contain our new vision of reality sometimes means that we have to find new words or expressions in order to communicate concepts or to give voice to experiences which simply were not a part of the patriarchal reality system. Some of these words may be old concepts which have been infused with new life and meaning. One such term is "sisterhood" which has been pulled out of obscurity to express the new kind of bonding among women. Sisterhood in this case is not analogous to its counterpart, "brotherhood." In many ways it is the foil which reveals the inconsequentiality and shallowness of the term "brotherhood." Interestingly enough, the *Standard College Dictionary* begins to reveal the distinction between the two concepts. "Brotherhood" is defined as a "society, fraternity, guild," or as "all the persons engaged in an enterprise or profession." Sisterhood, on the other hand, is defined as "a body of women or girls united by some bond of fellowship or sympathy."

As it has come to be understood in patriarchal culture, brotherhood connotes the weakest possible bonding between persons. "Brotherhood Sunday" with its pious generalities and lack of emotional feeling is but an indication of the disrepute into which what was once a noble concept has fallen. Sisterhood is the opposite of brotherhood. It connotes the strongest possible bonding among women—a bonding which is emotional, intellectual, intuitional, and sometimes physical and a bonding which is grounded in concrete and significant interaction. The concept of sisterhood cannot be explained fully in words, certainly not in a dictionary definition. In fact, it is not really a concept at all, but an experience. Here is one woman's description of it:

The experience of sisterhood is many sided. It has, first of all, both a general and a specific dimension. In affirming my own womanhood—or personhood as woman—I affirm it in all women. But I also and particularly affirm those women with whom I share the experience of affirmation. (The other side of this—sisterhood as presupposition—would be that in affirming all women I affirm myself as a woman.) This does not mean that, in community, I acknowledge in myself the characteristics of the "eternal feminine" or make peace with my assigned role. On the contrary, what I proclaim is precisely my freedom as a woman over these limiting stereotypes.

Thus this experience is, secondly, both deeply personal and intensely political. I affirm myself as a woman, but only as I enter into a new, and hitherto silent, community. In saying "yes" to myself, where I and my society had said only "no," I open the possibility of seeing other women as persons and friends; I discover a source of energy for personal and social growth and change. I acquire a sense of freedom which is rooted in my new consciousness of personal integrity and wholeness; I express it by uniting with other women in the common task of creating our future. I am freed to repossess or to try to free myself from parts of my past, but I can do this effectively only as I work for interpersonal and institutional change in the present.

But sisterhood, more than an experience of community, *is* a community. It is a place where women can "get ourselves together," begin to understand, and thus, begin to overcome, our common oppression. It is a place where we can begin to act out of our new sense of wholeness, making our own decisions for our own lives. Thus this non-hierarchically structured movement refuses to replace one set of authorities with another. Rather, women, rejecting among other myths that of our powerlessness, create in community, alternatives to a stunted past.[28]

Mary Daly has coined the phrase "sisterhood of man" to incorporate the vital meaning of community connoted by the term "sisterhood" with the generic "man." What such a jarring of images does is to lend generic weight to the word "sisterhood" while de-masculinizing the word "man." [29] Perhaps it is a phrase which can then be used by both sexes.

At other times women doing theology have found that traditional symbols or paradigms have been reborn among them. Women at one of the Grailville theology conferences, for example, rediscovered the meaning of Pentecost.

In women's liberation Pentecost is ours also because it concerns the empowering of the formerly scattered, isolated, obscure, and unheard. It is as women have come and spent time together that they have found released among them, like a great rush of wind from heaven and like the flames of a fire distributed to all, the utterance of new language and strange speech, as each has found courage to express her thoughts in her own authentic words. Across the barriers of age, social class, culture and race, they speak and are heard. The customary hierarchies collapse as the voiceless find voice and the powerless power.[30]

Occasionally, words or sounds in response to an experience erupt from among the group and are immediately coined as appropriate to the occasion. Sometimes these words last only as long as the life of the group which gave them voice. Or, they may find their way into the general parlance and remain there. One such expression is the "yeah,

yeah" experience. Usually, when women in groups begin to talk personally about themselves and their lives, others in the group will respond to the one who is talking with an excited, "Yeah, yeah!" The response of "yeah, yeah" indicates an instant recognition of the bond which links those women together as well as recognition of that which all women share. It is the moment at which the personal and the political come together. It can be a moment of great joy as well as an admission of pain and hurt. One woman has described it as the process by which we come to be "sisters." The "yeah, yeah" experience, or the "click," as it is sometimes referred to (i.e., the click of recognition, the click of the light bulb which suddenly illuminates), is to be contrasted with the kind of recognition which often takes place in groups operating out of the patriarchal world view. This recognition takes the form of a "yes, but" response. It affirms the logic of the other's statement; it assents intellectually to what is being said, but it rejects the experiential and emotional stance from which the speaker speaks. It fails to consider that the person and the word are one. It is essentially a nondialogical response.

In the "Introduction" to this book I suggested that with the demise of God, the Father, a new name for God may begin to emerge as the oppressed take up their own liberation. I believe that in the feminist movement not a new name, but a new *way of naming* is beginning to emerge. The contribution of feminists to god-talk is to topple the old idolatry in which God was enshrined in masculine, hierarchical, conceptual imagery. Instead, most feminists now see the question of god-talk as open-ended. To encapsulate ultimate reality in a limited formulation—God as Father, Son, and Holy Ghost, for example—is the real idolatry. Perhaps the ancient polytheistic world in which God took many different forms—masculine as well as feminine, animal and plant as well as human—was more faithful to the experience of ultimate reality which can never be fully grasped in any one set of symbols, icons, or concepts.

Feminist theologizers have come to believe, however, that the reification of God, the projection of anthropomorphisms onto a sacred deity, is idolatrous. Mary Daly finds objectionable the idea of God as noun.

Why indeed must "God" be a noun? Why not a verb—the most active and dynamic of all? Hasn't the naming of "God" as a noun been an act of murdering that dynamic Verb? And isn't the Verb infinitely more personal than a mere static noun? The anthropomorphic symbols for God may be intended to convey personality, but they fail to convey that God is Be-ing.[31]

As we participate in our own being and becoming, women indeed experience God as verb. A year and a half before Mary Daly's discussion of God as verb was published, a group of women at a Grailville theology conference decided to write down all the words which expressed for them a sense of the meaning of God in their lives. Almost all the words they came up with were verbs, such as "energizing," "empowering," "grounding," "being," "creating," "participating," etc. If God is conceived as a noun at all, it is usually a noun such as "force," a "power," a "liberator," or a "ground of being."

In spite of the efforts of existentialist and process philosophers and theologians to present alternative ways of imaging God, a residue of anthropomorphism continues to operate in our religious language and traditions. Because there are those in our culture who cannot seem to escape referring to God as "he" or as "Lord" or "Father," some feminists advocate the use of feminine imagery, pronouns, and symbolism for God, along with the traditional masculine imagery. Thus, God as Mother/Father, as He-She, as Mid-wife, or as Mother giving birth to her creation could become operative symbols. Carol Christ and Emma Trout favor the use of the idea of one God with double sexual imagery, but they hope that if this becomes operative, images drawn from female experience would not be limited to those of motherhood but, like the parable of the woman and the lost coin which Jesus used, would be drawn from the nonbiologically determined experiences of women as well. The use of double imagery, they point out, "would have the effect of breaking the hold of maleness on our image of God without, at the same time, legitimating sexual polarity."[32] Some persons have suggested that the third person of the Trinity can be seen as feminine, thus adding a feminine element to the Godhead. Most feminists reject this formulation because they feel it merely leaves intact the God as Father image, and the exclusivity of the male incarnation. In addition it perpetuates the idea of sexual polarity and complementarity rather than pointing to the idea of an androgynous fulfillment of creation.

The use of feminine imagery in religious language and liturgy is an important interim measure, for it breaks the exclusive identification of males with the Godhead. In doing so, it tends to open males and females to an awareness of the power and importance of women and thus it begins to reshape reality. If Catholic bishops were forced to think of God in female terms as well as male, to refer to God as he/she or alternately as he and she, they would no longer be able to justify their exclusion of women from the priesthood.

However necessary such symbolizations for God must be, they can only be provisional. They reveal the impoverishment of our language and methods of worshiping and they should lead, not to another fossilization of language but to a realization that we need to look for other ways to experience God and other forms in which to communicate that experience.

As I indicated earlier, the feminist movement is opening up other ways of experiencing and other forms of communication. The body is one such way. It has its own language, its own form of communication, its own understanding of the sacred; yet it was precisely this way to God which was denied throughout the history of Christianity.

Fortunately, body language was saved and cultivated in the black church. Almost more than anything that was *said*, it was the body language of the preacher in his exaggerated movements all around the nave of the church and in the emotionality and rhythm of his incantatory sermons which spoke most loudly about God to the black parishioners. And they responded in kind by swaying, "falling out," shouting, clapping, and sometimes dancing.

The feeble attempt of the white church to be "relevant" to today's world has seen the introduction of modern dance and drama into the worship service. While all such attempts are to be applauded, they fall short of the wholistic experience of worship found in the black church or in the women's consciousness-raising group, for such presentations only mask the fact that they are still spectator sports. The congregation, locked into the rigidity of the hard, forward-facing pews, cannot respond to the dance or drama other than through the intellect. Even applause, which is a minimal form of response, indicating only that what was seen was received and appreciated, is forbidden the average worshiper in the white, Christian church.

Feminist theology calls for the *participation* of the *total person* in the experience of Be-ing, of God worship. The body is and can be a locus of the sacred. The body utilizes form, space, and feeling, thus opening up the creative, intuitional possibilities of the right hemisphere of the brain with which body language seems to be connected.

An example of the way in which body language can be used to discover and then communicate theological understandings occurred at the Grailville Conference on Theology in 1972. In trying to reformulate a concept of God and God's relationship with human beings, the women rejected the old hierarchical "order of creation" paradigm in favor of a vision of God as the matrix or *grid of being.* Since the new paradigm could not be fully captured in words, they attempted to put it down on paper in the form of a diagram with an accompanying verbal explanation. Here is what the paradigm looked like:

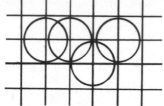

God is the grid of being rather than the pinnacle of authoritarian control.

Here is a close-up of one of the circles:

The number four symbolized perfection as well as the creative tension of opposites. The circle represented both individual human beings and God. As we participate in God, we participate in the interacting functions. Furthermore, if any one of the lines was extended to infinity, it would touch other people's circles of completeness, thus the basis for community.

But the above explanation and diagrams did not fully satisfy those who were seeking to understand God and themselves in a new way. The distancing and abstracting function of words was not adequate. Neither was the one-dimensional space utilized by diagrams. Thus, the women decided to try to experience the paradigm in a fuller way by using their bodies. Here is their explanation of what happened:

First the group placed themselves in the form of the hierarchical ladder of creation, with God at the head, then Jesus, men, women, children etc. . . . God sent Jesus to tell the men to get the women to behave because the women were beginning to move around on their own and were getting out of their spot in the diagram. They were also to be told to make the children behave. All at once the Spirit began to move swiftly among the group which made everyone uneasy so they forced her to stop.

At this point the group decided to try to make a transition into the [circular diagram, the new paradigm]. . . . The Trinity went off together to decide what they thought we ought to do next, for we found a transition is hard to make. While the Trinity was talking together, the "people" decided they had to wait. But the question was what do you do while you wait. It was decided that you support one another, so the group got into a circle of support [each person holding the other's hand]. . . .

The group then decided to assign the four poles [of the circular diagram] to four persons and let those four work their way into the meaning of the diagram. The person who had been God was Creating, Jesus Christ was Participating, the Spirit was Energizing and one of the "people" was Grounding. After some effort, the four spontaneously found themselves whirling together—and realized that they *felt* the meaning of the wholeness expressed in the diagram. . . . in a deep way. The rest of the group also felt what had happened and joyously leaped and shouted in recognition of understanding.[33]

Experiments, such as this, in exploring theology with the body indicate that there is a kind of understanding which can happen without the use of words and a kind of communication which can occur only through a participation of the total person in the experience. Even attempts, such as these, to explain what happened through the use of language cannot begin to capture the depth of insight or the emotional and spiritual excitement with which the women who participated in it were caught up. It is offered here merely as an indication of the possibilities for worship and theology which inhere in nontraditional ways of doing and understanding.

The language of space, light, and form, as used by the patriarchy, has served to prevent us from getting in touch with the nonrational ways of knowing. Think of what is communicated by the form in which most churches are built, by the light which is utilized, by the way space is allocated inside. Church sanctuaries are usually long and angular and emphasize height. They are products of the hierarchical mechanistic world view of the fathers with its awesome, transcending Father-God. The cross, symbol of death, sacrifice, and crucifixion, provides the dominant motif in most sanctuaries. All eyes are inevitably focused on it. Those who "lead" the service are usually elevated physically "above" the rest of the congregation, thus implying that they have some kind of authority over the others.

Think of what is being said about God, about the church, by the way in which space is allocated. The sanctuary is closed, shut off from the classrooms, the day-care center, the social hall, the kitchen, and the offices. God is worshiped (i.e., found) in a special place, away from the rooms in which our everyday lives are led. The sanctuary itself is a model of constriction and coercion. Pews screwed to the floor and facing forward make it almost impossible for any kind of spontaneous life and spirit to emerge, and utterly impossible for any kind of expressive body movement to take place. Moreover, pews prevent the development of community and real communication between people. One has to contort one's body in order to look someone else in the eye. It is impossible to hold hands or to embrace one another when sitting in pews, if it is not altogether socially inhibited; and it is difficult to gather a sense of what the total worshiping community looks like when all eyes are facing forward. At a Congregational church in New England which I visited recently, the parishioners were locked into their pews by the usher, each pew having a separate door by which it was entered! The sermons contained in church architecture speak louder than any words delivered on the subject of love and brotherly concern could possibly do.

Think also of the symbolism of light as it is used in Christian churches. Most church sanctuaries I have been in are dark. Windows are used not to let the light of the natural world in, but to filter it through the lens of orthodox symbolism depicted in stained glass. The world outside the sanctuary is considered a diversion, a distraction.

Until recently, Protestant churches contained very little color. Now those churches attempting to be relevant are beginning to employ colorful banners as an admission of the poverty of their previous vision. Still, in only one sanctuary have I seen the symbolism of organic growth taken seriously. If churches use plants at all, many of them use cut flowers from the florist. But how rich the symbolism and aesthetic beauty of a naturally growing plant! The necrophilic ethos of most traditional Christian theology comes through loudly in the dark, cross-centered, nature-denying world of church architecture.

Feminists have a very different conception of how space, light, and form are to be used. Through my observations of feminist-led worship services, feminist-oriented group meetings, and conversations with feminists about their ideas of what the church should be like, a new language and vision are arising.

For feminists, space is fluid and personal; it is not compartmentalized or seen as alien to the persons who occupy it or to the purposes for which it is to be used. Whether this conception of space is inherent in the feminine mode of understanding (you will remember that the right half of the brain, overly developed in women, specializes in spatial orientation) or whether it is a habit born out of necessity is hard to tell. There is probably truth in both explanations. Judy Chicago, a feminist artist, was struck by the differences in the way women and men used space when she set out to find all of the hidden women artists on the California coast, women who worked in their own homes, whose studios were often their own bedrooms. What she discovered was a fluid relationship between the women's art work and home life. There was no compartmentalization of studio from living quarters but both seemed to flow into each other. In fact, these women artists' homes could be considered as much a part of their art as the actual objects upon which they worked. Moreover, the homes and the art were active, fluid, full of variety and color, seemingly without a single guiding principle—anarchic.

In contrast to what she found among women artists, Ms. Chicago noticed that the studios of most male artists were either separate from their homes, or several miles distant. There was a sharp demarcation between their "work" as artists and their role as husband and father. Even their studios were often stark and compartmentalized. Work areas were separated from exhibit areas. The art works stood out as *objects* to be *looked at,* rather than as *subjects* to be interacted with in the context of a total environment.[34]

Ms. Chicago's observations of the differences between male and female artists might be borne out in the church if feminists had a chance to design their own forms of church life, worship, and architecture. My observations of feminist-led worship services as well as my discussions with feminists indicate that fluidity, variety, color, and lots of light characterize the feminist consciousness. Many of those feminists still committed to the church have to continue to work within the forms already established, but the more they attempt to fill old wineskins with new wine, the more they realize that it is an impossible task.

If feminists had their way, churches might take on an entirely different character. Worship would not take place in a room set aside but would occur in a multipurpose room, so as not to separate and compartmentalize it from other areas of the church's life. The church would be filled with natural light, and the symbolism of organic growth—perhaps in the form of living plants—would be prominent. Soft curves, comfortable chairs, and large pillows would take the place of angular lines and hard, cold pews or benches. People would have to face each other, rather than the priest or minister. There would be occasion for physical interaction as well as "spiritual contemplation."[35]

Feminist worship would accept and affirm the rights of anger, insecurity, pain, and sensuality to find expression and would provide occasions for their constructive release. Its emphasis would be on growth and affirmation rather than on guilt and self-abnegation. It would not overlook human evil and suffering but would point to the structural links between personal and systemic evil, denouncing that which is unjust, alienating, cruel, and dehumanizing in both spheres and pointing to a vision of wholeness which is both practical and possible.

As we exorcise the demon of patriarchy from our midst, rediscover women's herstory and the values inherent in the feminine mode of understanding and perception, we are able to find expression for that wholistic vision toward which we yearn. This chapter will close by offering you two examples of the way in which that wholeness has found expression among women.

The first is an unusual description of the process of moving from brokenness and alienation toward wholeness which came out of the Grailville Conference on Women and Theology, 1972. It was outlined in this fashion by Marcella Womack of Kansas City. The second is a poem written by Susan Ross Clewell of the St. Paul School of Theology, Kansas City, Missouri. In it she discovers a sense of wholeness through an appropriation of her newly discovered herstory.

WOMEN AND THEOLOGY CONFERENCE
GRAILVILLE, 1972
DEALT WITH

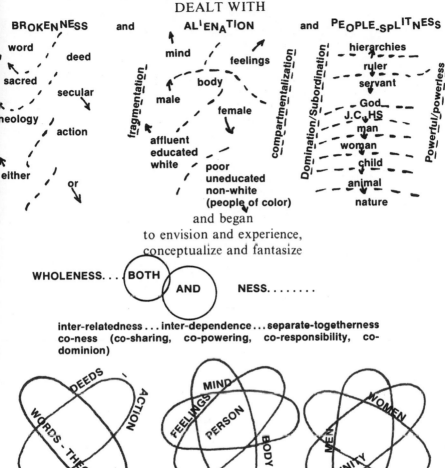

BROKENNESS   and   **AL¹ENₐᵀION**   and   **PEₒPLE-ₛₚLᴵᵀNESS**

word / deed

sacred / secular

ᵗheology / action

either / or

mind / feelings

body

male / female

affluent educated white / poor uneducated non-white (people of color)

fragmentation

compartmentalization

Domination/Subordination

Powerful/powerless

hierarchies

ruler

servant

God

J.C. HS

man

woman

child

animal

nature

and began
to envision and experience,
conceptualize and fantasize

WHOLENESS... (BOTH / AND) **NESS........**

inter-relatedness ... inter-dependence ... separate-togetherness
co-ness (co-sharing,   co-powering,   co-responsibility,   co-
dominion)

DEEDS · ACTION · WORDS - THEOLOGY

MIND · FEELINGS · PERSON · BODY

WOMEN · MEN · TRINITY

**dynamic
inter-action**

**dynamic
inter-action**

**dynamic
co-creators ...... RESTORING
CREATION!**

POEM BY SUSAN ROSS CLEWELL

I am woman
beginning
first life, first legend
first mystery

I am the ancient red-haired
mariner exploring a world
of my creation
        (justice, peace, wisdom)

I am ark, womb
cradle of life
I am milk and honey

I am the wise dweller of Anatolia
and the ruler resting in its tombs
painter of caves at Altamira

I am Tubal-Cain (daughter of Tibir
daughter of Tiamat)
sower of grain, tamer of animals
builder of towns
fire-maker

I neither war nor hunt
kill nor sacrifice
        (intelligence, devotion, liberty)

I am Mary-Isis called also
Athene, Venus, Diana
I am Proserpine, Ceres, Juno,
Minerva, Hera, Rhamnusia
I am the Queen of Heaven

I am Jezebel, loyal to my
Goddess, despiser of Yahweh

I am Iahu 'Anat
Sumerian female deity
murdered by the Israelites
        (mercy, nobility, concord)

I am Celtic Druid
possesser of all knowledge
builder of monolith mystery
at Stonehenge

I am Antigone, strong, courageous
Shubad, wife of no king
Sarah, Rebecca
Rachel, Leah
claiming my own from
Abraham-Isaac-Jacob
        (gentleness, generosity, dignity)

I am crescent moon
phasing in cycles
worshiped with Moloch
the golden calf
called abominable by your men of Law

I am intuition (merely)
knowledge of the universe
possessed for millenniums
            (spirit, soul, freedom)

I am wholeness
oneness with earth
and I must worship wholeness

Join me
Reclaim that within
you, earth-mystery
that is me
The One Who Frees
is not found
in separateness
in incompleteness

I am cycle, I am season
I am creation, I am life
I am woman

Postscript

The women's movement raises the question of whether institutionalized religion as it now exists is valid anymore. Certainly, as more and more women see through the cracks of the old reality system, they become less and less willing to spend time in it. Many of us have become mental or physical dropouts from institutionalized religion, not because we are irreligious, but because our religious impulses are being killed by the traditional Christian church.

Mary Daly suggests that sisterhood is antichurch in that it sets up a counterworld to the one upon which the major religions have been founded. But if sisterhood stands over against the church as we know it, refusing to accept its hierarchical, necrophilic, competitive world view, sisterhood at the same time points to the possibilities for a new kind of religious consciousness—one which is not defined by a set of beliefs or traditions but by its ability to include the full range of human experience in its purview, by its ability to generate life and a practical hope, by its ability to enable people to become self-actualized and to meet the problems of the world with courage, determination, effectiveness, and sensitivity to the plurality of creation.

Even as I write, the counterforces to this world view as a possibility are almost overwhelming. Coercive power is always at an advantage; and many people cannot abide the revelation that their gods have been so many Wizards of Oz, creating light shows of sound and fury, judgment and order to compensate for their own insecurities. And so, these people cling ever more tightly and fanatically to the old certainties: Catholic bishops reaffirm the law of celibacy and their faith in the Immaculate Conception; middle Americans cling to their faith in the "Christian principle of love" which would forgive and forget Richard Nixon's "peccadilloes" in favor of stability and "the American way of life"; men and women alike cleave to the notion that to destroy sex-roles is to destroy the family and thereby the very fabric of existence itself. In other cases, the young rush from the disillusionment with drugs or politics to the defense of new certainties: to the Jesus who demands total obedience and conversion to a regimented life, to a guru who tells them that the material world with its suffering and betrayal is only an "illusion."

Yet there is considerable evidence that more and more people are moving to the edges of patriarchal culture to work both rationally and intuitively, with confidence and optimism, and yet with a sense of perspective toward the coming into being of a new order beyond both the old securities and the new fanaticisms.

They are doing this both within and outside patriarchal institutions, including the institutional church. I think specifically of the thirty or more women's projects made possible through grants of seed-money from Project WIL (Women in Leadership), an endeavor of the United Presbyterian Women to stimulate new models for personal growth and social change by and for women. In these projects middle-class white women, Chicana women, black women, elderly women, rural Filipino women, women artists, women seminarians, gay women, and straight women are all demonstrating that leadership can arise from within rather than being imposed from without, that decision making can be consensual, that "process" is often more important than "product," that personal relationships are more important than structure or status, and that service means empowerment. I think also of the attempts of the National Commission on Women of the United Methodist Church to develop a completely open, honest collegial style of operation and shared leadership, and of the National Ecumenical Women's Coordinating Group to be concerned with the way in which church money is so carelessly lavished on travel budgets, hotel accommodations, and fancy meals and of their experiments in rotating leadership. I think of the Kansas City Church Women's Collective which is providing a model for an ongoing, supportive, theologizing community—a new kind of church—made up of young and middle-aged, clergy and lay, Protestant and Catholic, married, divorced, and lesbian. I think of the Women's Center at the Graduate Theological Union in Berkeley, California, which has become the hotbed of a number of innovative projects in the religious arena—women's liturgies and services which lift up the struggle and history of women, theology from a feminist perspective, and a Women's Bible project which will carry on a dialogue between modern feminists and Elizabeth Cady Stanton and her sister iconoclasts of the nineteenth century.

I think also of the Philadelphia Task Force on Women and Religion, a group composed of Protestants, Catholics, and Jews, for whom differences in religious dogma are of little consequence, as they seek together to humanize their respective churches and to provide a communications network with church women around the country who are attempting to make the church more responsive to women. I think of the numerous courses on women, given by women, in schools of mission, in churches, in colleges, and in seminaries across the country which are demonstrating that that knowledge is best which can be appropriated from within, that the teacher is a learner and the learner a teacher, and that education involves the total person in both reflection and action toward the humanization of the world.

Slowly the hierarchies are being eroded; slowly the polarizations are beginning to fuse. It may be that events themselves will force the acceptance of a new order. The world cannot live much longer with the continuing depletion of its natural resources, with the increasing pollution of land, air, and water, with the impending crisis of overpopulation, and with the development of more horrific overkill systems. A different set of priorities, a new way of assessing values is fast becoming a necessity of survival. "The world is now far too small," as Joseph Campbell has pointed out, "for any more of those old games of Chosen Folk (whether of Jehovah, Allah, Wotan, Manu, or the Devil) by which tribesmen were sustained against their enemies in the days when the serpent could still talk." [1]

Perhaps, as Octavio Paz has seen, "from the interplay of masculine and feminine a new and hitherto undreamed-of culture and creativity might arise." [2] It is to that possibility which this feminist perspective on theology has been offered.

Notes

INTRODUCTION

[1] Harvey Cox, *The Secular City* (New York: The Macmillan Company, 1968), p. 235.

[2] Joyce Carol Oates, "New Heaven and Earth," *Saturday Review,* vol. 55, no. 45 (November, 1972), p. 52.

[3] Lady Ward's address was reprinted in *Anticipation,* No. 11, July, 1972, pp. 27-32. Papers circulated for the information of participants in the ecumenical inquiry on "The Future of Man and Society in a World of Science-Based Technology," Dept. of Church and Society, World Council of Churches, 150 route de Ferney, 1211 Geneva 20, Switzerland.

[4] This booklet can be obtained from the Grail Book Store, Grailville, Loveland, OH 45140. The Packet is also available from Church Women United.

CHAPTER 1

[1] Lewis Carroll, *Alice's Adventures in Wonderland and Through the Looking-Glass,* ed. Martin Gardner (New York: The Macmillan Company, 1924), pp. 187-189.

[2] James Cone, *A Black Theology of Liberation* (New York: J. B. Lippincott Company, 1970), p. 30.

[3] From St. Theresa's *Way of Perfection,* quoted in Mary Daly, *The Church and the Second Sex* (London: Geoffrey Chapman, 1968), p. 57. Permission by Harper & Row, Publishers.

[4] Anais Nin, *The Diary of Anaïs Nin,* ed. Gunther Stuhlmann (New York: Harcourt Brace Jovanovich, Inc., 1966), p. vii.

[5] Richard Gilman, "Where Did It All Go Wrong?" *Life,* vol. 71, no. 7 (August 13, 1971), p. 48.

[6] Thomas Aquinas, *Summa Theologica* I, 92, Ic., as quoted in Mary Daly, *The Church and the Second Sex* (New York: Harper & Row, Publishers, 1968), p. 49.

[7] Karl Barth, "The Doctrine of Creation," vol. 3, part 4, *Church Dogmatics* (Edinburgh: T. & T. Clark, 1961), p. 171.

[8] Quoted in Eleanor Flexner, *Century of Struggle* (Cambridge, Mass.: The Belknap Press, 1959), p. 46.

[9] Quoted in Krister Stendahl, *The Bible and the Role of Women*, trans. Emilie T. Sander (Philadelphia: Fortress Press, 1966), p. 7.

[10] Flexner, *op. cit.*, p. 47.

[11] Peggy Ann Way, "An Authority of Possibility for Women in the Church," *Women's Liberation and the Church*, ed. Sarah Bentley Doely (New York: Association Press, 1970), pp. 79-82.

[12] Mary Daly, *op. cit.*, p. 137.

[13] The term is borrowed from Peter Berger's work on the sociology of religion, *The Sacred Canopy* (Garden City, N.Y.: Doubleday & Company, Inc., 1967).

[14] Peter L. Berger, *A Rumor of Angels: Modern Society and the Rediscovery of the Supernatural* (New York: Doubleday & Company, Inc., 1969), p. 7.

[15] *Ibid.*, p. 22.

[16] Way, *op. cit.*, p. 91.

[17] Anecdote related by Dr. Mary Daly to her class in the Theology of the Women's Liberation Movement at Union Theological Seminary, New York City, February, 1973.

[18] Yap Kim Hao, "Theology Workshop in East Asia: Reflection Within Struggle," *The Christian Century* (October 18, 1972), p. 1047.

CHAPTER 2

[1] Mary R. Beard, *Woman As Force in History* (New York: Collier Books, imprint of The Macmillan Company, 1946), p. 183.

[2] Mary Daly, "The Women's Movement: An Exodus Community," *Religious Education*, vol. 67, no. 5 (Sept.–Oct., 1972), p. 327.

[3] Elaine Magalis, in a book on the involvement of women in missions in the nineteenth century, entitled *Conduct Becoming to a Woman*, published by the Women's Division, Board of Global Ministries of the United Methodist Church, 1973, and read by this author in unpublished manuscript form, concludes that the biblical arguments against women's equality were taken seriously in this country by almost everyone, because of the fact that most of America subscribed to Christian belief.

[4] Mary Daly, "After the Death of God the Father," *Commonweal*, vol. 94, no. 1 (March 12, 1971), p. 8.

[5] See Berger's discussion in *The Sacred Canopy* (Garden City, N.Y.: Doubleday & Company, Inc., 1967), pp. 31-33.

[6] Theodore Roszak, in "The Hard and the Soft: The Force of Feminism in Modern Times," *Masculine/Feminine*, ed. Betty and Theodore Roszak (New York: Harper & Row, Publishers, 1969), presents a convincing case for viewing the nineteenth-century women's movement as perhaps *the* most powerful influence upon the cultural character and political style of the Western world in that era.

[7] Berger, *op. cit.*, p. 36.

[8] *Ibid.*, p. 39.

[9] Wolfhart Pannenberg, *Theology and the Kingdom of God* (Philadelphia: The Westminster Press, 1969), p. 69.

[10] Simone de Beauvoir, *The Second Sex*, trans. and ed. H. M. Parshley (New York: Bantam Books, Alfred A. Knopf, Inc., 1952), p. xvi.

[11] *Ibid.*, p. 52.

[12] E. O. James, *The Cult of the Mother-Goddess* (New York: Frederick A. Praeger,

Publishers, 1959), p. 80, copyright © Thames and Hudson, Ltd., 1959. Reprinted by permission of Praeger Publishers, Inc., New York.
[13] *Ibid.,* p. 84.
[14] Rosemary Ruether, "Male Chauvinist Theology and the Anger of Women," *Cross Currents,* vol. 21, no. 2 (Spring, 1971), p. 180.
[15] Rosemary Ruether, *Liberation Theology* (New York: Paulist Press, 1972), p. 120.
[16] Quoted in Mary Daly, *The Church and the Second Sex* (London: Geoffrey Chapman, 1968), p. 49.
[17] Ruether, *Liberation Theology,* p. 116.
[18] See Leonard Swidler's article, "Jesus Was a Feminist," *Catholic World* (January, 1971), for a fuller exposition of woman's role in ancient Hebrew society.
[19] Krister Stendahl, *The Bible and the Role of Women,* trans. Emilie T. Sander (Philadelphia: Fortress Press, 1966), p. 26.
[20] Theodore Roszak, *Where the Wasteland Ends* (Garden City, N.Y.: Doubleday & Company, Inc., 1972), pp. 143-144.
[21] Wolfhart Pannenberg, *Theology and the Kingdom of God,* ed. Richard John Neuhaus (Philadelphia: The Westminster Press, 1969), pp. 68-69, italics added.
[22] Karl Barth, *Church Dogmatics,* vol. 3, part 4, "The Doctrine of Creation" (Edinburgh: T. & T. Clark, 1961), pp. 151-156. Italics added.
[23] Rev. Daniel Wise, "The Sphere, the Duties and Dangers of Young Women," Swormstedt and Poe for the Methodist Episcopal Church, Cincinnati, 1855, pp. 91-92. Quoted in Elaine Magalis, *Conduct Becoming to a Woman: Bolted Doors and Burgeoning Missions* (Women's Division/Board of Global Ministries, The United Methodist Church, 1973), p. 2.
[24] Elaine Magalis, *op. cit.,* p. 33.
[25] Roszak, "The Hard and the Soft," *op. cit.,* p. 92.
[26] Quoted in Mary Beard, *Woman As Force in History* (New York: The Macmillan Company, 1946), p. 11.
[27] Elizabeth Cady Stanton, *The Woman's Bible,* reprint (New York: Arno Press, New York Times Company, 1972), p. 214. Reprinted by Arno Press, Inc., 1972.
[28] Ruether, *Liberation Theology,* pp. 96-97.
[29] Georgia Harkness, *Women in Church and Society* (Nashville: Abingdon Press, 1972), p. 198
[30] St. Augustine, *The Confessions of St. Augustine,* Books I-X, trans. F. J. Sheed (New York: Sheed & Ward, Inc., 1942), Book 3, chap. 1, p. 35.
[31] Ruether, *Liberation Theology,* p. 100.
[32] "On Female Dress," *The Writings of Tertullian,* vol. 1, in Ante-Nicene Christian Library, vol. 9, ed. Rev. Alexander Roberts and James Donaldson (Edinburgh: T. & T. Clark, 1869), pp. 304-305.
[33] Ruether, *Liberation Theology,* p. 101.
[34] *Ibid.,* p. 107.
[35] *Ibid.,* p. 102.
[36] Rosemary Ruether, "Misogynism and Virginal Feminism in the Fathers of the Church," an unpublished paper.
[37] J. Edward Carothers, Margaret Mead, Daniel D. McCracken, Roger L. Shinn, eds., *To Love or to Perish: The Technological Crisis and the Churches* (New York: Friendship Press, 1972), p. 36.
[38] John A. T. Robinson, *Honest to God* (Philadelphia: The Westminster Press, 1963), p. 82.
[39] Valerie Saiving Goldstein, "The Human Situation: A Feminine Viewpoint," *The Nature of Man in Theological and Psychological Perspective,* ed. Simon Doniger (New York: Harper & Row, Publishers, 1962), p. 162.
[40] *Ibid.,* p. 165.

[41] Phyllis Chesler, *Women and Madness* (New York: Doubleday & Company, Inc., 1972), p. 31.

[42] E. O. James, *Comparative Religion* (London: Methuen & Co., Ltd., 1938), p. 234.

[43] *Ibid.*, p. 251.

[44] Jane Ellen Harrison, *Epilegomena to the Study of Greek Religion and Themis* (New York: University Books, Inc., 1962), p. xvii.

[45] *Ibid.*, pp. xxiii-xxv.

[46] Joseph Campbell, *The Masks of God: Primitive Mythology* (New York: The Viking Press, Inc., 1959), p. 103.

[47] Rodney Stark and Charles Y. Glock, "Will Ethics Be the Death of Christianity?" *Trans-action,* vol. 5, no. 7 (June, 1968), pp. 7-14.

[48] G. W. Allport and J. M. Ross, "Personal Religious Orientation and Prejudice," *Journal of Personality and Social Psychology,* vol. 5, no. 4 (1967), pp. 432-443.

[49] Thomas Szasz, *The Manufacture of Madness* (New York: Harper & Row, Publishers, 1970), p. 262.

[50] "Kennedy, Agnew and Black America," *Harper's,* vol. 246, no. 1476 (May, 1973), p. 44.

CHAPTER 3

[1] Theodore Roszak, *Where the Wasteland Ends* (Garden City, N.Y.: Doubleday & Company, Inc., 1972), p. 132.

[2] *Ibid.*, pp. 132-133.

[3] Helen Diner, *Mothers and Amazons,* ed. and trans. John Philip Lundin (New York: The Julian Press, Inc., 1965), pp. 69-70.

[4] Robert E. Ornstein, "Right & Left Thinking," *Psychology Today,* vol. 6, no. 12 (May, 1973), p. 87.

[5] Descriptions of these early replicas of the Goddess can be found in Wolfgang Lederer, *The Fear of Women* (New York: Harcourt Brace Jovanovich, Inc., 1968); E. O. James, *The Cult of the Mother Goddess* (New York: Frederick A. Praeger, Publishers, 1959) copyright © Thames and Hudson, Ltd., 1959. Reprinted by permission of Praeger Publishers, Inc.; James Mellaart, *Catal Hüyük* (New York: McGraw-Hill Book Company, 1967); Elizabeth Gould Davis, *The First Sex* (New York: G. P. Putnam's Sons, 1971); Erich Neumann, *The Great Mother* (New York: Pantheon Books, Division of Random House, 1955).

[6] Gould Davis, *op. cit.,* pp. 73-81.

[7] "Figurines of a Phoenician Goddess Found in Wreck Off Israel," *New York Times,* January 15, 1973, p. 10.

[8] John Bright, *A History of Israel* (Philadelphia: The Westminster Press, 1959), pp. 141-142. © MCMLIX, W.L. Jenkins. © MCMLXXII, The Westminster Press. Used by permission.

[9] Gould Davis, *op. cit.,* p. 16.

[10] E. O. James, *The Cult of the Mother Goddess,* p. 180.

[11] *Ibid.*, p. 230.

[12] Diner, *op. cit.,* pp. 4-5.

[13] Stephen H. Langdon, *Tammuz and Ishtar: A Monograph upon Babylonian Religion and Theology* (Oxford: Clarendon Press, 1914), p. 43.

[14] Gould Davis, *op. cit.,* pp. 44-46.

[15] Joseph Campbell, *The Masks of God: Primitive Mythology* (New York: The Viking Press, Inc., 1970), p. 315.

[16] James, *op. cit.,* p. 231.

[17] Campbell, *op. cit.,* p. 86.

[18] See E. O. James, *Comparative Religion* (London: Methuen & Co., Ltd., 1938), p. 149.

[19] Langdon, *op. cit.,* p. 17.

[20] Quoted in Edith Hamilton, *The Greek Way* (New York: W. W. Norton & Company, Inc., 1942), pp. 294-295.

[21] Elizabeth Janeway, *Man's World, Woman's Place* (New York: William Morrow & Co., Inc., 1971), p. 61.

[22] Rosemary Ruether, "The Roots and Implications of Male/Female Duality," unpublished paper delivered to the Executive Staff Conference of Church Women United, Nov., 1971.

[23] See Simone de Beauvoir's analysis in Part 2, chapters 4 and 5 of *The Second Sex,* trans. and ed. H. M. Parshley (New York: Bantam Books, Alfred A. Knopf, Inc., 1953).

[24] Aeschylus, *The Eumenides,* trans. E. D. A. Morshead, in *The Complete Greek Drama,* ed. Whitney J. Oates and Eugene O'Neill, Jr. (New York: Random House, Inc., 1938), vol. 1, p. 301.

[25] Gould Davis, *op. cit.,* pp. 104-108.

[26] Euripides, *Medea,* trans. E. P. Coleridge (London: G. Bell & Sons, Ltd., n.d.) as quoted in *The Complete Greek Drama, op. cit.,* p. 728.

[27] Bruno Bettelheim, *Symbolic Wounds* (Glencoe, Ill.: The Free Press, 1954), pp. 139-140.

[28] Campbell, *op. cit.,* p. 60.

[29] Theodor Reik, *The Creation of Woman* (New York: George Braziller, Inc., 1960), p. 17.

[30] Margaret Mead, *Male & Female* (New York: Dell Publishing Co., Inc., 1949), pp. 88, 102-104.

[31] Una Stannard, "Adam's Rib, or The Woman Within," *Trans action* (Nov -Dec., 1970), pp. 24-35.

[32] John Money, "Sexual Dimorphism & Homosexual Gender Identity," *Readings on the Psychology of Women,* ed. Judith M. Bardwick (New York: Harper & Row, Publishers, 1972), pp. 3-7.

[33] Reik, *op. cit.,* see chapter 1.

[34] Emily C. Hewitt and Suzanne R. Hiatt, *Women Priests: Yes or No?* (New York: The Seabury Press, Inc., 1973), p. 43.

[35] Lederer, *op. cit.,* p. 159.

[36] The following delineation of the place of Asherah in ancient Israel is based on Raphael Patai's account in *The Hebrew Goddess* (New York: KTAV Publishing House, Inc., 1967), pp. 15-100

[37] *Ibid.,* p. 51.

[38] *Ibid.,* pp. 101-136.

[39] Anne Bennett, "Women in the New Society," *Journal of Current Social Issues,* vol. 11, no. 1 (Winter, 1972-1973), p. 27.

[40] *Ibid.*

[41] The following summary of Shekhina and Hokhmah is based on Patai's analysis in *The Hebrew Goddess,* pp. 137-156.

[42] *Ibid.,* p. 270.

[43] James, *op. cit.,* pp. 178-179.

[44] *Ibid.,* p. 180.

[45] Leonard Swidler, "Jesus Was a Feminist," *Catholic World,* vol. 212, no. 1270 (January, 1971), pp. 177-183.

[46] *Ibid.,* p. 179.

[47] Ruth Hoppin, "Games Bible Translators Play," *Women & Religion,* a packet of

materials printed by the National Organization for Women Ecumenical Task Force on Women & Religion.

[48] See Johannes Weiss, *Earliest Christianity*, ed. and trans. Frederick C. Grant, vol. 1 (New York: Harper & Row, Publishers, 1959), p. 150; Georgia Harkness, *Women in Church and Society* (Nashville: Abingdon Press, 1972), p. 70.

[49] James, *op. cit.*, p. 192.

[50] *Ibid.*, pp. 205, 225.

[51] Eric Neumann, *The Great Mother*, trans. Ralph Manheim (New York: Pantheon Books, Division of Random House, 1955), pp. 331-332.

[52] Henry Adams, *Mont-Saint-Michel and Chartres* (Boston: Houghton Mifflin Company, 1933), p. 250.

[53] *Ibid.*, p. 261.

[54] James, *op. cit.*, p. 208.

[55] Roland H. Bainton, *Women of the Reformation in Germany and Italy* (Minneapolis: Augsburg Publishing House, 1971), p. 45.

[56] Margaret A. Murray, *The Witch-Cult in Western Europe* (Oxford: The Clarendon Press, 1921), p. 273.

[57] Sybil Leek, *The Complete Art of Witchcraft* (New York: The World Publishing Co., 1971), p. 36.

[58] Barbara Ehrenreich and Deirdre English, *Witches, Midwives, and Nurses: A History of Women Healers* (New York: The Feminist Press, 1973), pp. 10-11.

CHAPTER 4

[1] Simone Weil, *The Need for Roots*, trans. Arthur Wills (New York: Harper & Row, Publishers, 1971), p. 225.

[2] *Christian Century*, vol. 90, no. 34 (September 26, 1973), p. 942.

[3] Mary White Harder, James T. Richardson, Robert B. Simmonds, "Jesus People," *Psychology Today*, vol. 6, no. 7 (December, 1972), p. 45.

[4] See Elizabeth Gould Davis, *The First Sex* (New York: G. P. Putnam's Sons, 1971), pp. 22, 48-59, 93.

CHAPTER 5

[1] See Phyllis Trible, "Depatriarchalizing in Biblical Interpretation," *Journal of the American Academy of Religion*, vol. 41, no. 1 (March, 1973), pp. 36-37.

[2] Theodore Roszak, *Where the Wasteland Ends* (New York: Doubleday & Company, Inc., 1972). See especially chapter 6, pp. 178-219. Roszak opposes the "single vision" which has dominated Western culture to the multidimensional world view which he finds among the ancients and certain primitives.

[3] In spite of the revolutionary changes one sees in physics in the last few decades—Einstein's relativity, Heisenberg's indeterminacy principle, Bohr's principle of complementarity, etc.—Roszak *(op. cit.)* continues to see the same objectifying psychology and sensibility with regard to nature at work in the scientific community.

[4] I am indebted to an unpublished paper by Margaret Maxey, entitled "Precis: The Secularization of Authority," for these insights into the authority of paradigms.

[5] Rubem A. Alves, "Christian Realism: Ideology of the Establishment," *Christianity and Crisis*, vol. 33, no. 15 (September 17, 1973), p. 176.

[6] Reinhold Niebuhr, *Man's Nature and His Communities* (New York: Charles Scribner's Sons, 1965), p. 22.

[7] Rosemary Ruether, "Women's Liberation, Ecology & Social Revolution," *WIN* (October 4, 1973), pp. 4-7.

[8] Shirley Hazzard, "The United Nations: Elderly Orphan," *The Nation*, vol. 217, no. 13 (October 22, 1973), p. 394.

[9] Hannah Arendt, *The Human Condition* (New York: Anchor Books, imprint of Doubleday & Company, Inc., 1959), pp. 24-34. Ms. Arendt points out that Athenian democracy rested on a base of authoritarian absolutism in the home.

[10] John Stuart Mill, *The Subjection of Women*, quoted in *Feminism: The Essential Historical Writings*, ed. Miriam Schneir (New York: Random House, Inc., 1972), p. 176.

[11] *Ibid.*, p. 177.

[12] Paul Tillich, *Systematic Theology*, vol. 2 (Chicago: The University of Chicago Press, 1957), p. 177.

[13] Arnold J. Toynbee, "The Genesis of Pollution," *New York Times*, Sept. 16, 1973, Section 4, p. 15.

[14] Ruether, "The Scope of Women's Liberation," unpublished paper presented at a conference on "Manhood and Womanhood in the Church," Yale Divinity School, March 4, 1970.

[15] Ellen Battelle Dietrick, "Comments on Kings," *The Woman's Bible*, ed. Elizabeth Cady Stanton (New York: European Publishing Company, 1895). Reprinted by Arno Press, Inc., 1972. pp. 74-76.

[16] Ruether, "The Scope of Women's Liberation."

[17] Maya Pines, "We Are Left-Brained or Right-Brained," *New York Times Magazine* (September 9, 1973), p. 122.

[18] *Ibid.*, p. 137.

[19] *Ibid.*, p. 126.

[20] *Ibid.*, p. 125.

[21] Roszak, *op. cit.*, p. 112.

[22] Phyllis Trible, *op. cit.*, p. 31.

[23] *Ibid.*, p. 36.

[24] *Ibid.*, pp. 32-48.

[25] Sam Keen, *To a Dancing God* (New York: Harper & Row, Publishers, 1970), pp. 141-160.

[26] Amitai Etzioni, "The Fetus: Whose Property?" *Commonweal*, vol. 98, no. 21 (September 21, 1973), p. 493.

[27] C. Eric Lincoln, "Why I Reversed My Stand on Laissez-Faire Abortion," *Christian Century*, vol. 90, no. 17 (April 25, 1973), p. 478.

[28] *Ibid.*, p. 478.

[29] Rosemary Ruether, "Male Chauvinist Theology and the Anger of Women," *Cross Currents*, vol. 21, no. 2 (Spring, 1971), p. 183.

[30] *Ibid.*, p. 184.

CHAPTER 6

[1] Andrew St. George, "The Cold War Comes Home," *Harper's*, vol. 247, no. 1482 (November, 1973), p. 75.

[2] James Cone, Inaugural Address given in James Chapel, Union Theological Seminary, New York City, Oct. 11, 1973.

[3] Sam Keen, *To a Dancing God* (New York: Harper & Row, Publishers, 1970), p. 99.

[4] Mary Daly, *Beyond God the Father: Toward a Philosophy of Women's Liberation* (Boston: Beacon Press, 1973).

[5] *Ibid.*; see especially chapter 1, "After the Death of God the Father," pp. 13-43.

[6] *Ibid.*, p. 8.

[7] Sally Gearhart, "She Who Hath Ears. . . ," *Women and the Word: Toward a Whole*

Theology (Berkeley, Calif.: Office of Women's Affairs, 2465 LeConte Ave., 1972), pp. 76-77.

[8] Elizabeth Cady Stanton, address to the National American Woman Suffrage Association, 1890, quoted in *Feminism: The Essential Historical Writings,* ed. Miriam Schneir (New York: Random House, Inc., 1972), p. 155.

[9] Eleanor Flexner, *Century of Struggle* (Cambridge, Mass.: The Belknap Press, 1959), p. 10.

[10] Mary R. Beard, *Woman As Force in History* (New York: Collier Books, imprint of The Macmillan Company, 1946), p. 57.

[11] Paulo Freire, *Pedagogy of the Oppressed,* trans. Myra Bergman Ramos (New York: Herder and Herder, Inc., 1970), p. 36.

[12] Paul L. Lehmann, "Editorial," *Theology Today,* vol. 29, no. 1 (April, 1972), p. 5.

[13] Freire, *op. cit.,* p. 33.

[14] Susan Eenigenburg, "Eve's Revolutionary Apple," *Women Exploring Theology at Grailville,* a packet prepared by Church Women United, 1972, 475 Riverside Dr., NY 10027.

[15] I am indebted to personal conversations with Nelle Morton for this material as well as to her article, "The Rising Woman Consciousness in a Male Language Structure," *Andover Newton Quarterly,* vol. 12, no. 4 (March, 1972), pp. 177-190.

[16] *Ibid.,* pp. 178-179.

[17] *Ibid.,* p. 180.

[18] *Ibid.,* pp. 180-181.

[19] Freire, *op. cit.,* pp. 45-46.

[20] Richard Sennett and Jonathan Cobb, "The Fascination of Sacrifice," *Intellectual Digest,* vol. 4, no. 2 (October, 1973), p. 68.

[21] Morton, *op. cit.,* p. 187.

[22] Eenigenburg, *op. cit.*

[23] Mary Daly, "A Call for the Castration of Sexist Religion," *Unitarian Universalist Christian* (Autumn/Winter, 1972).

[24] Barbara Deming, "Two Perspectives on Women's Struggle," *Liberation* (June, 1973), pp. 30-37.

[25] M. Corita Kent, *Footnotes and Headlines: A Play-Pray Book* (New York: Herder and Herder, Inc., 1967), p. 10.

[26] *Ibid.,* p. 13.

[27] The myth was developed by Judith Plaskow Goldenberg, Karen Bloomquist, Sister Margaret Early, and Elizabeth Farians and was written up in this form by Judith Goldenberg. Contained in *Women Exploring Theology* packet, *op. cit.*

[28] *Ibid.* Revised by Judith Goldenberg and used with her permission.

[29] Daly, *Beyond God the Father,* p. 9.

[30] Winsome Munro, "Pentecost as a Paradigm for Women's Liberation," *Women Exploring Theology, op. cit.*

[31] Daly, *op. cit.,* pp. 33-34.

[32] Carol Christ and Emma Trout, "Alternative Images of God: Communal Theology," unpublished paper.

[33] Adapted from the report of the Work Group on Singleness/Community as a Model for Theologizing, in the *Women Exploring Theology* packet, ed. Sally Bentley and Claire Randall, *op. cit.*

[34] Tape by Judy Chicago heard by this author on radio station WBAI, New York.

[35] Conversation with Davida Foy Crabtree.

POSTSCRIPT

[1] Joseph Campbell, *The Masks of God: Primitive Mythology* (New York: The Viking Press, Inc., 1959), p. 12.

[2] Interview with Octavio Paz, *Intellectual Digest,* vol. 3, no. 4 (December, 1972), p. 68.

Index